Class Struggles

History: Concepts, Theories and Practice

Series editor: Alun Munslow, University of Chichester

The New History
Alun Munslow

History on Film/Film on History
Robert A. Rosenstone

Imperialism
Barbara Bush

Class Struggles

DENNIS DWORKIN

PEARSON
Longman

Harlow, England • London • New York • Boston • San Francisco • Toronto
Sydney • Tokyo • Singapore • Hong Kong • Seoul • Taipei • New Delhi
Cape Town • Madrid • Mexico City • Amsterdam • Munich • Paris • Milan

Pearson Education Limited

Edinburgh Gate
Harlow CM20 2JE
United Kingdom
Tel: +44 (0)1279 623623
Fax: +44 (0)1279 431059
Website: www.pearsoned.co.uk

First edition published in Great Britain in 2007

© Pearson Education Limited 2007

ISBN-13: 978-1-4058-0138-6
ISBN-10: 1-4058-0138-7

British Library Cataloguing in Publication Data
A CIP catalogue record for this book can be obtained from the British Library

Library of Congress Cataloging in Publication Data
A CIP catalog record for this book can be obtained from the Library of Congress

10 9 8 7 6 5 4 3 2 1
10 09 08 07 06

Set by 35 in 11/13pt Bulmer MT
Printed in Malaysia

Contents

Preface to the series

History: Concepts, Theories and Practice is a series that offers a coherent and detailed examination of the nature and effects of recent theoretical, methodological and historiographical developments within key fields of contemporary historical practice. Each volume is open to the idea of history as a historicist cultural discourse constituted by historians as much as it is reconstructed from the sources available about the past. The series examines the discipline of history as it is conceived today in an intellectual climate that has increasingly questioned the status of historical knowledge.

As is well known, questioning of the status of history, indeed of its very existence as an academic subject, has been seen in several recent scholarly developments that have directly influenced our study of the past. These include the emergence of new conceptualisations of "pastness," the emergence of fresh forms of social theorising, the rise of concerns with narrative, representation and the linguistic turn, and a self-conscious engagement with the issues of relativism, objectivity and truth. All these are reflected in the appearance of new historical themes and frameworks of historical activity.

In acknowledging that history is not necessarily nor automatically authorised by one foundational epistemology or methodology and that history cannot stand outside its own genre or form, all volumes in the series reflect a multiplicity of metanarrative positions. Nevertheless, each volume (regardless of its own perspective and position on the nature of history) explains the most up-to-date interpretational and historiographic developments that fall within its own historical field. However, this review of the "latest interpretation and methodology" does not diminish the broad awareness of the "challenge to history as a discipline" reflected in the tensions between referentiality, representation, structure and agency.

Each volume offers a detailed understanding of the content of the past, explaining by example the kinds of evidence found within their own field as well as a broad knowledge of the explanatory and hermeneutic demands historians make upon their sources, the current debates on the uses to which evidence is put, and how evidence is connected by historians within their field to their overall vision of What is history?

Alun Munslow

Acknowledgments

In the course of writing this book, I have accumulated numerous debts. Colleagues and friends in the University of Nevada, Reno History Department have been especially important in helping me complete this project. Elizabeth Raymond gave generously of her time, closely reading the manuscript at all stages. She has helped make the book better in multiple ways. Scott Casper and Martha Hildreth also read the manuscript in its entirety, furnishing invaluable suggestions. I also want to thank Dee Kille for commenting on early versions of chapters. Many of the arguments in this book were first given in my cultural theory seminar, where my students gave helpful feedback. I am grateful for the support of friends and colleagues in the English Department as well – Stacy Burton, Jen Hill, and Aaron Santesso – but especially Mark Quigley, with whom I had several conversations involving the final chapters. Many of these conversations took place in Bibo Coffee Company, where I often wrote in the late afternoon and early evening. When I wasn't there at those times, I was usually at Walden's Coffeehouse. Both places provided friendly environments and welcome relief from the confines of my study.

The writing of the book also was shaped by wider contacts within my discipline. Eric Porter pointed me in the direction of pivotal American history texts pertaining to the relationship between race and class. Geoff Eley has not only been supportive of this project but also sent me manuscript versions of *The Crooked Line* and the coauthored (with Keith Nield) *The Future of Class in History: What's Left of the Social?* My chapter focusing on Gareth Stedman Jones was given as a conference paper at the 2005 meetings of the Pacific Coast Conference on British Studies. The commentator of my panel, Jeffrey Auerbach, provided thought-provoking remarks, and my fellow panelist Michelle Tusan – my counterpart in British history at the University of

Nevada, Las Vegas – offered encouragement at a time when I really needed it. A highlight of that conference was that Stedman Jones himself was a keynote speaker. During the conference we chatted about his work, and he subsequently shared unpublished writings. Both proved important to understanding his achievement. In addition, James Epstein kindly agreed to read the completed manuscript on a short timeline and offered invaluable criticism. I would never have written this book if it were not for the series editor, Alun Munslow, who has been supportive at every stage. The anonymous readers of the original prospectus on which this book is based made useful suggestions on how to proceed.

Since I began work on this book, my father has died and my mother's Alzheimer's disease has reduced her to an unrecognizable shell of her former self. I shall never forget their love and the support and faith that they had in me. I am also grateful that my in-laws – Caroline Musselman and Tom Miller – have shown such a keen interest in my work. I cannot say enough about my wife and partner, Amelia Currier, whose understanding and compassion were so important in helping me to complete this project. One of the few pleasures that I allowed myself while writing this book was to watch my son Sam play in countless baseball games. There are few 14-year-old guitar-playing third basemen that can match him.

July 2006

Introduction

We use the term "class" all the time, but we mean numerous things by it. Just for starters, it can involve our career path, the schools that we attend, the party that we vote for, the way that we speak, the car that we drive, the clothes that we wear, the food that we eat, the music that we listen to, the art that we enjoy, and the sports that rivet us. More abstractly, it can entail status or income, education or work, lifestyle or social position, group solidarities or conflicts. Class divisions have been attributed to productive relations, market access, a status hierarchy, or culture. Often it seems that they are hard to tell apart from other forms of division: racial, gendered, regional, ethnic, religious, and so forth. Class societies can be viewed as stable or conflict ridden. Our understanding of them is invariably political, but the political meanings that we derive from them vary greatly. Thus, for the poet Matthew Arnold (1822–1888), class divisions ultimately led to anarchy without the intervention of a cultural elite, while for the radical theorist and activist Karl Marx (1818–1883), class struggles ultimately signaled the triumph of communism. In short, it is difficult to define or place limits on what "class" means. I find the concept of class necessary but allusive.

We live in an age of accelerating globalization, proliferating multinational corporations, and unbridled free-market capitalism. If we read the newspapers, we are acutely aware of the impact of these on growing income and lifestyle inequities within particular societies, but also between different parts of the world as a whole. The economist Paul Krugman has written of the growing income disparities among Americans, arguing that the United States has entered a second "Gilded Age" (Krugman 2002). In 1970 the top 0.01 percent of American taxpayers had 0.7 percent of the total income, and they earned 70 times more than the average. In 1998 the same segment received more than

3 percent of all income. This meant that the 13,000 richest families made as much as the 20 million poorest and had 300 times that of the average. Meanwhile, according to a 1997 World Bank report, the global share of world income going to the top 20 percent of the wealthiest countries was 73.9 percent in 1970 and 82.7 percent in 1989. For the world's 20 percent poorest countries, it had diminished from 2.3 percent in 1960 to 1.4 percent in 1989 (Seabrook 2002: 79).

Since one common-sense definition equates class divisions with income disparities, we might think that, given these trends, class analysis in the past quarter century would have a growing appeal. In fact, the opposite is true: the concept of class, at least in the humanities and social sciences, is in crisis. If writing a book on gender, race, postcolonialism, or nationalism, I would probably focus on the expanding influence of my key concept. A book on class tells a different story. Within the field of history, class was a central organizing idea in the "new" social and labor history, a historiographical revolution highly influential in the 1960s and 1970s. It was also important for a group of prominent sociologists, who sought to understand the transformations of the post-World War II world. Among historians, class interpretations have recently been subjected (along with social history more generally) to multiple challenges. This has also been true in sociology, with a title such as *The Death of Class* (Pakulski and Waters 1996a) dramatically capturing, if not the demise of class itself, something important about the moment in which the book was conceived. The title of my book has a double meaning. It refers to a key idea in class theory – the Marxist notion of class struggle – while suggesting that it is the concept, rather than what it seeks to describe, that is doing the struggling. I believe that pronouncements regarding the death of class are exaggerated. Yet I accept that class's status within history and sociology – as well as anthropology, philosophy, cultural studies, and political science – is greatly diminished. How and why this has happened is a major theme of this book.

Class crisis

This crisis is rooted in the declining appeal of Marxism and other clusters of ideas that shared some of its assumptions. While certainly all writers who developed postwar class theory and analysis were not Marxists, the Marxist tradition had a powerful sway on the shape of their scholarly work. It was by no means the orthodox Marxism associated with the Soviet Union and Communist parties around the world. Their authoritarianism and narrow economic view of society and history – often referred to as "economism" – was often an object of scorn and attack. It was a critical Marxism: it developed, revised, and questioned Marx's ideas, often crossing them with ideas from other intellectual traditions. The cultural theorist Stuart Hall has captured the spirit of this critical dialogue with the Marxist tradition, describing it as "working within shouting distance of Marxism, working on Marxism, working against Marxism, working with it, working to try to develop Marxism" (Hall 1992: 279).

Whether derived directly or indirectly from Marx's writings, class theory and analysis in the humanities and the social sciences has been dualistic, founded on the distinction between an objective socio-economic structure and forms of consciousness and action shaped by it. Scholars working in various disciplines by no means agreed about the extent to which this material foundation determined consciousness and action. Indeed, we shall see that Marx's own version of the relationship via the metaphor of base and superstructure proved highly controversial, contentious, and problematic. Nonetheless, there was a consensus that, to use Marx's terminology, "social being," mediated by experience, provided the foundation for "social consciousness," or, more specifically, that society (and the economic relationships that sustained it) provided the key to understanding culture and politics, not the reverse. Within this framework class was viewed dualistically as well. Just as being shaped consciousness, the class structure of a society produced forms of inequality and hierarchy that provided a key to understanding behavior. One's position in the class structure shaped self-interest. The development of class consciousness emanated from the awareness of this interest via experience and was manifested in collective action. Among the scholars responsible for class theory and interpretation in the 1960s and 1970s, there was never a question that particular forms of class consciousness could be derived from class relationships in a straightforward, mechanical, or automatic way. Indeed, they held that culture and politics played central roles in mediating them. Yet they assumed that the class structure was ultimately determining. And many felt compelled to implicitly and explicitly explain why – especially in the case of the working class – forms of class consciousness (as imagined within Marxism) were frustrated.

The distinction between structure and consciousness has been fundamental to the development of this model, but it has also raised difficulties, as the dualism does an injustice to the potential range of meanings involved. We can glean some of the complexities by considering Ira Katznelson's exploration of the meanings of class in his introduction to *Working-Class Formation: Nineteenth-Century Patterns in Western Europe and the United*

States (1986). Katznelson offers four definitions. The first signifies the purely unequal structural relationship between capital and labor intrinsic to capitalism (or potentially other modes of production) as a system. It is an abstraction from the multitude of relationships that individuals and groups encounter in their daily lives. Katznelson describes it as "experience-distant." The second definition refers to "the social organization of society" as experienced by actual people in concrete social formations. It is still structural, but it is less abstract, involving, for example, workplace social relations, the structures of labor markets, connections between home and work, and the organization of space, for example, working-class neighborhoods. It is by specifying the patterns of these relationships that it is possible to differentiate say the class structures of Britain, France, and the United States. Where the first two definitions of class, though distinct, are analytical constructs, the last two signify the disposition of "formed groups" to act in class ways. The third captures the process whereby groups of people develop a common understanding of the social system or come to share a set of values as a result of their experience of class relationships (definition two). The fourth defines classes through the modes of collective action that emerged out of these shared values. In putting forward this four-tiered scheme, Katznelson is by no means suggesting that class proceeds through "a series of necessary stages of natural progression." As he observes: "Questions about the content of each level and about the connections between the levels constitute the very heart of the analysis of class formation" (Katznelson 1986: 22).

If Katznelson's approach is an advance over a purely dualistic one, it simultaneously retains some of its problematic assumptions. As Kathleen Canning observes, Katznelson views production, defined exclusively in economic terms, as providing the foundation for class formation. As a result, "the state, culture, ideology, gender, law, and religion are viewed as intervening variables rather than constitutive elements of production" (Canning 1992: 743). In addition, human agency and collective action are regarded only as responses to material social conditions, thus ignoring their potential role in shaping those very conditions. Canning's reflections give a taste of the criticisms launched at the binary model of class and society.

In the 1960s and 1970s, historians and sociologists, responsible for expanding and reworking class theory and interpretation, shared the assumptions of this dualistic model, but they explored its ramifications in different ways. Crudely put, some of the most creative work in sociology was the development of sophisticated mappings of objective class relationships (definitions one and two) as a precondition for answering questions about the connections between structural location, life chances, consciousness, and collective action.

Sociologists – most importantly John Goldthorpe and Erik Olin Wright – elaborated and refined their theoretical models on the basis of conducting large-scale surveys.

Historians, on the other hand, studied the process of class formation and experience (definitions three and four). This work helped define the new social and labor history, whose aspiration to write "total history" was grounded in a "bottom-up" or "history from below" perspective. This conception of history was greatly indebted to the inspiring example of E. P. Thompson's *The Making of the English Working* Class ([1963] 1968), which aspired to recover the history of the working class within a materialist and Marxist understanding of society and history. Thompson's insistence that the material foundation could not explain the particular shape that class consciousness assumed was founded on an unshakable faith in the power of human agency. The impact of Thompson – and other historians working in the same vein – helped reshape the priorities of the historical profession. Here, class relations and class struggle produced new objects for historical analysis. They significantly enlarged the scope of who counted as historical actors. And they provided the foundational concepts for understanding the historical narrative as a whole, expanding on Marx's famous contention in *The Communist Manifesto* that all history was class struggle.

I am not suggesting that historians and sociologists, who did so much to further the study of class and class formation, were in a fluid dialogue with each other. There were certainly conflicts and tensions between them. Few sociologists appear to have considered historians' understanding of class to be sufficiently theoretical; historians often saw sociological writings on class as ahistorical. What I am suggesting is that, overall, historians and sociologists in the 1960s and 1970s made decisive (though different) contributions to a more nuanced and sophisticated understanding of class and class consciousness. Accordingly, when the consensus regarding this binary model began to crumble, its shockwaves registered in both disciplines.

In general, two types of criticism have been leveled against this binary understanding of society. First, critics have argued that the centrality accorded to class narratives has marginalized other forms of identity. This view is implicitly and explicitly connected to the political, social, economic, and cultural changes of the past 35 years. A quick inventory of those changes includes the shift in advanced capitalist societies from manufacturing to service economies; the decline of the industrial working class; and the rise of the new right and the crisis of the left accompanying it. Most important is the increasing centrality of feminism, environmentalism, gay rights, antiracism, and various assertions of religious, national, and ethnic rights. In this emerging postmodern and globalized world, the rise of such politics has been inseparable from changes in how identity itself is understood. There has been a shift from perceiving identity as being fixed and stable to conceiving of it as multiple, hybrid, and in flux. Scholars in sociology and cultural studies have been in the forefront of theorizing many-sided notions of identity; historians have similarly argued that identities in the past are more complex than allowed for by class narratives. Scholars in all these fields have argued that individuals might belong to a class because of their structural location, and they may participate in practices that have been shaped by, or result in, class consciousness. Yet they are likewise defined and constructed by their gender, race, ethnicity, region, and nationality, among other things. Class is thus one form of identification among many: it can not be viewed in isolation and nor does it have a privileged status. Its resonance depends on the various forces in play in a given historical situation.

Second, a growing number of scholars have challenged the epistemological foundations of the class model and the broader understanding of society on which it is founded. Critical here has been the influence of the "linguistic turn," especially in cultural studies, history, and literary criticism. The linguistic turn is a shorthand description for several strands of structuralist and, most importantly, poststructuralist thought. It often, but not always, forms part of a postmodern sensibility. According to this position, language is not simply a reflection of human experience: it plays a constitutive role in constructing it. It challenges the notion that an objective structure gives rise to interests and ultimately particular forms of consciousness. In effect, the logic of the linguistic turn is to subvert the binary model's common sense. It is through the linguistic ordering of experience and consciousness that our understanding of our interests is derived in the first place. What we perceive as an objective structure turns out to be the effect of (what Cornelius Castoriadis calls) the "social imaginary." Poststructuralists advocate that we shift our emphasis from seeking to understand society to attempting to grasp how historical actors have come to represent it.

The implications of this thinking for social history have been particularly pronounced, for it challenges the very foundation on which the field is based. When their influence was paramount, social historians talked of producing "total history" based on a material understanding of society. In many ways that dream was in decline independent of the linguistic turn, as social history divided into countless subdisciplines. But the shift from the "social" to the "cultural" – from social to cultural history – speeded up this fragmentation, as many scholars shifted their attention to how historical actors produced meaning. As class was frequently the organizing category within social-history narratives, the ramifications of this trend in thinking for class theory and analysis were dramatic. Rather than class consciousness being conceived as ultimately rooted in an objectively verifiable structure, the new cultural history, where it emphasized it at all, saw class as having been produced by language and discourse; that is, it was ultimately a cultural construct, a form of representation.

The two critiques that I have sketched out are analytically distinct, but in practice they frequently overlap. This is particularly true in the case of feminist scholars who, influenced by poststructuralism, go beyond seeing identity as simply multidimensional. They view it as being produced by systems of difference, the product of language and culture and the power relations governing them (Joyce 1995a: 5). Accordingly, identity is continually made and remade, riddled by contradictions, never entirely stable. Such a notion undermines the tendency of social historians to view groups as coherent and fully formed with clearly articulated goals and aspirations. It also makes it possible to argue that culturally produced discursive systems create interwoven class and gender identities.

The road ahead

In the following chapters I elaborate on these critiques and their implications for scholarly work. My primary focus is on their impact in the field of history. Since other disciplines have played pivotal roles in elaborating postwar class theory, since they have been affected by the same kind of challenges, and since, in our increasingly interdisciplinary world, the lines between disciplines have become increasingly blurred, I look at other fields – notably sociology and cultural studies – as well. I explore various kinds of work: specialized studies that shed light on the theory of class, work that uses new theoretical ideas to think about class in original ways, and scholarly debates that provide opportunities to better appreciate what is at stake. My goal throughout is to allow readers the opportunity to make up their own minds about the importance of class to the contemporary humanities and social sciences, to develop their own understanding on whether – and if so how – it should be rethought. To this end, I have often let the major figures speak for themselves, while showing the limits of their thought by exploring critiques and discussions of their work. I have not hesitated to make my own views known when I think it is appropriate.

A few words about my position as a writer hopefully provide a context for what follows. Like so many historians of the left, reading E. P. Thompson

(1924–1983) changed my life. I am an intellectual (rather than a social) historian, and, as it turns out, it was not his *magnum opus*, *The Making of The English Working Class*, which first aroused my interest. It was his theoretically and historically informed critique of fellow British Marxists, Perry Anderson and Tom Nairn, "The Peculiarities of the English" ([1965] 1978) and the debate that surrounded it. I was drawn to Thompson's socialist humanism, cultural Marxism, political activism, utopian yearnings – in short, his sustained effort at fusing theory and practice. My interest in Thompson provided the impetus for my dissertation, published in revised form as *Cultural Marxism in Postwar Britain: History, the New Left and the Origins of Cultural Studies* (Dworkin 1997). Much of what I have to say about British left-wing scholars comes from this book.

How I originally imagined my dissertation project ended up bearing little resemblance to the end result. About half way through working on it, I attended a series of lectures in 1983 given by Stuart Hall (1932–), one of the pioneering figures in cultural studies, which affected me no less deeply than my first encounter with Thompson. Hall, himself influenced by Thompson, had developed a style of intellectual engagement that seemed (at least to me) appropriate to grappling with the tumultuous last decades of the twentieth century. His engagement with Marxism was, among other things, an adaptation of the ideas of Louis Althusser (1918–1990) and, especially, Antonio Gramsci (1891–1937). His work provided a space for creatively confronting the momentous intellectual and political shifts that were taking place: feminism, postmodernism and postmodernity, poststructuralism, multiculturalism, the new right, critical race theory, post-Marxism, postcolonial theory, globalization, and so forth. At the same time he was no less politically active than Thompson, although the form of his activism was different.

The point of this highly compressed and streamlined account of my intellectual trajectory is that I have been a fellow traveler to both social history and cultural studies: I have viewed them somewhat from a distance, from the perspective of an intellectual historian. In what follows I continue to write from this position. My goal is not simply to summarize historical and other scholarly writings and to encapsulate theoretical and historiographical debates. It is to write an intellectual history of the present that situates the new work on class within its historical context, although I am well aware that I lack the sources that historians often find in archives. I view class theory, and the assumptions on which it is based, as an important dimension of the representation of (what may be loosely conceived of as) modernity; but I also view it as part of the history that it seeks to understand. From this point of view, shifts in conceptions of class (and critiques of those conceptions) have been informed by broader economic, social, political, and cultural change. These shifts have also taken place as a result of intellectual argument that is internal to class discourse. In short, I see ideas about class and the reality that those ideas seek to describe and often transform as being deeply intermingled.

In conceiving of this intellectual history, I have embraced a broad view of what comprises the relevant body of work. This allows me, for instance, to look at scholarship on "subaltern" groups (see Chapter 8). The concept of the subaltern is in some ways a reworking of class in situations where modern industrial conditions are not predominant. It was originally used by Gramsci to understand social and political dynamics in rural Italy, and more recently by South Asian scholars to understand analogous circumstances within a colonial context (see below and Chapter 8). In addition, given that I look at class in relationship to other social and cultural dimensions – notably race and gender – it has been a challenge to discern the limits of my subject, since these other dimensions comprise extensive literatures on their own account. My goal has been to analyze texts and debates from the perspective of their importance for class theory and analysis, which sometimes entails an abbreviated, focused, and strategic exploration of them. Sometimes I have discussed work that tests the limits of class theory in order to better show what those limits in fact are.

Conceptions of class are, of course, deeply embedded in broader views of society and history, and thus to focus on them involves considering the status of the "social" in sociological and historical work. For historians, to think about these connections entails considering the trajectory of the new social history and the challenges it has faced. In what follows I am as interested in looking at how social history has fared as at the class model that often underpins it. As I am a British historian – and since British scholars have been so important to formulating class interpretations – British social and cultural history assumes a central position in my narrative. I also look beyond Britain, focusing (to various degrees) on scholarly work on France, India, Ireland, Latin America, and the United States. In the course of writing this book, I have been intellectually humbled, as I have discovered whole literatures of which I was barely aware and that I could hardly hope to master. Ironically, as I have extended my geographical reach, I have become more cognizant of the continuing importance of British cultural Marxists to scholarship inside and outside of Britain. Thompson's legacy, in particular, is a major theme of this book. At the same time, I am aware that British social and labor history – and British history more generally – no longer play nearly as central a role in historical discussions as they once did – in part the result of British decline and the decentering of

European historical narratives, including Marxist ones. My attempt at grappling with South Asian historiography signifies my acknowledgment of this trend. I have learned much from this encounter, but I certainly do not claim expertise.

In addition to this introduction, the book has eight chapters and a conclusion. It is divided into three sections. The first section consists of two chapters that provide a historical context for understanding current debates and trends. The first chapter explores the emergence of ideas about class in the eighteenth and nineteenth centuries, focusing on the ideas of Karl Marx and Max Weber (1864–1920) – the two most influential theorists of class. My principal goal here is for readers to better understand conceptions of class that provided the ground for future developments, setting "limits" and "pressures" on class theory. I argue that, though Marxist and Weberian approaches have been the two principal axes in class theory, they share common assumptions about the nature of the social. They distinguish between objective or structural relations and the subjective or group-related activities resulting from them. The second chapter centers on the reworking of class theory as embodied in post-World War II sociological studies that map class in conditions of postwar capitalism and in the new social history, notably history from below. As suggested earlier, I see these two trends as exploring different dimensions of the class structure–class consciousness model, while sharing implicit common assumptions about society as a whole.

The second section of the book focuses on postmodern and poststructuralist critiques of class interpretations. Chapter 3 provides an overview of the new intellectual and political landscape that produced these critiques, with particular reference to the challenges that they provided for Marxist-inspired scholarship. Chapters 4 and 5 both focus on historical writing. In Chapter 4 I look at the impact of cultural, linguistic, and other revisionist perspectives as they played themselves out in French history – concentrating on recent trends in nineteenth-century labor and French-revolutionary historiography.

Chapter 5, the book's longest, focuses on a more than 15-year debate prompted by Gareth Stedman Jones's essays collected in *Languages of Class: Studies in English Working Class History, 1832–1982* (1983), especially his reinterpretation of Chartism, the first working-class political movement on a national scale. Stedman Jones's work was pivotal to a broader challenge to Thompsonian social history as well as being crucial for scholars who embraced new cultural and political approaches. Another central figure in this chapter is the social-turned-cultural historian Patrick Joyce, who has been in the forefront of championing a postmodernist perspective in British history.

Joyce's importance has been to challenge historians to reconsider (in some cases consider) the epistemological assumptions of their work as well as to suggest an alternative model – what he calls the "history of the social." The understanding and relative importance of class is accordingly overhauled in the process.

Section three looks at efforts within history and cultural studies to examine class in relationship to other determinations and identities – notably gender, race, colonialism/postcolonialism, and nationality/nationalism. The relationship among these is deeply intertwined, so the chapter divisions are somewhat artificial. Chapter 6 traces the contribution of feminist historians – principally those that study Britain – to understanding class, from their original preoccupation with recovering the history of women, dominant in the 1970s, to their more recent explorations of gender relationships. I focus on Leonore Davidoff and Catherine Hall's historical treatment of class and gender in *Family Fortunes: Men and Women of the English Middle Class, 1780–1850* ([1987] 2002). I also pay close attention to the writings of Joan Scott. Her book, *Gender and the Politics of History* (1988), a poststructuralist critique of the new social history (including feminist versions of it), has been remarkably influential and controversial. I end the chapter by looking at scholarship that has used the notion that class is gendered to rethink the experience of the English/British working class, the privileged domain of the new labor history.

In Chapter 7 I look at the work of cultural-studies scholars and historians who have transformed our conception of the relationship between race and class, arguing that race is not reducible to an effect of exploitative productive relations and that class is mediated by racial struggles. The chapter includes a discussion of work produced within British cultural studies (Stuart Hall and Paul Gilroy) and American sociology (Michael Omi and Howard Winant). It looks at scholarship in American social and cultural history, notably Robin Kelley's contribution to the history of African-American radicalism and the African-American working class. And it explores the recent explosion in scholarship on "whiteness" in the United States, in which David Roediger – a social and cultural historian critical of Marxism's tendency to reduce race to class antagonisms – has been so pivotal.

The focal point of Chapter 8 is the connection between theories of class and the colonial/postcolonial experience. It is concerned primarily with the Subaltern Studies collective, a group of South Asian historians who, in the 1980s, sought an alternative to neocolonialist, nationalist, and orthodox Marxist understandings of the Indian past. These scholars produced a history of subalterns – a broader category than class yet conceived within Marxist class theory. Their original work extended British Marxist historical work on preindustrial societies. However, many of them also were drawn to poststructuralist and postcolonial theory: they explored the idea of the subaltern as a discursive construct and grappled with the Eurocentric nature of historical discourse. Although made up of historians, the Subaltern Studies group was more influential in fields outside of the historical discipline. Subaltern Studies has been particularly influential in literary and cultural studies. I look at these scholars' influence in Irish and Latin American studies.

Conclusion

What is most important for me about recent debates and scholarly contributions pertaining to class is their vitality. I have no doubt that historians, working in the tradition of the new social history, can continue to make valuable contributions without undergoing epistemological soul searching. I also believe that the various forms of critique, and the new directions of which they are harbingers, have enriched (rather than undermined) class theory and analysis, even if they force us to see class as a less certain, stable, and dominant phenomenon. Most important, while some may speak gloomily of the future of "class," I am impressed by the intellectual energy resulting from new ways of thinking, the innovative rethinking of settled positions, and the liveliness of recent discussions. Despite contentious and polarizing debates, there has been a group of scholars who have attempted to carve out positions that are intermediate. As the dust begins to settle, it might just be possible that a new conceptual space, bringing together the insights of social and cultural approaches to class, may be surfacing.

Section One

Classical foundations

Chapter 1

The making of class

In this chapter I discuss the idea of class from its ancient origins to its first modern usages. Most importantly, I examine the pioneering efforts of Karl Marx and Max Weber to theoretically articulate the idea of social class and place it within a broader understanding of society and history. By the time that Marx and Weber reflected on and deployed class in their work, they already had a body of meanings on which they could draw. Yet their ideas are not only fundamental to subsequent thinking about class but also important for assumptions about the nature of society and the social more generally. While they approached class from different points of view, Marx and Weber shared common assumptions: they believed that class was rooted in economic activity and that it played a pivotal role in shaping modern capitalist societies (Crompton 1998: 50). These two men helped establish the foundation for understanding structured inequality and its consequences – especially in its modern form. Since in recent debates, foundational concepts – such as class, society, and the social – have been called into question, it is important that we understand how they were framed in the first place.

Origins of an idea

"Class" comes from the Latin word *classis*, which had multiple meanings. It referred to either a ship or a navy (a definition without modern implications). It was also used to describe what the *Oxford English Dictionary* (*OED*) calls "a division of the scholars or students of an institution, receiving the same instruction or ranked together as of the same standing." This is the basis for the division of English grammar schools into "six forms" and for American university students belonging to the "freshman class" or the "class of 2006." From the point of view of social theory, the most important connotation of *classis* was its deployment to describe the division of the Roman people according to their age and property holdings. An early king of Rome, Servius Tullius, undertook this initiative, which divided society into six armies or bands. The highest-ranked group was the *Classici*, from which the later idea of "classic" developed. The Servian system was not based on divine law: it was a constructed system of difference and hierarchy, a hallmark of modern conceptions of class society.

The Roman understanding of class was slow to develop in English. According to the *OED*, class was first mentioned by Thomas Blount, a seventeenth-century English Catholic, who, in his *Glossographia*, which appeared in 1656, described it, among other things, as "an order or distribution of people according to their several Degrees." Blount had in mind Roman society rather than his own, however, which at the time was conceived as divinely ordained, consisting of various ranks and orders. A prevalent view was that society consisted of three estates – the clergy, the nobility, and the common people. Being part of an estate bestowed upon individuals specific qualities and legal rights, while each estate – in the words of Ferdinand Toennies, "like the organs or limbs of a body" – performed a unique function necessary for sustaining society (quoted in Calvert 1982: 45).

Whether class is conceived as an objective dimension of society and politics or as part of an emerging social imaginary or both, its materialization as a discourse is connected to a series of eighteenth- and nineteenth-century transformations – the Industrial Revolution, an expanding public sphere, growing urbanization, transformations in notions of political representation associated with the American and French Revolutions, and intensifying centralization and state power – changes that we often associate with the coming of modernity. Let's examine some of the principal meanings of class that developed, focusing on those that helped shape the language of classical social theory.

It was during the nineteenth century that the language of class achieved prominence, even if older social categorizations – rank, order, and station, for example – continued to be used and only gradually receded. As historians sensitive to how gender operated at the time have argued, this language, while speaking as if it pertained to all of society, represented the public world dominated by men, suppressing women's differential class experience. However, it was possible for the intertwined relationship of class and gender to manifest itself. This is clear from an extract of the diaries of A. J. Munby, who devoted himself to photographing working-class girls and had a long-term relationship with a domestic servant, Hannah Cullwick, whom he photographed in numerous class and gender roles and whom he married after a nearly twenty-year courtship. "In short, what, in the Equation of Life," he once wrote, "is the respective value of the terms *sex* and *station*[?]" (quoted in Davidoff [1979] 1995: 142).

Arguably the most influential representation of class in the public world is the tripartite division: upper, middle, and working classes. Yet, as Raymond Williams suggested, this way of dividing up society actually involves two concepts. On the one hand, the logical extension of "upper" and "middle" is a "lower" rather than a "working" class. On the other hand, a working class presupposes a nonworking other. Here, the division hinges on economic productivity: between productive and unproductive laborers – those who sell their labor power and those who exploit it.

We find both concepts of class articulated during this period. The tripartite conception (high, middle, and low) reworked and expanded upon older ways of conceiving social status, a notable innovation being the idea of the middle class(es). Penelope Corfield (1991) attributed the emergence of the middle class as a category – what Daniel Defoe referred to as "the middle station of life" – to social change and the perception of it: expanding forms of wealth other than land, the more conspicuous visibility of the middle rank, and the growing perception that greater wealth entailed a changing lifestyle. In contrast, Dror Wahrman (see Chapter 5) argued that politics, rather than the social process, helped bring about particular forms of understanding that produced the middle class as a central social category. He accordingly credited the Reform Bill of 1832 – a reform of the British parliamentary electoral system enfranchising a wide swathe of middle-class men – as "cementing" the middle class's "invention" as a social category (Wahrman 1995: 18). However the idea of the middle class as a key social description emerged, over time it was accorded an independent and elevated status by its supporters and defenders that proved influential, as when Henry Brougham stated in 1831: "by the people, I mean the middle classes, the wealth and intelligence of the country, the glory of the British name" (quoted in Williams 1983: 63). It was not long before the middle classes were conceived in the singular.

The second conception of class (that which hinged on productivity) developed in texts such as Constantin François de Volney's *The Ruins, or A Survey of the Revolution of Empires* (1795) – a French text widely read in English translation. Volney distinguished between two classes: "the people" – "labourers, artisans, tradesmen and every profession useful to society" – and the privileged or idle class of "priests, courtiers, public accountants, commanders of troops, in short, the civil, military or religious agents of government" (quoted in ibid.: 63). As it developed in England, this division of society had implications for the emerging working class(es), its demands for just compensation being based on the fruits of its labor. Historically, most social and labor historians have held that the fundamental expression of this division was in terms of capital and labor (Briggs [1960] 1985). Gareth Stedman Jones has challenged this idea, suggesting that Chartism – the first nationwide working-class political movement, its rallying cry universal manhood suffrage and electoral reform – typically deployed different language (see Chapter 5) (Stedman Jones 1983: 90–178). He argued that Chartists distinguished productive laborers from a rapacious and corrupt establishment of landowners, moneylenders, crooked officials, and capitalist middlemen. This fraudulent social and political order simultaneously oppressed laborers and honest masters.

If we allow that we can find in Chartist writings the deployment of language more reminiscent of Volney than of Marx, there were also those who attributed this polarizing social division to the opposition of capital and labor – both inside and outside the developing labor movement. Writing in 1834, Peter Gaskell observed:

> Since the Steam Engine has concentrated men into particular localities – has drawn together the population into dense masses – and since an imperfect education has enlarged, and to some degree distorted their views, union is become easy and from being so closely packed, simultaneous action is readily excited. The organisation of these [working-class] societies is now so complete that they form an "imperium in imperio" of the most obnoxious description . . . Labour and Capital are coming into collision – the operative and the master are at issue, and the peace, and well-being of the Kingdom are at stake (quoted in Briggs [1960] 1985: 16–17).

Furthermore, in the novel *Hard Times* ([1854] 2001), Charles Dickens manifested similar anxieties, portraying the manipulative union organizer Sleary as fomenting class warfare rather than the more desirable alternative of class harmony:

> Oh my friends, the down-trodden operatives of Coketown! Oh my friends and fellow countrymen, the slaves of an iron-handed and a grinding despotism! Oh my friends and fellow-sufferers, and fellow-workmen, and fellow-men! I tell you that the hour is come, when we must rally round one another as One united power, and crumble into dust the oppressors that too long have battened upon the plunder of our families, upon the sweat of our brows, upon the labor of our hands, upon the strength of our sinews, upon the God-created glorious rights of Humanity, and upon the holy and eternal privileges of Brotherhood (Dickens [1854] 2001: 106)!

Gaskell's and Dickens's observations are noteworthy because, though they opposed the militancy of the working-class movement, they privileged the class struggle no less than Marx. The latter's ideas were rooted in an already existing social imaginary rather than being spontaneously created like Athena out of the head of Zeus. It was a social imaginary that was far from neutral: it was replete with political connotations.

Here the manuscript breaks off . . .

The *Economist*'s lead article in its 2002 Christmas issue, "Marx after Communism" (*Economist* 2002), assesses Marx's legacy following the demise of the Soviet empire. The magazine is, of course, a zealous advocate of the free market; and, not surprisingly, it uses the article as an occasion to rehash old arguments regarding Marx's wrong-headedness. That it feels compelled to acknowledge a renewed interest in Marx, more than ten years following the collapse of a system that presumably relegated his ideas to the dustbin of history, speaks volumes. We are more recently reminded of Marx's continued relevance by a BBC Radio 4 survey, in which he was voted the greatest philosopher ever, receiving 28 percent of the 30,000 votes, defeating David Hume by a handy margin (Higgins 2005; Seddon 2005).

The *Economist* describes Marxism as a "broad church" that lives on. While its effort at linking Marxism to religion rather than science is meant to be uncomplimentary, there is more than a shred of truth to it. Like a broad church, Marxism is complex, contradictory, and heterogeneous. Its breadth is enormous. Undoubtedly, part of the antagonism towards Marxism is attributable to the tragic political practices associated with it. And like any major thinker, Marx has given rise to a tradition – Marxism – that has creatively read and misread him, frequently going beyond what he himself imagined. He has been appropriated and adapted, borrowed and stolen from, made and remade. Given the importance of Marxist social theory for class analysis, it is important that we begin by grappling with Marx himself.

Born in Germany, Karl Marx (1818–1884) was from a Jewish middle-class family that had a long line of rabbis on both sides. The Marx family converted to a Protestant domination, the Evangelical Established Church, before Marx's birth, probably to advance his father's professional career. While attending the University of Berlin, Marx was influenced by the philosopher Georg Wilhelm Friedrich Hegel (1770–1831), participated in the liberal and reformist Young Hegelian movement, and began his career as a political activist, editing the *Rheinische Zeitung*. After the government shut down the newspaper, Marx emigrated to Paris in 1843, where he became a revolutionary communist and met Friedrich Engels (1820–1895), who became his life-long friend and collaborator. To escape political reaction on the European continent, following the suppression of the 1848 revolutions, Marx moved to London, where he lived until his death. In London, Marx continued his career as a revolutionary activist and thinker. He helped found the International Working Men's Association, the first worldwide socialist organization, in 1864. He produced his unfinished, three-volume masterpiece of economic theory and political analysis, *Capital* (1867–1894). And he wrote numerous shorter political and historical essays.

In the 1859 preface to *A Contribution to the Critique of Political Economy* (henceforth referred to as the Preface), Marx recalled how he discovered the "guiding thread" of his intellectual project. He was nurtured in Hegelian philosophy, but he came to believe that the Hegelians had misconstrued the relationship between consciousness and society. Rather than viewing the evolution of law and the state as an autonomous realm or "the so-called general development of the human mind" as the Hegelians had, Marx concluded that they had their roots in "the material conditions of life." He described the totality of these conditions as "civil society" and argued that "the anatomy of civil society is to be sought in political economy" (Tucker 1978: 4).

Before discussing Marx's views on society and history, I want to make a couple of comments regarding his privileging of political economy and civil society. First, Marx subverted the categories of political economy, but he also was indebted to English and French thinkers, culminating in Adam Smith (1723–1790) and David Ricardo (1772–1823), who first fleshed out the fundamental importance of economic life. It is the early economists, beginning with the French Physiocrats, who first maintained that forms of production were responsible for shaping social relations and class divisions. Believing that agriculture was the only legitimate source of wealth, François Quesnay (1694–1774), economist and physician to Louis XV, saw social classes as arising from the fact that agricultural producers failed to receive the full benefit of their labor. In addition to the agricultural or productive class, there were two others: the class of landowners or proprietors and the sterile class, which he defined as "all the citizens who are engaged in providing other services or doing other work than that of agriculture, and whose expenses are paid by the productive class, and by the class of proprietors, which itself draws its revenue from the productive class" (quoted in Calvert 1982: 20). Similarly, Anne Robert Jacques Turgot (1727–1781), though not one of the Physiocrats *per se*, likewise believed that class divisions originated in the relationship of individuals to the productive process. And like them, he believed that workers of the land were the only real producers. However, Turgot pushed these ideas further, arguing that social divisions were founded on the unequal distribution of capital. Artisans (industrious but not productive) and agricultural producers were only compensated for their labor. A third class, the proprietors, transformed the surplus into accumulated capital as a consequence of investments made in agriculture and manufacturing. Marx believed that such insights did not get to the heart of the matter, but he clearly drew from them.

Second, neither Marx nor other thinkers responsible for exploring the world of civil society – whether John Locke (1632–1704), Jean-Jacques Rousseau (1712–1778), Adam Ferguson (1723–1815), or Hegel – discovered something that was simply out there. Civil society signifies the space of individual interaction between the realm of the family, on the one hand, and of the state, on the other. But it is not to be taken for granted. Here, I borrow generously from Keith Tester, who points out that the "civil" in "civil society," with its connotations of "civility" and "civilization," is being contrasted with the "primitive" and the "barbaric" (Tester 1992: 9). By the same token, the idea of society itself entails "nature" as an assumed other. Thus, "civil society" is produced through human effort in the course of history as well as an ideal that is furthered through the process of its articulation. Its development as a concept is itself part of the historical process that it seeks to describe. It is therefore inherently self-reflexive, a construction, created through an act of the imagination. As Tester aptly puts it, civil society – as society more broadly – is "only intelligible through the imaginative (non-natural, epistemologically synthetic) construction of categories which are used *as if* they were directly derived from something called reality" (ibid.: 14). While Marx undoubtedly would have found the idea that civil society was a product of the imagination foreign, it is not hard to see that he himself thought of it as a construction. He derived his idea of civil society from Hegel, who saw it as the post-feudal separation of society and state, but Marx went beyond this, seeing it as being historically produced by the bourgeoisie. For Marx, as for Engels, civil society was not merely a description of what existed but was, to cite Tester again, an "emergent condition," historically conditioned, and transient. "Marx examines civil society and sees it as a valley of tears and shadows, and the tossing of man into a cauldron of selfishness where each individual struggles against others to meet material needs. He uses man as man is to look forward to man as man should be" (ibid.: 20).

Marx anatomized civil society within the framework of his philosophy of history – historical materialism. For him, the historical process consisted of a series of epochs, each defined by its dominant mode of production. The mode of production coincided with (what we would call) economic life and played a crucial role in defining human existence:

> This mode of production must not be considered simply as being the repro-
> duction of the physical existence of the individuals. Rather it is a definite
> form of activity of these individuals, a definite form of expressing their life,
> a definite *mode of life* on their part. As individuals express their life, so they
> are. What they are, therefore, coincides with their production, both with
> *what* they produce and with *how* they produce. The nature of individuals
> thus depends on the material conditions determining their production
> (Tucker 1978: 150).

Modes of production were made possible by the development of the productive forces (materials, tools, and labor), but they were founded on the "social
relations of production"; that is, the patterns of ownership and control in a
given society.

According to Marx, in any given historical epoch, the relations of production at first facilitated the growth of the productive forces. But they eventually
came into conflict with them and hindered their development. The continued
growth of the productive forces was contingent upon the surfacing of new
relations, which evolved in the bosom of the old society but only became dominant as a consequence of a revolutionary transformation. Marx viewed the
interaction between the forces and the relations as taking place in all historical
epochs. Yet his understanding of their dynamic relationship was founded on
a specific case – the transition from feudalism to capitalism. The revolutions
in seventeenth-century England and eighteenth-century France constituted
the pivotal upheavals that broke the back of feudal society and ushered in the
bourgeois capitalist era.

For Marx, the relations of production played a "determining" role in shaping
the institutions and ideas of society. He used an image derived from design to
conceive of the connection between them: "The sum total of these relations of
production constitutes the economic structure of society, the real foundation,
on which rises a legal and political superstructure and to which correspond
definite forms of social consciousness. The mode of production of material life
conditions the social, political and intellectual life process in general" (ibid.: 4).
In what amounts to an inversion of the Hegelian privileging of consciousness,
Marx stated that transformations in the relations of production (the economic
structure) were responsible for corresponding shifts in the superstructure:
"With the change of the economic foundation the entire immense superstructure is more or less rapidly transformed" (ibid.: 5). Economic transformations,

rather than law, politics, religion, aesthetics, and philosophy – the ideological expressions through which people manifested their consciousness of these transformations – elucidated the real movement of history.

Marx's conception of the social formation, as described here, commonly referred to as the "base–superstructure" model, is one of his most original, influential, flawed, and controversial ideas. It is the foundation of Marxist cultural theory, although ironically Marx himself never claimed that culture was part of the superstructure. Rather, subsequent Marxist thinkers believed that Marx's description of the superstructure logically included it. The base–superstructure model has subsequently given rise to wide-ranging debates, not least because many have viewed it as being rigidly deterministic, static, and reductive; as paying insufficient attention to human agency; and as failing to appreciate either the potential autonomy or the causal impact of the superstructure itself.

Yet before rejecting it on such grounds, it is important to consider that elsewhere Marx (and Engels) demonstrated a more complex understanding of the historical process and the social dynamics underpinning it. For instance, in an often quoted passage in *The Eighteenth Brumaire of Louis Bonaparte*, published in 1852, Marx wrote: "Men make their own history, but they do not make it just as they please; they do not make it under circumstances chosen by themselves, but under circumstances directly found, given and transmitted from the past. The tradition of all the dead generations weighs like a nightmare on the brain of the living" (ibid.: 595). This formulation suggested a more nuanced understanding of historical actors' capacity to shape their destiny than contained in the Preface. It likewise recognized that historical moments were produced by numerous determinations, not just the dominant mode of production. In addition, Engels, in a famous letter to Joseph Bloch, written in 1890, asserted that he and Marx never meant to say that economic relations alone shaped historical outcomes. They might constitute "the *ultimately* determining element in history," but the superstructure likewise played an influential role. Engels's warning that a rigid and mechanical application of Marx's historical materialism "would be easier than the solution of a simple equation of the first degree" now seems prophetic, given the simplistic versions of Marxism that triumphed in the Soviet-dominated, orthodox Communist movement (ibid.: 760–61).

Marx does not make it easy for us to decipher his views on class. In the Preface, arguably the most succinct articulation of historical materialism, he does not concern himself with class structure and class struggle. In fact, "class" is not mentioned at all there, aside from references to specific groups, for instance the ruling class. What is more, there is no place in the entire body of Marx's work where he ever defines what he means by class. In the unfinished third volume of *Capital*, edited by Engels and published after Marx's death, there is a subheading called "Classes"; and Marx asks the question: "What constitutes a class?" After just five paragraphs the section ends abruptly followed by an insertion by Engels: "Here the manuscript breaks off" (ibid.: 441–42). There is no doubt that class is a central category in Marx's work. In fact, it is everywhere. It is just not systematically addressed, which provides us with all kinds of challenges as readers.

In response to this theoretical lacuna, commentators inevitably acknowledge that Marx's theory of class must be constructed rather than discovered. A good place to start is the short fragment before "the manuscript breaks off." In this text Marx discussed class in two ways. First, he used it to describe groups produced by the relations of production: "The owners merely of labour-power, owners of capital, and landowners, whose respective sources of income are wages, profit and ground-rent, in other words, wage-labourers, capitalists and landowners, constitute then three big classes of modern society based upon the capitalist mode of production" (ibid.: 441). Marx did not assert that these were the only classes, only that they were the "big classes." (This formulation is at variance with the assertion in *The Communist Manifesto* [1848] that capitalist social relations produced two main classes – the bourgeoisie and the proletariat.) Marx attributed the development of these classes to the historical logic of capital. He defined it as follows:

> the continual tendency and law of development of the capitalist mode of production is more and more to divorce the means of production from labour and more and more to concentrate the scattered means of production into large groups, therefore transforming labour into wage-labour and the means of production into capital. And to this tendency, on the other hand, corresponds the independent separation of landed property from capital and labour, or the transformation of all landed property into the form of landed property corresponding to the capitalist mode of production (ibid.: 441).

Second, Marx acknowledged that this understanding of class operated at a level of abstraction that did not necessarily correspond to that which was historically specific. As he stated it: "In England, modern society is indisputably more highly and classically developed in economic structure. Nevertheless, even here the stratification of classes does not appear in its pure form. Middle and intermediate strata even here obliterate lines of demarcation everywhere (although incomparably less in rural districts than in the cities)" (ibid.: 441).

Marx thus not only acknowledged that class in practice deviated from its "pure form" but also implied that great variation was possible. Even though England was the historical case on which the model was founded, in its cities, where a more complex division of labor existed than in the countryside, classes were less likely to conform to it. Marx thus suggested that class in the social world as lived and experienced was complex and frequently ambiguous. However, he did not specifically address the numerous elements that produced these historically specific classes. He stated that the three great classes were distinguished on the basis of their livelihood – labor power, capital, or landed property. Yet he admitted that this criterion yielded any number of classes. He gave the examples of doctors or officials. Whether Marx become distracted or frustrated or stymied is unclear. But this is the point at which the fragment ends.

What emerges from it though is a multilayered conception. On the one hand, class refers to the objective relations that individuals enter into independent of their will, arising from the social relations of production. On the other hand, it entails the more ambiguous and untidy world of everyday life, where other determinations play their role. In *Capital*, which recasts the categories of political economy and, in crucial respects, holds historical specificity in abeyance, Marx finds this second understanding of class "immaterial." It becomes more central when he grapples with the numerous levels of the historical process.

Let's turn our attention to these more historically specific writings. In *The Communist Manifesto* Marx argued for the universality and privileged position of class struggles in history. In his words: "The history of all hitherto existing society is the history of class struggles" (ibid.: 473). We have already seen that social theorists as early as the French Physiocrats regarded class divisions as a key dimension of the social formation, while nineteenth-century English writers envisioned a deepening class conflict. And Marx himself never claimed that he was the first to proclaim the centrality of class and class struggle. "Long before me," he wrote, "bourgeois historians had described the historical development of the struggle of classes, and bourgeois economists the economic anatomy of the classes" (quoted in Calvert 1982: 84).

Marx's understanding of class struggle bore the imprint of Claude Henri de Rouvroy, Comte de Saint-Simon (1760–1825), a founding father of sociology and an early theoretician of socialism. Saint-Simon situated class struggles within a macro view of history. He believed that societies were driven by their own internal dynamic, passing through periods of growth, maturity, and decline. He saw his own age as a period of transition where remnants of feudalism persisted and the new industrial society had not yet achieved dominance. The result was conflicts between the new manufacturing and the old feudal classes.

Sometimes Saint-Simon saw capitalists and proletariats as forming different classes. At other times he regarded them as forming a separate industrial class distinct from those clinging to feudal privilege. The triumph of this industrial class ultimately meant the advent of a classless society (Giddens 1975: 14–15). Marx saw the transition from feudalism to capitalism similarly. Yet he privileged capitalism, rather than industrialism, and hence rejected the idea of an industrial class made up of capitalists and workers. In *The Communist Manifesto* Marx argued that there were two major classes in capitalist society: the bourgeoisie, who owned and controlled the means of production, and the proletariat, who possessed only their labor power and were thus compelled to sell it to sustain themselves.

Marx viewed the class struggle as the central narrative in history:

> Freemen and slave, patrician and plebeian, lord and serf, guild-master and journeyman, in a word, oppressor and oppressed, stood in constant opposition to one another, carried on an uninterrupted, now hidden, now open fight, a fight that each time ended, either in a revolutionary re-constitution of society at large, or in the common ruin of the contending classes (Tucker 1978: 473–74).

At first glance this formulation is crude. Writing to inspire proletarian political action, in the full flush of the 1848 revolutions, Marx placed working people at the center of a historical epic: a war between two armies – the ruling class and the oppressed. However, such confrontations were infrequent at best, even in revolutionary situations. Marx seemed aware that this notion of bipolar struggle needed qualifying, for he portrayed it as "hidden" as well as "open." He likewise admitted that only during the "epoch of the bourgeoisie" did class antagonisms reach such a polarized state:

> In the earlier epochs of history, we find almost everywhere a complicated arrangement of society into various orders, a manifold gradation of social rank. In ancient Rome we have patricians, knights, plebeians, slaves; in the Middle Ages, feudal lords, vassals, guild-masters, journeymen, apprentices, serfs; in almost all of these classes, again, subordinate gradations (ibid.: 474).

As in the fragment from *Capital*, Marx conceived of class at different levels of abstraction, distinguishing the pure form of class struggle from its manifestation in specific historical contexts. At the same time, in *The Communist Manifesto* there is an homologous fit between economic and political change, a fit that political events following the defeat of the 1848 revolutions would prove difficult to justify.

We learn a great deal regarding Marx's understanding of class in historical situations from his analysis of the major political events of his day – the French Revolution of 1848, the coup d'état of Louis Bonaparte, the Paris Commune of 1870, and so forth. Marx understood these events from the point of view of his pure model, but he never succumbed to the simplistic notion that their meaning could simply be deduced from it. He developed a more nuanced understanding of the many determinations operating in a given historical situation. Engels reiterated this when he wrote to Bloch:

> The economic situation is the basis, but the various elements of the super-structure: political forms of the class struggle and its results, to wit: constitutions established by the victorious class after a successful battle, etc., juridical forms, and then even the reflexes of all these actual struggles in the brains of the participants, political, juristic, philosophical theories, religious views and their further development into systems of dogmas, also exercise their influence upon the course of the historical struggles and in many cases preponderate in determining their *form*. There is an interaction of all these elements in which, amid all the endless host of accidents (that is, of things and events, whose inner connection is so remote or so impossible of proof that we can regard it as non-existent, as negligible) the economic movement finally asserts itself as necessary (ibid.: 760–61).

The Eighteenth Brumaire of Louis Bonaparte, published in 1852, is a compelling example of what Engels had in mind. Marx grappled with the dramatic defeat of the working-class movement in the French Revolution of 1848, as well as seeking to understand why Napoleon's nephew, Louis Bonaparte, an outsider to the struggle between the bourgeoisie and the proletariat, politically triumphed. Marx argued that working-class defeat in June 1848 "haunts the subsequent acts of the drama like a ghost." The working-class movement was decimated by the betrayal of its middle-class allies, the incarceration of its leaders, and political repression. As the bourgeoisie lashed out at its enemies, its unity fragmented, and the basis of its regime disintegrated. Bonaparte came to power on the backs of the lumpenproletariat, a class that Marx scorned, describing it as the "scum, offal, refuse of all classes":

> Alongside decayed *roués* [a lecherous dissipated man] with dubious means of subsistence and of dubious origin, alongside ruined and adventurous offshoots of the bourgeoisie, were vagabonds, discharged soldiers, discharged jailbirds, escaped galley slaves, swindlers, mountebanks, *lazzaroni* [declassed lumpenproletariat], pickpockets, tricksters, gamblers, maquereaus [procurers], brothel keepers, porters, *literati*, organ-grinders,

rag-pickers, knife grinders, tinkers, beggars – in short, the whole indefinite, disintegrated mass, thrown hither and thither, which the French term *la bohème*; . . . (Marx and Engels 1969: 442).

Marx's hostility towards the lumpenproletariat anticipated (and helped shape) the later disdain that many traditional Marxists felt for the counterculture of the 1960s and 1970s and the identity politics that it helped pioneer. It likewise foreshadowed the later theoretical difficulties that many Marxists would have in incorporating marginalized groups that did not fit into its production-oriented view of society and hence did not conform to its understanding of political resistance, fashioned in the image of the industrial proletariat.

Why did the conflict between the bourgeoisie and the proletariat end up producing a regime that, as Marx admitted, "seems to be settled in such a way that all classes, equally impotent and equally mute, fall on their knees before the club" (Tucker 1978: 606)? In other words, why did the class struggle produce such an unforeseen result? Marx gave a twofold answer. First, Bonaparte's support came from the largest class, the French peasantry. The peasants lacked the political organization to represent themselves. They could only be represented.

Their representative must at the same time appear as their master, as an authority over them, as an unlimited governmental power that protects them against the other classes and sends them the rain and the sunshine from above. The political influence of the small peasants, therefore, finds its final expression in the executive power subordinating society to itself (ibid.: 608).

Second, the bourgeoisie may have been politically defeated, but Bonaparte saved them from themselves. His regime preserved the interest of capital at a moment of acute political crisis. "After the *coup d'état*," Marx wrote, "the French bourgeoisie cried: Only the chief of the Society of December 10 can now save bourgeois society! Only theft can now save property; only perjury, religion; only bastardy, the family; only disorder, order" (ibid.: 614).

Marx's understanding of Louis Bonaparte's rise to power thus explores those very ambiguities of class relationships and those very historical contingencies that he bracketed off in *Capital*. It confronts the fact that intermediate social groups, parties, factions, and the state must all be taken into account. Their role in historical outcomes cannot be reduced to class interest in any simple way. Elsewhere in the same text, Marx's ability to confront social complexity is evidenced in his theoretical reflections on the peasantry's class status. The peasants shared a common way of life, but their mode of production hindered the growth of the division of labor, their productive forces, and collective social relationships. They consisted of a "simple addition of homologous magnitudes." Marx likened the peasants to a sack of potatoes, since as a totality they were no more than the sum of their parts. At one level they formed a class: "In so far as millions of families live under economic conditions of existence that divide their mode of life, their interests and their culture from those of the other classes, and put them in hostile contrast to the latter, they form a class" (ibid.: 608). At the same time they did not possess class consciousness and in a sense were not a class at all: "In so far as there is merely a local interconnection among these small peasants, and the identity of their interests begets no unity, no national union and no political organisation, they do not form a class" (ibid.: 608).

Marx's contention that the peasantry *did* and *did not* form a class is only an apparent contradiction. As a result of their common relationship to the means of production, the peasants formed (what Marx called elsewhere) a "class in itself." These objective relations likewise hindered the growth of class consciousness and political action, that is, "class for itself." Marx thus defined class both as a structural location and as the various forms of consciousness – organizations, parties, movements – that were likely to be produced from collectively experiencing that location.

The working class's relationship to its location on the class map could not have been more different than the peasantry's:

> Economic conditions first transformed the mass of the people of the country into workers. The combination of capital has created for this mass a common situation, common interests. The mass is thus already a class as against capital, but not yet for itself. In the struggle, of which we have noted only a few phases, this mass becomes united, and constitutes itself as a class for itself. The interests it defends become class interests. But the struggle of class against class is a political struggle (ibid.: 218).

Massed in factories and densely populated urban neighborhoods, the working class's mode of life lent itself towards shared forms of consciousness, organization, and struggle. Marx was confident that his reading of historical trends guaranteed that these struggles would result in the working class's political triumph. He believed that he had demonstrated "that the class struggle necessarily leads to the *dictatorship of the proletariat*"; and he was convinced that he had shown "that this dictatorship itself only constitutes the transition to the *abolition of all classes* and to a *classless society*" (quoted in Calvert 1982: 84). Yet Marx was likewise aware that these struggles were sometimes "open," sometimes "hidden," that they were mediated and shaped by politics and ideology, and that in practice they deviated from the "pure" abstract model. Ultimately, class struggle revealed itself in the laboratory of history.

Class, status, party

As I was preparing to write this section, I came across a relevant article in the *New York Times*. Entitled "Forget Lonely. Life is Healthy at the Top," it discusses the work of a group of British and American researchers who argue that social status – not just money, education, nutrition, and so forth – is a major indicator of the health and life expectancy of individuals. Sir Michael Marmot, a British epidemiologist and a leading researcher in the field, attributes this to the "psychological" impact of inequality: "Your position in the hierarchy very much relates to how much control you have over your life and your opportunities for full social engagement" (quoted in Cohen 2004). Aside from the important theoretical and empirical issues that this trend in research raises, I was struck by its intellectual debt to Max Weber (1864–1920), who powerfully shaped the modern understanding of social inequality, conceiving it in terms of "class" and "social status." Weber's ideas have not been nearly as influential on historians as they have on sociologists. They are worth recounting, for they have surfaced as the major alternative to Marx, while at the same time being indebted to him as well.

Weber was from a bourgeois background and part of the German academic elite. He held positions at universities in Berlin, Freiburg, Heidelberg, and Munich. An intellectual of enormous erudition and scholarly productivity, he suffered from consistently poor health, eventually being forced to give up his post at Heidelberg, following a mental illness precipitated by the death of his father. Weber made contributions to economic history, comparative sociology, and the study of religion. He helped shape the emerging field of sociology, defining it as a value-free discipline based on the comparative method and the use of ideal types. He was active in politics as well. A left liberal, he helped draft the 1919 constitution of the Weimar Republic just prior to his death.

Weber was influenced by Marxist thought, yet he simultaneously criticized it as well. He endorsed Marx's contention that economic structures and transformations helped shape social and political outcomes, but he believed that this was only part of the story. In *The Protestant Ethic and the Spirit of Capitalism* ([1920] 1976), he sought to show how the values of Protestant worldly asceticism shaped modern capitalist society. His broader vision maintained that political, military, and administrative structures had important determining effects on historical outcomes. For Weber, Marx's thought was not materialist enough. As Hans Girth and C. Wright Mills stated:

> Part of Weber's own work may thus be seen as an attempt to "round out" Marx's economic materialism by a political and military materialism . . . This attention to the control of the material means of political power is as crucial for grasping the types of political structure as is attention to the means of production in the case of Marx for grasping economic structures (Gerth and Mills [1946] 1958: 47).

Both Marx and Weber grappled with what made capitalism unique, but they offered different answers. Weber accepted Marx's contention that capitalism was based on wage labor and the intensification of market relationships. However, he viewed this process more broadly, as part of the sweeping rationalization of the organization of human life. In this, he equated the worker's loss of control over his/her means of production with the supplanting of informal modes of administration by the impersonal procedures of the modern bureaucratic state. In short, economic shifts were one dimension of a more thoroughgoing transformation.

Whereas Marx believed that a socialist transformation was an outcome of the logic of history and would put an end to an oppressive state apparatus and economic system, Weber regarded socialism more contingently, as a real but not immediate possibility. He viewed it, with its emphasis on centralized planning, as extending the rationalizing process and producing further bureaucratic expansion. That Weber regarded the drift of modernization with dismay can be gleaned from his conclusion to *The Protestant Ethic and the Spirit of Capitalism*. He portrayed "the technical and economic conditions of machine production which to-day determine the lives of all individuals who are born into this mechanism, not only those directly concerned with economic acquisition" as an "iron cage." And of this "last stage of cultural development" he wrote: "Specialists without spirit, sensualists without heart; this nullity imagines that it has attained a level of civilization never before achieved" (Weber [1920] 1976: 181–82).

Weber's thinking about class bore the imprint of Marxist theory. Like Marx, Weber distinguished between class as a structure and as a form of consciousness and action. However, he believed that a purely contingent relationship existed between what he called the "class situation" and "class politics":

> That men in the same class situation regularly react in mass actions to such tangible situations as economic ones in the direction of those interests that

are most adequate to their average number is an important and after all sim-ple fact for the understanding of historical events. However, this fact must not lead to that kind of pseudo-scientific operation with the concepts of class and class interests which is so frequent these days and which has found its most classic expression in the statement of a talented author, that the individual may be in error concerning his interests but that the class is infallible about its interests (Joyce 1995a: 34).

Weber's critique seems more apropos to reductive forms of Marxism than to Marx himself, which complicates the relationship between Marx's and Weber's thought. As Anthony Giddens suggests:

> What is often portrayed in the secondary literature as a critique of "Marx's conception of class" actually takes a stilted and impoverished form of crude Marxism as its main target of attack. But this sort of determinist Marxism was already current in Germany in Weber's lifetime, and since Weber himself set out to question this determinism, the true lines of similarity and difference between his and Marx's analysis of classes are difficult to disentangle (Giddens 1975: 42).

Weber's writings on history and society are fragmentary and incomplete. At the time of his death, he left behind a considerable body of unfinished work that was subsequently edited and published by his students. When it came to class, however, Weber explicitly defined it, although not necessarily consist-ently. In one context he defined classes as being produced by existing eco-nomic relationships, but he did not see them as having consciousness or being active groups: "'classes' are not communities; they merely represent possible, and frequent, bases for social action" (Joyce 1995a: 31). However, elsewhere he regarded "class status" as being defined not only by the "external condition of life" but also by the "subjective satisfaction or frustration" that "is pos-sessed by an individual or a group" (quoted in Calvert 1982: 96). Here, at least, he regarded a class as being simultaneously defined by objective and subjective components, though still not as constituting a group.

Weber offered three criteria by which classes were defined: "(1) a number of people have in common a specific causal component of their life chances, insofar as (2) this component is represented exclusively by economic interests in the possession of goods and opportunities for income, and (3) is repre-sented under the conditions of the commodity or labor markets" (Joyce 1995a: 31–32). Whereas Marx viewed classes as being rooted in productive relations, Weber regarded them as being entrenched in the sale of property or services and the returns that they produced. Thus, for Weber, the market defined class relationships. "But always this is the generic connotation of the concept of class: that the kind of chance in the *market* is the decisive moment which presents a common condition for the individual's fate. Class situation is, in this sense, ultimately market situation" (ibid.: 32–33).

In contrast to Marx's contention that capitalist social relations produced a limited number of classes, Weber's more elastic view allowed for numerous class positions. Yet this potential proliferation was undercut by what he described as "social class" – the interconnection of various classes whose level of mobility in the marketplace was roughly equivalent. In all, Weber identified four main social classes: the working class, the petty bourgeoisie, white-collar workers, and a highly educated and privileged propertied class. He further designated the working class, white-collar workers, and the privileged class as being the most important of these.

What is more, rather than believing that the class structure will become simpler over time, Weber believed that classes would become more fragmented, diffuse, and numerous. Anthony Giddens offers two examples of what Weber had in mind (Giddens 1975: 47). First, trade unions' ability to limit the number of workers with specific marketable skills produced divisions within the working class, lending itself to fragmentation. Second, and most important, an ever-expanding bureaucracy meant a higher percentage of non-manual workers in the labor force with different class interests than manual workers, thus producing further impediments to unified action.

Weber's reflections on class were deeply intertwined with his ideas about "status." He did not argue that class was unique to capitalism, only that in earlier societies status was typically the basis for social hierarchy and that it existed (in competition with class) under modern capitalist conditions as well:

> In contrast to classes, *Stände* (*status groups*) are normally groups. They are, however, often of an amorphous kind. In contrast to the purely economic-ally determined "class situation," we wish to designate as *status situation* every typical component of the life of men that is determined by a specific, positive or negative, social estimation of *honor* (Joyce 1995a: 36).

Where class referred to objective situations and need not lead to group awareness and action, status by definition involved interpersonal subjectivity. It was "normally expressed by the fact that above all else a specific *style of life* is expected from all those who wish to belong to the circle. Linked with this expectation are restrictions on social intercourse (that is, intercourse which is not subservient to economic or any other purposes" (ibid.: 36–37). It brought privileges with it but also responsibilities. According to Weber, the most extreme form of a status system was one defined by "caste": it achieved legitimacy not only through tradition and law but also through religious sanctions.

What is the relationship between class and status? Weber's main point was not that class and status systems were incompatible or unrelated: indeed they could be deeply intertwined. It was that one or the other was likely to prevail in a given situation. Thus, in a precapitalist society, where rank was determined by noneconomic factors, status frequently conveyed a privileged access to goods and property. Yet a society founded on a status system was unlikely to develop free competition and market relationships. Correlatively, in a society where the market system prevailed, status groups found themselves under threat, as "the social estimation of honor" played a diminishing role in the distribution of wealth. Weber generalized regarding the circumstances under which a class or a status system was likely to prevail:

> When the bases of the acquisition and distribution of goods are relatively stable, stratification by status is favored. Every technological repercussion and economic transformation threatens stratification by status and pushes the class situation into the foreground. Epochs and countries in which the naked class situation is of predominant significance are regularly the periods of technical and economic transformations. And every slowing down of the change in economic stratification leads, in due course, to the growth of status structures and makes for a resuscitation of the important role of social honor (ibid.: 39).

It is unclear whether Weber believed that capitalism by its very nature continually transformed itself and thus was always likely to breed a class system, or whether he conceived of a time when this economic system would eventually produce forms of hierarchy more characteristic of a status system.

For Weber then, class and status systems were different but entangled forms of the distribution of power. A third dimension of power that interested him was political parties. As opposed to class and status groups, parties always involved association. They represented goal-oriented activity, whether it was the actualization of an ideology or the establishment of a patronage system. Parties were based on either class or status or a combination of the two. They might even be immune to the influence of both. Once again, Weber's understanding of the relationship between class, status, and parties highlights his distance from Marx. For if Marx never assumes an automatic relationship between political parties and the class structure, he views class relationships as defining the environment in which a party or parties operate.

Conclusion

Marx's and Weber's ideas on class therefore, like their views on society and history more generally, are notably different. Where Marx situated class relationships and class struggle within a philosophy of history, Weber rejected philosophies of history altogether. For Weber, classes were derived from market (as opposed to productive) relationships, which were not nearly as likely to produce group consciousness and action. Status rather than class was frequently more likely to have consequences for group behavior. Most important, where Weber's views were to play an important role in shaping our ideas about modern society, Marx's ideas – via the Marxist tradition's simultaneous contributions to theoretical analysis and political and economic transformation – were a historical force in their own right. As Gramsci stated it, Marxism was itself part of the superstructure: "it is the terrain on which determinate social groups become conscious of their own social being, their own strength, their own tasks, their own becoming" (Forgacs 1988: 196). In other words, Marxism simultaneously understood and transformed the world, which meant that the political stakes in theoretical discussions over the Marxist theory of class were always close at hand.

Yet if Marx and Weber approached class from different perspectives, they also shared common assumptions. They believed that class was rooted in economic activity and that it played a pivotal role in shaping modern capitalist societies. They laid the groundwork for understanding structured inequality and its consequences – especially in the context of modernity. Their achievement reworked a class vocabulary that first surfaced during the eighteenth century and by Marx's time constituted an influential social imaginary. As I have suggested, the idea of civil society itself was a crucial part of this imagined world. From this point of view, the view of society contained in Marx was always something of a construction.

Most important, Marx's and Weber's thinking about class was dualistic: they distinguished between objective or structural relations and the subjective or group-related activities associated with them. Subsequent writers placed greater weight on one or the other of these. But it was this dualistic model that inspired post-World War II sociological investigations and the new social history. It was likewise the model that has recently given rise to controversies and challenges.

Chapter 2
_____

Class and class consciousness

In the 1960s and 1970s, historians and sociologists pursued new directions in class theory and analysis. In sociology a small contingent of scholars had pursued class analysis prior to the 1960s. They were joined by a new generation who believed that society was grounded in structural inequalities and conflicts and regarded class as being produced by social relationships that can be understood via the employment structure. Within history, a contingent of historians associated with the "new" social and labor history pioneered new directions in class analysis. Building on older traditions of left-wing scholarship, often enthusiastic about social-scientific ways of thinking, and inspired by the politics of the emerging new left, they developed a highly influential mode of historical understanding, which captured the imagination of more than a generation of scholars. Their ultimate goal was to produce total history, while some of the most notable figures among them were committed to "a history from below," written from a bottom-up perspective.

The historical and sociological investigations discussed in this chapter were responsible for helping produce an enormous body of work in numerous fields and subfields and influenced other disciplines in the social sciences and the humanities as well. The majority of historians would probably reject the idea that either social history or the class narrative provides a key to the historical process as a whole. Sociologists are divided regarding the relevance of class in today's society. Indeed, there are scholars in both of these disciplines who question whether class remains a useful concept at all. Yet the scholarship discussed here remains the point of departure for contemporary approaches to class analysis as well as being a continual point of reference for current debates. Despite important disciplinary differences, historians and sociologists shared a dualistic conception of class founded on the distinction between social being and social consciousness, and they held to a constructionist view of the relationship between theory and evidence.[1]

Mapping class

My aim in this section is to sketch out some of the main features of post-World War II sociological studies of class. I do this by considering two types of contribution to what by any definition is a vast quantity of theoretical and empirical work: the neo-Weberian approach of John Goldthorpe (1935–) and David Lockwood (1929–) and the structural Marxist approach of Erik Olin Wright (1947–). I consider the contributions of these sociologists to class theory, situating their work in its historical context and in relationship to the intellectual and political debates in which it was constituted.

There are good reasons for discussing Goldthorpe and Lockwood in tandem. As lecturers in the Department of Applied Economics at Cambridge in the 1960s, they collaborated on an ambitious research project on affluent workers. Funded by the forerunner of the Social Science Research Council, the research resulted in numerous articles and papers, culminating in a monumental three-volume study, beginning with *The Affluent Worker in the Class Structure* (Goldthorpe *et al.* 1969). Lockwood himself gives us a glimpse into the closeness of this collaboration: "John Goldthorpe and I have worked together so closely on the wider problem of which this paper is a part that I find it difficult to say where my thoughts end and his begin" (Lockwood 1966: 262).

Goldthorpe and Lockwood's analysis of class developed in an intellectual and political atmosphere initially inhospitable to it. In the 1950s sociology was dominated by an "orthodox consensus" that, despite claims to objectivity and detachment, was politically motivated. Under the spell of the unprecedented capitalist boom of the 1950s and 1960s, it took the postwar settlement of Western industrial states – the mixed economy and the welfare state – as the universal norm of history. While it spoke in terms of "the end of ideology," it was oblivious to its own neoliberal foundations. The consensus had three principal components (Crompton 1998: 25; Giddens 1982: 1–3). First, sociology was positivist (or constructionist); that is, it derived general laws from empirically verifiable facts. Second, it was functionalist: it viewed society as a social system with an intrinsic tendency to cohere through a process of normative integration. Third, sociologists believed that economically advanced societies – capitalist or communist – would eventually converge. This viewpoint, "pluralistic industrialism," was conceived as a theoretical alternative to Marxism.

Within the parameters of the orthodox consensus, class theory had little place. It was historically connected to ways of thinking that privileged conflict. Marxism, class theory's most developed form, was regarded as dogmatic and tainted by its association with totalitarianism. It is true that, under Stalinism, Marxist theory had atrophied into a inflexible system, closed off from the kind of intellectual debate necessary for creative development, although not as completely as is usually assumed. Most importantly, whereas Marxists considered class struggle as the precondition for an egalitarian society, functionalists and neoliberals believed in a society stressing the equality of access – not the equality of outcomes associated with socialism.

The orthodox consensus dominated sociology as well as, to some degree, the social sciences in general. Yet it never went uncontested. There was a minority of sociologists who believed that structural inequalities tended to produce instability and crisis. They typically insisted that class divisions produced the major political conflicts in modern society, and they were particularly critical of American work on stratification, which, they argued, focused on status or prestige rather than on class (Crompton 1998: 13–14). Distancing themselves from an older tendency within sociology, which regarded classes as groups of occupational aggregates, the critics of normative functionalism returned to the writings of Weber and Marx. They viewed class dualistically – as a form of structured inequality and as an expression of consciousness and political action. They charted the relationship between the two forms of class in ambitious empirical studies drawing on new, sophisticated survey techniques. And they took advantage of advances in data processing, made possible by rapidly changing computer technologies. In general, their work explored the impact of postwar economic changes on class relations, paying particular attention to the impact of mobility (or the lack of it) on class consciousness and action.

Goldthorpe and Lockwood never questioned the positivist foundation underlying the orthodox consensus. They were constructionists, for whom the deployment of theoretically informed models made it possible to see the objective pattern underlying the seemingly endless contingencies of the social world. But in other respects they emerged as important critics of the orthodox consensus. As early as 1958, Lockwood critiqued Parsonian functionalism for ignoring the "structuring of interests in the substratum" (Lockwood 1956: 137). Similarly, Goldthorpe attacked the thesis of "pluralist industrialism": "contrary to what would be supposed by liberal theorists, the idea of capitalist society is not outmoded or rendered problematic by that of industrial society; and further, that an analysis of the course of change in modern Western societies in terms of the functional imperatives of industrialism is no substitute for one in terms of the political economy of capitalism" (Goldthorpe 1984: 316–17). Yet despite Goldthorpe's insistence that researchers recognize capitalism's specificity, he did not align himself with Marxism, of which he was highly critical. Writing with Gordon Marshall, he stated: "Although exponents of class analysis in our sense would certainly see conflict as being inherent within class relations, this does not require them to adhere to a labour theory of value, or indeed any other doctrine entailing exploitation as understood in Marxist discourse" (Goldthorpe and Marshall [1992] 1996: 100).

To appreciate these sociologists' contribution to class analysis, let's take a step back and consider the larger issues that they – as other defenders of the class concept – confronted. As the contours of the postwar world began to emerge, it became clear that the dark days of the Great Depression would not return – at least in the same form. The welfare state promised working-class people unprecedented access to basic social services and educational opportunities. The capitalist boom of the 1950s and the 1960s held out the potential for an unprecedented boost to the standard of living for the majority of the population. The rapid growth of a consumer economy and mass culture, with its greater emphasis on leisure, seemed likely to reshape social outlooks across the board. The question that was being asked was this: did an improved standard of living and the greater potential for social mobility result in a blurring of class lines or even "classlessness"?

The idea that affluence might undermine class conflicts is traceable to at least the late nineteenth century, when the German socialist Eduard Bernstein (1850–1932) argued that a higher standard of living for the working class undermined Marx's prediction of intensified class antagonism and hence the idea that the class struggle is the motor of history (Lee and Turner 1996: 4). Ideas regarding classlessness further developed in twentieth-century America, where there were relatively high incomes among working-class people, where there were comparatively weak expressions of working-class consciousness and politics, and where ethnic and racial conflicts were arguably of greater salience than those of class. Economists, political scientists, and sociologists, for whom the managerial revolution and a spreading meritocracy were reducing inequalities, championed the idea of an emergent classless society. Such ideas began to take hold in Britain in the late 1950s. Despite British traditions of class affiliation, academics and political pundits nonetheless argued that classlessness was on the rise there as well. The issue was of particular relevance for the Labour Party, where "revisionists" ascribed its third consecutive electoral defeat in 1959 to its image as a class party. They wanted the Party to reinvent itself along pluralist lines.

Goldthorpe and Lockwood rejected arguments that regarded working-class affluence as leading to classlessness. They believed that classlessness implied more interaction between, and integration among, middle- and working-class people, a trend that empirical studies did not bear out.

A variety of studies carried out in different parts of Britain over the last ten years or so have pointed to a marked degree of status segregation in housing, in informal neighbourhood relations, in friendship groups, in the membership of local clubs, societies and organisations and so on. And in all cases the division between manual and non-manual workers and their families has proved to be one of the most salient (Goldthorpe and Lockwood 1963: 138).

They acknowledged that rising incomes and housing improvements helped produce a greater sense of self-esteem and heightened expectations. However, they rejected the idea that working-class people were becoming more middle class.

For Goldthorpe and Lockwood, a major problem in the various attempts to link affluence and classlessness was the assumption that the working class was homogeneous. For instance, in "Sources of Variation in Working Class Images of Society" (1966), Lockwood argued that working-class life was variable, coinciding with three distinct types of experience: proletarian, deferential, and privatized. Proletarian and deferential workers were most frequently found in declining industries. Where the former understood class relationships as dichotomous, "us" versus "them," the latter thought of society as organized hierarchically, according to status or prestige. In contrast, privatized or affluent workers were typically a product of postwar changes. They worked in the new industries, lived in new urban settings, and resided in the newly built, government-subsidized housing or council flats. They had less of a collective sense of working-class identity and were calculative and opportunistic voters. They were likely to switch their vote if their expectations of continuing improvement were frustrated. Indeed, Goldthorpe and Lockwood argued these working-class voters might potentially develop a more radical political outlook if their aspirations for rising social status were frustrated (Goldthorpe and Lockwood 1963: 156). Their assertion defied the predictions made by defenders of the classlessness thesis as well as serving as a warning to the Labour Party of the possible consequences of deserting class politics.

Underpinning Goldthorp and Lockwood's work on working-class affluence was a broader preoccupation with the relationship between class structure and consciousness. In *The Blackcoated Worker* (1958), Lockwood described three determinants informing class consciousness: the market situation (the amount of mobility, job security, and the source and level of income), the work situation (the degree of autonomy and authority at the workplace), and the status situation (one's location in the status hierarchy of society as a whole). Here, Lockwood clearly drew on Weber's distinction between class and status. Elsewhere, Goldthorpe and Lockwood registered their debt to Weber, when they argued that "certain forms of class formation and status group stratification may co-exist in the same society and may be jointly affected by the same underlying processes of change" (Goldthorpe and Lockwood 1963: 157). For Lockwood, class position was experiential: "the raw materials of class ideology are located in the individual's various primary social experiences" (Lockwood 1966: 249). Yet his thought entailed an analytical separation of class between structure and consciousness that turned out to be highly influential. According to Crompton, it gave rise to a wave of neo-Weberian studies of the class structure based on empirically definable occupation groups (Crompton 1998: 38–39).

Responsible for the most ambitious and influential of such attempts, Goldthorpe originally built on Lockwood's distinction between the market and work situation.[2] In addition, he considered the impact of employment status: whether workers were self-employed, in a supervisory position, or earning wages. Using these criteria, he and his fellow researchers developed the "Hope–Goldthorpe occupational scale," which recognized seven classes (ibid.: 64–65). Two categories of professionals and three working-class ones served as bookends for three others: white-collar workers, the self-employed, and lower-grade technicians and foremen.[3] Goldthorpe regarded these categories as more than just sociological abstractions: they formed the basis of demographic and socio-cultural identities, family life playing a decisive role in mediating between structural location and consciousness. A major thrust of his research was to chart the relationship between class as a structural location, a form of consciousness, and a type of political action, especially in relationship to social and economic mobility (Milner 1999: 80).

Goldthorpe and Lockwood framed their research and writing in relationship to mainstream sociological debates. In contrast, Erik Olin Wright's work (particularly early in his career) contributed to an emerging Marxist intellectual culture outside the confines of orthodox Communism. It was produced by the generation of new left and radical intellectuals, whose political consciousness was a product of the student movement of the 1960s and 1970s, as well as by older Marxist writers and scholars energized by the intellectual and political projects of those younger. This regeneration of Marxist thought took place at a time when rapid transformations worldwide challenged many of official Marxism's positions, particularly prophecies regarding the imminent collapse of capitalism and the widening polarization of classes. It benefited from the breakdown of the postwar consensus in liberal capitalist democracies, exemplified by the French events of May 1968, which momentarily gave birth to a coalition of radical students and disenfranchised industrial workers who fleetingly challenged the political order of the Fifth Republic. From this point of view, the resurgence of Marxist theory was part of a broader revival and expansion of radical thought, but the Marxism that materialized was in some ways as adverse to the theory and practice of orthodox Communism as it was to liberal capitalism. It consisted of recovering and developing the insights of Marxist theorists at odds with Stalinist orthodoxy and thus hitherto accorded marginal status. Equally important, it comprised new theoretical directions, made possible by dialogues with modes of thought outside of the Marxist tradition – existentialism and structuralism being two important examples.

Wright first developed his ideas on class as a sociology graduate student at the University of California, Berkeley, a major center of the new Marxist thinking. He did so in conjunction with a group of radical scholars, who produced the journal *Kapitalistate*, and as part of an informal organization, the Union of Marxist Social Scientists. Like many radical intellectuals of the 1970s, Wright fell under the influence of the Marxist structuralism of Louis Althusser (1918–1990), whose attempt at creating a rigorous and scientific "theoretical practice" was the subject of impassioned debate. Althusser's ideas are complex and wide-ranging, but for our purposes his importance is twofold. First, he argued that although the social formation was shaped ultimately by the "economic," it was, most importantly, also "overdetermined" by it, the implication being that the "political" and the "ideological" levels were relatively autonomous and potentially manifested their own determining effects. At any given historically specific moment, or "conjuncture," either the "political" or the "ideological" levels might have the greatest impact. Second, he saw classes in a given conjuncture as being produced by the confluence of the three levels. Within Marxism, Althusser distanced himself both from Marxist humanists (thinkers such as György Lukács [1885–1971] and Lucien Goldmann [1913–1970]), who viewed classes as collective subjects struggling to fulfill their historical mission, and from orthodox Marxists, who equated classes with the social relations of production.

Of particular importance for Wright was the political theorist Nicos Poulantzas (1936–1979), who critically adapted Althusser's ideas to explore class transformations in contemporary society. Marxists in France (as elsewhere) not only confronted why Marx's prediction of class polarization and capitalist collapse appeared mistaken, but also sought to redraw the class map in light of the massive transformations experienced by capitalist societies in the postwar world. For Serge Mallet and Alain Touraine, changes in capitalist society were actually producing a new working class (Milner 1999: 46). In opposition to such views, Poulantzas argued that capitalist transformations had created a new petty bourgeoisie. His argument was founded on a strict definition of the working class: it comprised wage laborers who were "productive" or directly involved in the production process. By this criterion he was able to exclude workers who worked for firms that were "unproductive" or distributed commodities. Further, even when workers were part of the productive process, Poulantzas regarded them as petty bourgeois if they played supervisory or managerial roles.

Wright's early work, culminating in *Class, Crisis, and the State* (1978), responded to numerous Marxist class theories, but most importantly Poulantzas's, which he deemed important but problematic. He rejected Poulantzas's distinction between productive and unproductive labor, arguing that the resulting classes did not have fundamentally different economic interests. And he found equally unwarranted the lumping together of unproductive wage laborers and self-employed capitalists into a new, broadly conceived petty bourgeois class. Wright calculated that when Poulantzas's class categories were brought to bear on data from a 1969 survey on American working conditions, the working class constituted less than 20 percent of the American workforce, the new petty bourgeoisie 70 percent (Wright 1978: 55). By any accounting this defies our common-sense understanding of the class map in contemporary society, constituting a virtual inversion of Marx's understanding of the class dynamic. Ironically, it confirmed what many Americans already cheerfully believed: they lived in an overwhelmingly middle-class society. This is clearly not the portrait of society that either Poulantzas wanted to create or Wright was interested in promoting.

Wright thought that the problem with Poulantzas's class model was that its sensitivity to class complexities was undermined by molding new phenomena into traditional Marxist categories. Alternatively, Wright's class map acknowledged the growing trend of individuals to inhabit ambiguous positions, what he called "objectively contradictory locations within class relations" (ibid.: 61). Classes, he claimed, were defined according to their ability (or inability) to control three aspects of the labor process: capital, the physical means of production, and the labor power of others. These criteria yielded six classes. The bourgeoisie controlled all three aspects of the labor process and the working class none of them. The petty bourgeoisie controlled their own means of production but not the labor power of others. Three other intermediate class strata inhabited "contradictory" class locations between these three traditional ones. Supervisors and managers, who did not own the means of production but controlled them as well as the labor power of others, inhabited a contradictory class location between the bourgeoisie and the proletariat. Semiautonomous employees, who neither owned nor controlled the means of production but retained control over their own labor power, occupied a space between the proletariat and the petty bourgeoisie. Small employers' contradictory position was between the bourgeoisie and the petty bourgeoisie. In subsequent years Wright revised this map within an analytical Marxist framework, a conscious attempt to mold his work into a form that mainstream social scientists could easily interrogate. Drawing on game theory, he treated exploitative relations of production as various situations where players would be better off withdrawing rather than playing (Wright 1985). Despite the shift in emphasis, the result represented a modification rather than a overhaul of the original model.

Goldthorpe and Lockwood's neo-Weberian approach and Wright's structural Marxist perspective are landmarks in the class analysis of postwar society. As such, they have been at the center of heated debates, politics always simmering close to the surface. Yet from the vantage point of the present, the differences do not seem so pronounced. After all, both approaches accord a privileged position to economic relationships, particularly the employment structure. And they both represent a broadening of how class is to be conceived. This is true of Goldthorpe and Lockwood, for, in addition to the market situation, they consider the work and the status situation as well. It is also true for Wright, since he considers authority and autonomy in the workplace, a widening of the classical Marxist perspective. Indeed, as class analysis in general has come under attack, Goldthorpe and Wright increasingly seem to share a common ground. They have staked out different and even overlapping segments of the same intellectual territory rather than facing each other across an unbridgeable divide.

Historians interested in understanding the class dynamic tended to regard such models with suspicion. In so far as they attempted to understand the underpinnings of group practices, sociological models were germane, and many were attracted to quantitative methodologies characterizing sociological studies. In a sense, no less than sociologists, historians had the same assumptions regarding structure and agency, framing consciousness and action in terms of a frequently implicit understanding of class relations. But for historians there was always something static and abstract about sociological models: they often seemed to eliminate process, historical specificity, and the dynamics of power. If there were sociologists sensitive to what Pierre Bourdieu called "the symbolic work of fabrication of groups, of group making" (Bourdieu 1987: 10), historians regarded it as a central focus. That is, it was for those scholars who reshaped historical practice in what became known as the new social and labor history.

History from below

In this section I discuss the new social and labor history of the 1960s and 1970s, viewing it as part of an intellectual trajectory going back before World War II. There were certainly social historians that did not privilege class or who did not identify themselves (however loosely) with the Marxist tradition. But Marxist historians played a prominent role in explicating class formation, inspiring more than a generation of scholars to write "history from below." In seeking to understand their contribution to class theory and analysis, I call attention to the materialist or socio-economic underpinnings of their work, widely shared by social historians generally.

Social history is as old as historical writing itself, traceable to the ancient Greek writer Herodotus, who described numerous kinds of social customs and popular beliefs (Stearns 1998: 844–45). In the nineteenth century, when the idea of the social was being fleshed out, historians of society and social change produced some of the most innovative work of the time, although this was truer of continental Europe than of Britain and the United States. Here, I have in mind Jacob Burckhardt (1818–1897) on the Italian Renaissance, Jules Michelet (1798–1874) on the French Revolution, and Alexis de Tocqueville (1805–1859) on the French Revolution and nineteenth-century America – a list easily expandable. As the historical profession evolved in the twentieth century, it gravitated towards high politics, diplomacy, and (to a lesser extent) "great ideas." There were, however, several historians who paved the way for social history's rise to prominence. These include R. H. Tawney (1880–1962), Beatrice (1858–1943) and Sydney Webb (1859–1947), and Barbara (1873–1961) and J. L. Hammond (1872–1949) in Britain; Georges Lefebvre (1874–1959) and Marc Bloch (1886–1944) in France (to be discussed further below); and Charles Beard (1874–1948) and Frederick Jackson Turner (1861–1932) in the United States. In the 1960s the "new" social history began to overcome its marginal status. What was new about it was (1) the claim that the history of society provided the key to understanding the historical process as a whole, and (2) the contention that ordinary and dispossessed people – whether workers, peasants, slaves, housewives, radicals, or gays – played a central role in shaping the historical process. The result was a remarkable expansion of history's subject matter, which grew to include private life, the family, gender relationships, sports and leisure, popular culture, and the social context of medicine among other things. G. M. Trevelyan once defined social history as "history with the politics left out." The new social history challenged the hegemony of high politics in historical writing, yet left the politics very much in.

The achievement of the French *Annales* school represents a landmark in social history's development. The group derived its name from the journal that championed its scholarship, *Annales d'histoire économique et sociale*, first published in 1929 (later renamed *Annales: économies, sociétés, civilisations* in 1946). *Annales* historians – notably Marc Bloch, Lucien Febvre (1878–1956), and Fernand Braudel (1902–1985) – were interdisciplinary in their orientation. They drew on the latest findings in anthropology, demography, economics, and geography, often using quantitative evidence to make their case. They championed "total history," an understanding of the historical process focusing on deep structures rather than surface events, economic and social (as opposed to political) life. In Braudel's famous formulation, there were three structural levels of determination (Braudel [1949] 1972; 1981). The deepest level, or *longue durée*, involved geography, climate, demographic patterns, deeply held values, the rhythms of economic life, and so forth. The intermediate stage, or *conjunctures*, signified the life of economic systems and state structures. The third plane, or *l'histoire événementielle*, comprised the traditional domains of the historian – the world of high politics, diplomacy, and affairs of state. In what constituted a virtual inversion of the historian's conventional outlook, it was now deemed the most superficial and ephemeral dimension of the historical process. Furthermore, rather than emphasizing the deeds of great men, a contingent of *Annales* historians aspired to uncover the "*mentalités*" of social groups, those taken-for-granted assumptions that structured the meanings of everyday life. The idea bears the imprint of the French sociologist Emile Durkheim's (1858–1917) notion of "collective representations." It also might be thought of as an alternative to the Marxist concept of ideology, which, though an attempt to capture a group's world-view, privileged formal thought – political and economic theory, literature, and philosophy – and implied a dimension of false consciousness.

The *Annales* school's privileging of the economic and the social over the political, the weight given to structures over events, the aspiration to write total history, the interest in making arguments based on quantitative evidence, the attraction to models drawn from the social sciences, and the emphasis on recovering popular mentalities provides a window into the themes, pre-occupations, and concerns that were to be found in the new social history. As it developed, the new social history represented the confluence of the *Annales* approach, methodologies derived from American social science, and the "history from below approach" being simultaneously developed in Britain. Writing in 1980, Peter Burke observed that social history could be variously defined "as the history of social relationships; the history of the social struc-ture; the history of everyday life; the history of private life; the history of social solidarities and social conflicts; the history of social classes; the history of social groups 'seen both as separate and as mutually dependent units'" (Burke 1980: 31).

Given the rising prestige of cultural approaches, the declining appeal of social history, and the attenuated relationship between history and the social sciences in the past 25 years, it is beginning to be difficult to recall just how widely applauded quantitative methods in social history once were. But as William Sewell Jr. (1940–) – among the most influential voices in the "new" cultural history, but who originally made his mark as a social historian – reminds us, quantitative approaches signified the innovative and progressive nature of social history's aspirations:

> The kinds of people social historians studied were often illiterate, and even those who could read and write rarely left papers that revealed much about their lives. But such people came into contact with public authorities when they paid taxes or tithes; when they were drafted; when they registered births, marriages, and deaths; when they got counted by the census or were arrested by the police. It was largely by aggregating the rather thin and stereotypic information contained in the records of such encounters between ordinary people and the state that social historians were able to reconstruct the patterns of their lives (Sewell 2001: 210).

Writing about European historical practice, the historical sociologist, Charles Tilly has argued that social history resembles a "strongpoled magnetic field" that pivots around a single core: "reconstructing ordinary people's experience of large structural changes" (Tilly 1985: 15). What Tilly specifically had in mind was an influential body of historical writing that sought to understand people's experience of the major structural transformation producing the modern world, the transition from feudalism to capitalism. This transition culminated in the industrial revolutions of the nineteenth century, modern class society, and, most importantly, the rise of the industrial working class. The importance of class for this body of work is manifest in the genre of historical writing known as "history from below."

It is perhaps possible to distinguish two types of such historical writing, although there is considerable overlap. One consists of situating preindustrial protests – from peasant uprisings and millenarian movements to deer poaching and urban rioting – in relationship to epoch-defining class conflicts. Here, the social interpretation of the French Revolution – which materialized during the interwar years, became the dominant paradigm in the years following World War II, and was widely influential outside of its original domain – may serve as an example. This interpretation looked back to an earlier nineteenth-century tradition of social approaches, while developing in reaction to the political histories that dominated historiographical discussions in the early twentieth century. In one respect, it echoed the approach of the *Annales* school, viewing the French Revolution as being rooted in deep structures. But it was also specifically Marxist, viewing the French revolutionary turmoil as a "bourgeois revolution" – a class conflict whereby the capitalist bourgeoisie supplanted the old nobility and aristocracy and established a new social order.

Georges Lefebvre, and subsequently his student Albert Soboul (1914–1982), played a pioneering role in advancing this interpretation. Lefebvre, while sympathetic to the Marxist theory of history, was not wedded to it as a system, seeing it more as a guide to research. He once remarked that it was not enough for historians to describe: they had to count. As George Iggers argues, Lefebvre's importance is threefold (Iggers 1975: 146–49). First, he was perhaps the first Marxist historian to base his generalizations on exhaustive archival research rather than on the authority of the classical texts – the writings of Marx, Engels, and Lenin. Beginning with his self-published thesis, *Les Paysans du Nord pendant la Révolution française* (1924), Lefebvre drew on surviving documents from numerous rural municipalities and mined notarial, tax, and manorial records. Second, on the basis of his findings, Lefebvre argued that the traditional Marxist account of class relationships in the French Revolution, which emphasized the bourgeois class's successful challenge to aristocratic dominance, was too simple. In addition to this dynamic, he stressed the aristocracy's role in triggering the revolution and the peasantry's in challenging aristocratic privilege. Moreover, he regarded the peasants as internally divided between two elements: a "bourgeoisie," who saw the traditional privileges of landowners as a barrier to their own advancement, and a "proletariat," who fought to preserve the collective rights that these privileges entailed. Third, Lefebvre played a pioneering role in shaping the contours of history from below – most importantly in his landmark study *The Great Fear* ([1932] 1973). An account of peasant insurgency in the countryside, stemming from an imagined conspiracy among the landed classes and their supporters, the book sympathetically recreated the peasant's worldview and actions in (1) the immediate context of poor harvests, widespread unemployment, and rising homelessness, and in (2) longstanding, deeply rooted, and structurally based class antagonisms.

A second type of history from below – the "new labor history" – focused on working-class culture and politics, particularly in the nineteenth century (Childs 1998). This type of historical writing did not appear out of nowhere: it was built on the achievements of scholars of earlier generations. While there were important exceptions – particularly among Communists and historians such as the Hammonds, G. D. H. Cole (1889–1959), and John R. Commons (1862–1945) – most labor history concentrated on the institutional development of trade unions and political parties and their relationship to the capitalist state. Frequently written by those with close connections to these organizations, labor history was teleological, explaining the emergence, expansion, and triumph of organized labor. It focused on labor leaders, party politics, electoral campaigns, and trade-union conferences.

While "new" labor historians – not to be confused with supporters of Tony Blair – often acknowledged their elders' achievement and built on its foundations, they also distanced themselves from it. They were often older than the 1960s student generation, but they thrived in the new radical political climate and frequently shared – even influenced – the grassroots and communitarian "new left" politics of those younger. Politically, they frequently defined themselves against the mainstream labor movement – now viewed as being entrenched in the capitalist system and as having hierarchical and centralized structures that stifled democratic, collective, and local initiatives. Accordingly, new labor history rejected the earlier stress on the rise and triumph of organized labor. This historical approach sought to recover the lives of activists and militants, dreamers and utopians, ordinary men and women, losers and cranks. The imaginative vision of the marginalized was regarded as crucial to bringing about a radically different future. New labor historians enlarged the scope of *what* counted in labor and working-class history, taking account of such things as family life, leisure, and popular culture, but also *who* counted, including those who were not necessarily "respectable."

The new labor history stressed the centrality of class consciousness and struggle. A recurrent theme was the process whereby skilled artisans became class conscious in the attempt to resist transformations in the labor process that threatened to reduce the value of their skills and make them into proletarians (Berlanstein 1993a: 2). Such work often focused on the role of the shop-floor experience in shaping working-class identity, action, and struggle. The new labor history, produced through a multitude of case studies, asked questions that led to a dramatic expansion of what counted as primary sources. Yet it paid scant attention to the epistemological assumptions that governed its construction of historical narratives or its views of the relationship between concept and evidence. Unusually self-reflective among social and labor historians, E. P. Thompson vigorously defended historians' capacity to deploy critical methods that gleaned knowledge from determinate, objective evidence and their ability to develop models for giving this evidence narrative form. In his words: "At the best . . . we must expect a delicate equilibrium between the synthesizing and the empiric modes, a quarrel between the model and actuality" (Thompson [1965] 1978: 288).

Thompson is responsible for the most influential version of the class dynamic within the field of history, its impact being felt throughout the humanities and social sciences. In Crompton's *Class and Stratification* (1998), the most complete survey of contemporary class theory, Thompson is virtually the only historian deemed worthy of inclusion – a sign not only of his importance but also of the indifference of the sociological literature on class to historical work. Thompson was a historian, a poet, and a political writer and activist. Following in his brother Frank's footsteps, he joined the Communist Party while a Cambridge undergraduate and remained a loyal Communist until the "crisis of 1956," although retrospectively he would see his biography, *William Morris: Romantic to Revolutionary* ([1955] 1977), as a work of "muffled revisionism." Nikita Khrushchev's 1956 speech, which admitted to crimes committed by Stalin's regime, precipitated an international crisis in the Communist movement. Thompson emerged as the most vocal critic within the British Communist Party, which he subsequently left following the Soviet invasion of Hungary in November. Thompson then helped found the British new left, a "third way" alternative to both Communism and social democracy. At a time of widespread political apathy, the new left advocated "commitment," which struck a chord with the emergent student movement and countercultures. Thompson also began his long association with the Campaign for Nuclear Disarmament (CND), which initially was intertwined with the rise of the new left. Thompson's longstanding CND activism eventually led to an internationally prominent leadership role in the 1980s.

In the late 1950s Thompson described himself as a socialist humanist: he sought to extend the libertarian communist tradition, while repudiating Stalinist dogma and "economism" (the simplistic and mechanical understanding of the determinative role of the economic realm in society and history). His espousal of this position coincided with a growing interest in the early writings of Marx, some of which were being published and translated in English for the first time. These writings, which discussed the alienation of workers under capitalism, were producing a view of Marx as a thinker steeped in the humanistic tradition. In the 1960s and 1970s, with the cultural theorists Stuart Hall (1932–) and Raymond Williams (1921–1988), Thompson articulated British cultural Marxism. It was a tradition of theoretically informed writing, emphasizing the constitutive role of the cultural realm within the context of material social relations and insisting upon the centrality of human agency in the historical process.

Thompson's historical writing was deeply influenced by his new-left experience, but it was also part of a tradition of British Marxist historiography, which grew out of the Communist Party's Historians' Group, active between 1946 and 1957 (Dworkin 1997: 10–44). Several important social and economic historians were associated with the group: Maurice Dobb (1900–1976), Christopher Hill (1912–2003), Rodney Hilton (1916–2002), Eric Hobsbawm (1917–), Victor Kiernan (1913–), George Rudé (1910–1993), Raphael Samuel (1934–1996), John Saville (1916–), and Dorothy Thompson (1923–). Despite blinkers regarding Stalin's regime and the nature of their own party, the historians openly debated Marxist theory, critically examined historical issues central to the study of British and European history, and with a group of non-Marxist historians founded the pioneering social history journal *Past and Present* in 1952.

Historians' Group discussions resulted in a distinctive style of scholarship that only revealed its breadth and scope in later years. This scholarship stressed the complex relationship between class relations and class consciousness, emphasized the centrality of conflict and struggle in the historical process, and was founded on a "commitment" to the political advance of ordinary people. There is nothing specifically Marxist about emphasizing the role of "the peo ple" in history. But the historians framed their analysis within the context of a wider class struggle, and they implicitly claimed that the view at the bottom of society (unlike the top) was free from mystification. Hilton's writings on medieval peasant uprisings in *Bond Men Made Free: Medieval Peasant Movements and the English Rising of 1381* (1973), Hill's recovery of the radical fringe of the English Revolution in *The World Turned Upside Down: Radical Ideas During the English Revolution* (1972), and Hobsbawm's analysis of the labor movement in *Labouring Men: Studies in the History of Labour* (1964) and preindustrial forms of resistance in *Primitive Rebels: Studies in Archaic Forms of Social Movement in the 19th and 20th Centuries* ([1959] 1965) and *Bandits* ([1969] 2000) provided exemplary models for history from below.

But no text put its stamp on the new social and labor history like Thompson's *The Making of the English Working Class* (Dworkin 1997: 105–9). Thompson conceived of the book as an alternative to established labor-history writing, which represented early working-class agitation as meaningful only insofar as it facilitated the development of the mainstream labor movement. Rejecting such teleological thought, Thompson aimed to recover agitation as their creators saw it, although he arguably created an alternative teleological narrative linking radical and militant voices, hitherto suppressed and marginalized, to the new left politics in which he was engaged. In a famous formulation Thompson provided a rallying cry for history from below:

> I am seeking to rescue the poor stockinger, the Luddite cropper, the "obsolete" hand-loom weaver, the "utopian" artisan, and even the deluded follower of Joanna Southcott, from the enormous condescension of posterity. Their crafts and traditions may have been dying. Their hostility to the new industrialism may have been backward-looking. Their communitarian ideals may have been fantasies. Their insurrectionary conspiracies may have been foolhardy. But they lived through these times of acute social disturbance, and we did not. Their aspirations were valid in terms of their own experience; and, if they were casualties of history, they remain, condemned in their own lives, as casualties (Thompson [1963] 1968: 13).

A more submerged dimension of *The Making of the English Working Class* was its relationship to contemporary debates on class. Here, Thompson was responding (like Goldthorpe and Lockwood) to Labour Party revisionists, for whom postwar changes implied classlessness and an erosion of working-class consciousness. Thompson acknowledged the long-term ramifications of these shifts and that working-class life was in transition, but he resisted the idea that these changes meant that class consciousness was disappearing or that socialism was no longer on the historical agenda. In "Revolution Again!" (1960), he argued that this thinking assumed

> that the working-class is a given entity with a "fixed" characteristic consciousness which may wax or wane but remains essentially the same thing – a working-class which emerged as a social force somewhere around 1780, with steam and the factory system, and which has thereafter grown in size and organisation but has not changed significantly in form or in relationship to other classes (Thompson 1960: 24).

Bearing this in mind, it is possible to see *The Making of the English Working Class* as refuting revisionists' analysis of contemporary trends by showing it was inadequate when deployed to understand the early Industrial Revolution. The original working class could not be solely understood as resulting from industrialization; its consciousness was not reducible to economic changes. Its evolving experience was rooted in hundreds of years of resistance to agrarian capitalism and political oppression. Correlatively, the working class's experience of contemporary transformations was mediated by modern labor and socialist traditions. Those who assumed an erosion of working-class consciousness as a result of affluence were employing an economically reductionist point of view.

Given the affinity between Thompson's and Goldthorpe and Lockwood's critique of revisionism, it might be asked: what did he think of their work or, more importantly, the sociological approach to class in general? Like Goldthorpe and Lockwood, Thompson criticized the orthodox consensus. Indeed, structural functionalism was one of his principal intellectual targets. While he never (to my knowledge) explicitly commented on Goldthorpe and Lockwood's work, his observations regarding Ralf Dahrendorf, one of the pioneers of sociological class analysis, are telling. He described Dahrendorf as being "obsessively concerned with methodology" and attacked him for failing to include "the examination of a single real class situation in a real historical context" (Thompson [1963] 1968: 11).

Another intellectual opponent at whom the book takes aim is orthodox Marxism, which Thompson portrayed as equating working-class people with the productive relations in which they were embedded. "Once this is assumed," he wrote, "it becomes possible to deduce the class-consciousness which 'it' ought to have (but seldom does have) if 'it' was properly aware of its own position and real interests" (ibid.: 10). In opposition to this reductionist understanding, Thompson argued that the working class should be understood in relationship to a historical and cultural process founded on evolving experience and consciousness: "The working class did not rise like the sun at an appointed time. It was present at its own making" (ibid.: 9). It made itself as much as it was made. His book charted the process whereby "English working people came to feel an identity of interests as between themselves, and as against their rulers and employers" (ibid.: 12). In short, the working class made itself through the process of class struggle.

What is the more general understanding of class underpinning Thompson's analysis of working-class formation? Thompson accepted Marx's binary class theory. He acknowledged that class is founded on exploitative relations of production. His emphasis, however, was on class consciousness: how these relations "are handled in cultural terms: embodied in traditions, value-systems, ideas, and institutional forms" (ibid.: 10). The experience of these relations might be determined but, not the cultural handling of them. Class was a process and was relational. Classes changed over time and in relationship to other classes:

> By class I understand a historical phenomenon, unifying a number of disparate and seemingly unconnected events, both in the raw material of experience and in consciousness. I emphasize that it is a *historical*

phenomenon. I do not see class as a "structure," or even as a "category," but as something which in fact happens (and can be shown to have happened) in human relationships (ibid.: 9).

For Thompson, classes were not born out of whole cloth but defined themselves through the process of conflict and struggle. Classes were the result rather than the cause of class struggles.

As discussed here, Thompson's understanding of class was based on the historical case of working-class class formation. His subsequent historical work concerned eighteenth-century English society prior to the Industrial Revolution, a time when pronounced forms of class consciousness had yet to materialize (Dworkin 1997: 211–14). To use the categories employed in this chapter, Thompson's historical work, following *The Making of the English Working Class*, was closer to the first type of history from below (preindustrial protests) than the second (working-class culture), which suggests just how fluid the categories in fact are.

For Thompson, eighteenth-century popular culture was both defiant and conservative. In the name of tradition, "the people" persistently fought the encroachments of capitalism. Yet they never actually envisioned overthrowing the political order. Thompson viewed this popular culture from a class perspective. Subservient groups in the eighteenth century did not develop the class consciousness typical of industrial workers; nor were their political practices attributable only to their role in the productive process:

> But one cannot understand this culture, in its experiential ground, in its resistance to religious homily, in its picaresque flouting of the provident bourgeois virtues, in its ready recourse to disorder, and in its ironic attitudes towards the Law, unless one employs the concept of the dialectical antagonisms, adjustments, and (sometimes) reconciliations, of class (Thompson 1978a: 151).

Thompson viewed this society through the metaphor of a "field-of-force." The gentry and the people stood at polar opposites; in between them there was the emerging middle class "bound down by lines of magnetic dependency to the rulers, or on occasion hiding their faces in common action with the crowd" (ibid.: 151). This metaphor helped explain not only the existence of frequent rioting and the rioters' limited aspirations, but also why ruling-class coercion had prescribed bounds. Hence, eighteenth-century England could be understood through the perspective of class struggles, but not class consciousness, what Thompson describes as "class struggle without class." Indeed, he argued (echoing Marx) that class struggle, rather than class consciousness, was historically universal.

Thompson's innovative understanding of class, through a framework emphasizing conflict and struggle is by no means unique, as a comparison with fellow-Marxist historian Eric Hobsbawm demonstrates. From a British and Austrian Jewish background, Hobsbawm grew up in Vienna and Berlin before moving to England in the 1930s. A lifelong Communist, he has been a leading advocate of a unified and pluralist left. He spent most of his academic career at Birkbeck College, University of London, and, following his retirement there, he was an emeritus professor at the New School for Social Research in New York. Hobsbawm grew up in the now largely extinct culture of Central European middle-class Jewry, a milieu that even then was disintegrating. Though one of the most accomplished British historians of his time, his "outsider" status helps explain his exploration of historical terrain well beyond the British Isles, most prominently in his three-volume global history of modern times: *The Age of Revolution, 1789–1848* (1962); *The Age of Capital, 1848–1875* (1975); *The Age of Empire, 1875–1914* (1987); and *The Age of Extremes: A History of The World, 1914–1991* (1994).

Hobsbawm's analysis was founded on Marx's familiar distinction (certainly for readers of this book) between class as objective relations, produced by the relations of production, and as a form of consciousness and action resulting from them (Hobsbawm [1971] 1984). Hobsbawm viewed class relations as an abstraction providing unity to the historical process as a whole. However, he made it clear that class consciousness in its fully developed form only appeared with the appearance of the modern labor movement, and even here it was subject to numerous contingencies. The working class was likely to spontaneously evolve class consciousness, owing to its place in the production process, but its consciousness only became fully developed, that is, socialist, when it found an effective leadership and organization and in the course of political struggle. What historians were mostly likely to encounter in the historical process as a whole were class-inflected political expressions, opposition movements that had a class component, or acts of rebellion and resistance that were rooted in class relations but deployed vocabularies without an explicit class content. Indeed, the last of these were frequently conservative in nature, looking to restore what was conceived as lost rights (Hobsbawm [1972] 1997). Thus, for Hobsbawm, like Thompson, class struggles were rooted in objective class relations but were not necessarily articulated in class terms; nor did they produce explicit forms of class consciousness.

Thompson's theoretical defense of the dynamic process of class struggle in the eighteenth century was indebted to the founder of the Italian Communist Party, Antonio Gramsci (Dworkin 1997: 212). While wasting away in an Italian fascist prison, Gramsci recast Marxist theory, viewing power relations in advanced capitalist societies as being irreducible to the relations of production. Political dominance or "hegemony" was won and lost on the cultural and political battlefield. It was never homogeneous, total, or all encompassing. It was always subject to forms of passive and active resistance. Though Gramsci's thought was known in Britain as early as the 1950s, it did not become an important point of reference for intellectual work until the following decade. Its growing influence in the 1970s and 1980s was part of the Marxist renaissance that was gathering steam during these years. A particularly influential reading of Gramsci came from the cultural critic and literary scholar Raymond Williams, one of the pioneers of the field of cultural studies, which was emerging in the 1970s as a major contributor to left-wing scholarly culture (see Chapters 3 and 7). Williams adopted Gramsci's idea of hegemony to enrich ideas that he had been exploring since the 1950s. He defined hegemony as "a whole body of practices and expectations, over the whole of living: our senses and assignments of energy, our shaping perceptions of ourselves and our world. It is a lived system of meanings and values – constitutive and constituting – which as they are experienced as practices appear as reciprocally confirming" (Williams 1977: 110). For Williams, hegemony entailed cultural domination, but it was never static or total. It was an incomplete process: continually defended and reformulated by the power bloc, challenged and opposed by subservient groups. Hegemony was always threatened by "alternative" and "oppositional" forces: "residual" cultural forms of earlier historical periods, challenging the dominant values by evoking an older set of values, and "emergent" ones – new practices, new significances and experiences. Emergent practices either were incorporated by the dominant culture or adumbrated new social forms.

For Thompson, Gramsci's thought provided a vocabulary for understanding class conflicts as forms of cultural politics. He used the Gramscian idea of hegemony to understand the power relationships governing eighteenth-century English society. The gentry's hegemony limited protest and criticism to either constitutional channels or sporadic gestures of direct action. Violent popular outbursts placed limits on the gentry's actions but did not contest its authority. The gentry's power ultimately rested on coercive force or the threat of it, but it was largely manifested through symbolic manipulation, theatrical gesture, and the legal system. Yet if Thompson believed that the gentry was a hegemonic class, he rejected the idea that the popular classes absorbed ruling class values or assented to the worldview disseminated from above. The popular classes shaped and safeguarded their own way of life. Hegemony did not mean that those who were ruled were robbed of their human agency; it was a way of grasping modes of class struggle in historical moments of relative tranquility.

For the emerging generation of radical intellectuals and their older colleagues, whose sympathies lay with the popular, student, and countercultural movements of the sixties, Thompson's work had a remarkable impact. As the American historian Alan Dawley observed, *The Making of the English Working Class* "resonated perfectly with the hopes of a generation of radical scholars that common people could make their own history, and that sympathetic historians could write it" (Dawley 1978–1979: 39). This interest was intensified by Thompson's own efforts at fusing intellectual work and political activism, as the book was written when he was a teacher of working-class students. In Britain, Thompson's book, and the tradition to which it belonged, were a major inspiration for the History Workshop, founded at Ruskin College, Oxford University in 1966. A group of socialist and feminist historians (created in large part because of the galvanizing efforts of Raphael Samuel), the Workshop played a central role in spreading the gospel of the new social and labor history, particularly through *History Workshop Journal*, launched in 1976. In the 1970s Workshop historians celebrated the lives of the popular classes, extending Thompson's method to capture smaller slices of regional and local history and the rhythms of working-class daily life.

Thompson's book was influential not only on historians in Britain. American new left, feminist, and radical historians also enthusiastically received it. It is difficult to recall a work in European history that has affected American historians so deeply or so immediately. Of the numerous social historians who fell under Thompson's influence, perhaps the most important was Herbert Gutman (1928–1985). His *Work, Culture and Society in Industrializing America* (1976) was written in opposition to the dominant, economistic modes of American labor history. Their stress on trade unionism excluded many working people, and their institutional emphasis separated workers from their subcultures and from the national culture as a whole. Following Thompson, Gutman saw working people as authors of their own history; and he viewed working-class history from the point of view of the institutions, beliefs, traditions, and ideas that American workers (many of whom were recent immigrants) created and recreated in their adaptation to the harsh realities of the new industrial system. A second historian worth noting in this context is Eugene Genovese (1930–). His *Roll, Jordan, Roll: The World the Slaves Made* (1974) achieved for the world of African-American slaves what *The Making of the English Working Class* had done for early industrial workers. In addition, Genovese's treatment of the master–slave relationship was in important respects analogous to Thompson's understanding of the connection between patricians and plebs in eighteenth-century England. Like Thompson, yet a few years earlier, Genovese deployed Gramsci's ideas. For Genovese, the slaveholding society of the Old South was rooted in exploitative class relationships, but most important was the cultural hegemony of the slaveholders, their paternalistic ideology establishing both the potential and limits for a semiautonomous slave culture of resistance.

Conclusion

Thompson's meteoric rise from an adult education teacher at the margins of the historical profession to an internationally prominent scholar who helped shape the scholarly interests of a generation of social and labor historians represents in miniature the trajectory of the new social and labor history as a whole. From a tangential position in the historical discipline, social and labor history redefined *what* counted and *who* counted, and it radically transformed the nature and scope of the historical archives, as it set out to answer previously unposed questions. Writing in 1972, Hobsbawm observed that it was a "good moment" to be a social historian. "Even those of us who never set out to call ourselves by this name will not want to disclaim it today" (Hobsbawm [1972] 1997: 93). Twenty years later the number of historians who embraced the social history label expanded dramatically. In the United States, for instance, where social history was slow to establish itself, 35 percent of practicing historians described themselves as social historians by 1990 (Stearns 1998: 847).

The new social history developed in dialog with the rapidly developing social sciences – particularly sociology. But at least when it came to the sociologists and historians discussed in this chapter, their approach to class was conspicuously different. Whereas sociologists were concerned exclusively with contemporary class relationships, historians were interested in both these and preindustrial conflicts, where the language of class did not yet exist. Such explorations were prefigured in Marx's own work but were greatly elaborated on by social historians. Not only did they see such conflicts as being informed by the relations of production (although not reducible to them), but they also viewed them as endemic, rather than tangential or contingent, to their societies. Social historians often used a binary model of class that pitted the poor against the rich, the peasants against the landlords, and the people against the powerful. From this perspective, class provided the thread running through the historical narrative as a whole.

Historians emphasized class consciousness and action, class as a historical formation that developed relationally and through the process of struggle. Sociologists mapped class relations as a precondition for understanding how class consciousness and action were produced. Yet despite their disciplinary and methodological differences, historians and sociologists operated ultimately under the same assumptions. They both conceived of class in terms of the binary model originally developed by Marx and Weber. It is as if historical and sociological work were different sides of the same coin.

Sociologists and historians who deployed the class motif shared some assumptions about methodology as well: a faith that the dialog between theory and evidence resulted in the production of objective knowledge. In addition, they explored class relationships at a time when conventional notions of class society were under pressure. This is clearly evident in the classlessness debate, to which historians such as Thompson and sociologists such as Goldthorpe and Lockwood participated. But class was also being challenged from a different quarter; that is, from the cultural and identity politics that emerged beginning in the 1960s, first from the radical student movement and later on from feminist, environmentalist, antiracist, gay and other forms of progressive politics. For some, the new labor history glorified the role of white male skilled workers at the expense of others. And it did so at a time when the labor movement was declining and working-class culture was arguably fragmenting and breaking up. It was possible to see the new social and labor history as clinging to a representation of the working class that was no longer viable. Indeed, some critics argued that it never was.

In sum, historians' deployment of class theory could be construed as being immensely creative or wishful thinking or both. Yet if committed Marxists might argue that bourgeois intellectuals always denounced class perspectives – and thus not much had changed – there was something different in the air. By the 1980s many of the most thoughtful attacks originated from within the left: those in various stages of abandoning Marxism but who still considering themselves leftists, post-Marxists as it were. Responding to a rapidly changing and increasingly multicultural and globalized world, one in which the socialist left itself seemed to be one of the casualties, they sought after new ways of grasping the relationship between the economy, society, culture, and politics. The modes of thought expressing such aspirations were many, but certainly an important one was the turn to language and culture, one of whose major expressions was the emergence of a postmodern sensibility. This was first felt in cultural studies, literary studies, political theory, and sociology – especially among scholars and critics explicitly concerned with understanding the implications of contemporary change. But this shift had consequences for history as well: for thinking about the past as well as the present, for historical practice as well as theory. These ideas challenged the very foundations of the new social and labor history as well as the assumptions about class that often accompanied it.

Notes

1. According to Alun Munslow, historians fall into one of three epistemological traditions. The "reconstructionist" position holds that historical truth will emerge from a study of the relevant sources. "Constructionists" believe that the deployment of theories and concepts will divulge meaningful patterns from the maze of evidence that exists. And the "deconstructionist" genre suggests "the content of history, like that of literature, derives its meaning as much by the representation of that content, as by research into the sources" (Munslow 2003: 5–6).
2. In subsequent work Goldthorpe abandoned the category of "work situation" and described class locations as originating from "employment relations," the major distinction being between "service" and "labor" employment. The former referred to work with the potential for salary increases and promotion possibilities; the latter was based on a contract that exchanged a specific quantity of work for a wage.
3. More specifically, the seven categories were: (1) higher-grade professionals (including managers of large businesses), (2) lower-grade professionals (including managers of small businesses and supervisors of white-collar workers), (3) routine non-manual workers (mostly clerical, white-collar), (4) the self-employed (petty bourgeoisie), (5) lower-grade technicians (the blue-collar elite), (6) skilled manual workers, and (7) semi-skilled and manual workers.

Section Two

Culture against society

Chapter 3

The cultural turn

In the 1980s and 1990s, class theory and analysis – and social approaches more generally – came under serious attack. They were being critiqued not only by the usual suspects – conservatives and neoliberals – but also by leftist scholars, including those in various stages of abandoning Marxism but still committed to radical projects of participatory democracy. In this chapter I begin to look at these critiques and the alternative ways of thinking that they engendered within cultural studies and sociology. (I subsequently devote all of Chapters 5 and 6 to how these trends manifest themselves in French and British social and labor history.)

I look at critiques of class theory and social interpretations in their historical context, seeing them in terms of the seismic shifts in the contemporary scene – what often has been described as a transition from a modern to a postmodern world. Sociologists, political scientists, and cultural theorists sought to specify the nature of these transformations (by no means an easy or straightforward task) as well as understand how they were reshaping contemporary life. (Historians did so as well but were primarily concerned with the implications of these transformations for understanding the past.) For critics, the transformations undermined the viability of the class narrative and the privileged position given to the working class in the making of history. Some saw themselves as going beyond Marxism, seeing their previous advocacy of it as a necessary but transient stage in their intellectual and political development. This position was often accompanied in relationship to the advocacy of one or more of several versions of identity politics. Others either adopted, or continued to champion, class theories, but the version that they advocated was often shorn of Marxist baggage. Here, Weberian class analysis proved a particularly attractive option. However, in view of the simultaneous importance it accorded to status and the emphasis it gave to historical contingency, it lent itself to denying the importance of class altogether in given situations. In some cases it was a stepping stone to the abandonment of class as a central concept.

I also draw connections between the scholarly understanding of this changing landscape and the development of theoretical challenges to the conceptual underpinnings of social approaches and class analysis. In this, I am predominantly interested in fleshing out the legacy of the "linguistic" and "cultural" turn, a shorthand description for several strands of poststructuralist and postmodern thought in the humanities and the social sciences. Such thinking was manifest in sociology and cultural studies before it made its way into history, but its impact on the historical field was no less important. Rather than viewing classes as produced by a structure that is objectively verifiable, scholars who advocated this approach viewed them as being produced by language and discourse. The logic of this position was a shift in overall focus – from the social to the cultural.

Language and culture

In this section I introduce concepts that are indispensable to understanding recent discussions regarding class and the social. First, I begin by considering the cultural or linguistic turn, which, although it developed independently of postmodernism, sometimes seems to have all but merged with it. I trace it through the interdisciplinary field that in some way exemplifies recent shifts in the humanities – contemporary cultural studies. This field's object of study is the rapidly changing social, political, and cultural world, understanding it through an eclectic mix of critical methods – poststructuralism and postmodernism being among them – that in critical respects are part of those very changes. Second, I discuss the terms postmodernism and postmodernity in their historical context, tracing their development from literary and architectural criticism to their broader deployment in the humanities, as found in the work of the philosopher Jean-François Lyotard (1924–1998).

Cultural studies originally developed in Britain. Its initial formulation took place in the context of the British new left of the 1950s and 1960s and in working-class adult education (see Chapter 2). Cultural studies was part of a broader effort to critically evaluate the impact of growing affluence, a spreading mass media, and a burgeoning consumer capitalism on cultural, political, and social life. Scholars who originally defined this new intellectual field were interested in analyzing the impact of these changes on working-class life and emerging youth subcultures (many of which were themselves working class) and were directly and indirectly involved in the "classlessness" debate of the time (see Chapter 2). Over time cultural studies scholars analyzed a wide array of contemporary practices – from punk rock and soap operas to museums and television news. Cultural studies is now an international phenomenon, although its strongest presence remains in the English-speaking world. A pivotal moment in its development and expansion was when it was accorded an institutional setting. The Centre for Contemporary Cultural Studies (now defunct) opened its doors at the University of Birmingham in 1964. The Centre's first director was Richard Hoggart (1918–). Stuart Hall succeeded him in the late 1960s. Under his direction the centre developed an explicitly cultural Marxist direction (see Chapter 2), with E. P. Thompson and Raymond Williams (as well as others discussed below) being formative influences.

"Culture" was undergoing important transformations. On the one hand, it was being liberated from its monopolization by elites. In Raymond Williams's famous phrase (adapted from T. S. Eliot), it signified "a particular way of life, which expresses certain meanings and values not only in art and learning but also in institutions and ordinary behavior" (Williams 1961: 41). On the other hand, the cultural was accorded a primary position in the social process itself: it was the realm in which meaning was made. This perspective represented a critique of the base–superstructure model that portrayed culture and ideology as being reflections of the economic base (see Chapter 1). Indeed, when a service economy was beginning to supplant a manufacturing one, when cultural production – whether music, movies, radio, clothes, or television – was a major part of advanced capitalist society, the distinction between culture and economics became blurred. The economy was infused with culture and vice versa.

From the onset cultural studies was interdisciplinary and eclectic, drawing from literary criticism, sociology, and history, though not in its formative stages (curiously enough) anthropology. It had a long and fruitful dialog with critical versions of Marxism – Althusser and Gramsci being the most important influences. No less important was cultural studies' encounter with French structuralist and poststructuralist theories of language and culture – originally developed by Ferdinand de Saussure (1857–1913), Claude Levi-Strauss (1908–), and Roland Barthes (1915–1980), and later by Michel Foucault (1926–1984) and Jacques Derrida (1930–2004). What follows is a highly compressed version of what those theories consist of, just enough to follow the arguments made by the various authors covered in this book.

Undoubtedly, the point of departure for any such discussion is the original insights into language developed by Saussure in his *Course in General Linguistics*

([1907–1911] 1959), a book compiled from student lecture notes. In opposition to language studies that emphasized the study of speech or *parole* (content) from a diachronic or historical point of view, Saussure advocated studying linguistic structure or *langue* (form), looking at it synchronically, as it existed in a slice of time. To illustrate with an analogy, Saussure was suggesting that, rather than considering baseball or cricket as a series of unique games (parole), we look at the rules that made them possible in the first place (langue) – that is, their structure. For Saussure, as for all subsequent structuralists, the crucial question was not "*what* does it mean?": it was "*how* does it mean?"

Saussure used this structuralist perspective to consider the constitution of the sign – the most basic unit of linguistic communication. His most important insight was that, in fact, signs were arbitrary, their meanings made possible through convention. Signs were made up of two components. The "signifier" consisted of the sign's material representation, whether visual, oral, or written. The "signified" constituted its meaning, not to be confused with its "referent," the actual thing that the sign represented. Thus, if the signifier was c-a-t, the signified was the idea that it conjured up – "catness" – and the referent was the little furry creature that rubs up against you when you're trying to read. For Saussure, the meaning of a sign was not simply given. It was relational, defined by its differences, what it was not. As he put it: "Language is a system of inter-dependent terms in which the value of each term results solely from the simultaneous presence of the others" (quoted in Hawkes 1977: 26).

Structuralists deployed these insights to investigate all kinds of practice – novels, films, myths, fairy tales, and so forth – attempting to connect ostensibly diverse manifestations to the underlying forms that governed them. Yet they always presumed whatever practice it was had a center or foundational principle, allowing for a hierarchy of meanings. In this sense at least, Marx's base–superstructure model can be viewed as a precursor to what structuralists had in mind, as its socio-economic foundation created a ladder of practices, beginning with the most material (the base), progressing through various levels of politics, ideology, law, religion, and philosophy (the superstructure). Indeed, it was because of such proclivities that the philosopher Althusser was able to transform Marxism into a full-blown structuralist system.

However, by the 1960s and 1970s, structuralists attracted a bevy of critics, who attacked the very foundations on which structuralism had been based. One of the two most important (the other, Foucault, will be discussed in Chapter 4), Derrida pushed Saussure's contention that meaning was created by the relationship between signs in the language chain to the point that it began to crumble in his hands. Derrida's logic can be illustrated with an example. Say we look up "cat" in the dictionary; that is, we want to derive the signified or the idea of "catness" from the signifier c-a-t. What we find, in fact, is nothing but a series of new signifiers, including s-m-a-l-l, c-a-r-n-i-v-o-r-o-u-s, and m-a-m-m-a-l. Of course, when we look up these signifiers, we find even more, thus getting farther and farther from realizing our original task. This exercise illustrates Derrida's concept of *différance*, by which he has in mind both "difference" and "deferral." According to Chris Weedon, Andrew Tolson, and Frank Mort:

> Meaning is no longer a function of the difference between fixed signifieds. It is never fixed outside any textual location or spoken utterance and is always in relation to other textual locations in which the signifier has appeared on other occasions. Every articulation of a signifier bears within it the *trace* of its previous articulations. There is no fixed transcendental signified, since the meaning of concepts is constantly referred, via the network of traces, to their articulations in other discourses: fixed meaning is constantly *deferred* (Weedon *et al.* 1980: 199).

While this only constitutes the first glimmers of Derrida's deconstructive method, it is important insofar as it points to the instability and fluidity of the language that we use. It implies that the apparent fixity of language is produced through a cultural act, one that (as it is often argued) is political as well. It undermines the idea that language reflects a pregiven, already known reality. "Reality" is itself a cultural effect. Basing his method on this volatility of meaning, Derrida deconstructed the "secure" binary oppositions upon which structuralism and Western philosophy relied on, demonstrating their "undecidability." More specifically, his deconstructive method entailed taking apart hierarchical notions – speech/writing, reality/appearance, and nature/culture – which excluded and devalued the "inferior" part of the binary while simultaneously depending on it (Barker 2000: 19).

What was the impact of such ideas on cultural studies? When Raymond Williams suggested that culture represented a way of life, he assumed a certain relationship between cultural producers and the culture that they created. We were the authors of culture, which represented the embodiment of our experiences. However, in later cultural studies there was a shift away from this humanist understanding towards one inflected by structuralist/poststructuralist insights. Here, culture represented the unconscious assumptions that made specific and concrete meanings possible. From this point of view, it was not experience that produced culture: it was the other way around. For there was no such thing as experience outside of culture's reach. For Stuart Hall, our understanding of reality was produced through acts of representation, mediated by cultural assumptions. This did not mean that there was no world independent of our imaginative appropriation of it, but it was only knowable through language and discourse. In Hall's words:

events, relations, structures do have conditions of existence and real effects, outside the sphere of the discursive; but that it is only within the discursive, and subject to its specific conditions, limits, and modalities, do they have or can they be constructed within meaning. Thus, while not wanting to expand the territorial claims of the discursive infinitely, how things are represented and the "machineries" and regimes of representation in a culture do play a *constitutive*, and not merely a reflexive, after-the-event, role. This gives questions of culture and ideology, and the scenarios of representation – subjectivity, identity, politics – a formative, not merely an expressive, place in the constitution of social and political life (Hall [1989] 1996: 443).

Representation was a political question, mediated by power relationships, relationships of dominance and subservience. What representations became dominant or hegemonic depended on the array of forces at play in a given historical moment.

Consider, in this context, Hall's analysis of "blackness" in the essay "What is This 'Black' in Black Popular Culture?" ([1992] 1996). To be black, in his view, was not the embodiment of an already known essence. It was produced through representation. Its meaning changed in relationship to "whiteness" and was mediated by shifts in politics and culture. In the 1960s "black" served to unify diverse groups – responding to the racism of a white culture that equated "black" with not being "white." This "essentialist" perspective (associated with the black power movement) simply inverted white racism – being black was equated with being good. The political benefits of this move proved enormous. The costs were the suppression of ethnic and gender differences.

Since then much had changed. For Hall, identities – whether based on class, race, gender, or a combination thereof – were conceived as resulting from signification. They were produced through the play of difference, fixity being produced by acts of suppression, which continued to remain present in a submerged way as well. Yet shifts in identity were not arbitrary. At a time when the West was being decentered, when the binary opposition of high/low culture was dissolving, and when modernist universals were being supplanted by a postmodern insistence on difference, the earlier binary "black/white" needed to be deconstructed, allowing for more fluid notions of how "blacks" defined themselves. In the end, Hall was not simply describing a change in what it meant to be black; he was intervening in its transformation. Human agents under determinate historical conditions produced cultural identity. Hence, if Hall's position was inflected by poststructuralism and postmodernism, it owed a debt to the tension between structure and agency found in the Marxist tradition, particularly Gramsci's understanding of politics in advanced capitalist societies as a "war of position," but also the historian E. P. Thompson and cultural theorist Raymond Williams (see Chapter 2).

As I have introduced the term "postmodern" in my discussion of Hall, it might be an appropriate juncture to explore what it is. I would like to make two observations before beginning this discussion. First, upon close examination the "postmodern" is not nearly as radical a break as is often assumed by enthusiastic and overly zealous critics. This is prefigured in the word itself, insofar as "modern" remains an integral part of it. "Postmodern" simultaneously implies continuity as well as discontinuity, a break with the past as well as its continuation. Second, while the postmodern debate took off in the 1980s, in practice, scholars and critics for several decades had grappled with the meaning of transformations now recognized as part of postmodernity. These include a growing culture of affluence, an emerging information society, the spread of a service economy and consumer capitalism, the decline of working-class militancy, the rise of new social movements, and the globalization or Americanization of the popular media. Recent attempts to define the postmodern and specify its consequences were built on these earlier efforts. The postmodern then came to signify a cluster of trends, many of which had been explored for decades. The full scope of its implications was coming into sharper relief.

The postmodern is notoriously difficult to define, in part because it has encompassed so much: the privileging of surface over depth, the triumph of the image, identity politics, the intermingling of high and popular culture, the reign of the simulacrum and pastiche, the fragmentation of the subject and the end of metanarratives, and the decentering of the West. An important reason for the term's elasticity is that it has been ferociously contested. I think of the "postmodern" – as well as "postmodernism" and "postmodernity" – as part of a contested social imaginary. I thus regard the postmodern as various interrelated constructions rather than an independently existing object. Most importantly, a crucial element of its definition is how the "modern" – its binary "other" – is itself defined. We usually think of the "postmodern" as a response to, or as emerging out of, the "modern." That is certainly true. It is likewise true that writers' definition of the postmodern implicitly or explicitly is founded on a construction of the modern.

Initially, literary and art critics used the terms "postmodern" and "postmodernism" to represent artistic styles and movements that distinguished themselves from the aesthetic principles of modernist orthodoxy. It was used in this way as early as the 1930s but began to gain currency in the 1960s and 1970s (Jencks 1987: 8). Literary critics described – and championed – postmodernism: an emergent artistic sensibility that rejected the academicism, elitism, and conservatism of the modernist-dominated literary establishment. Leslie Fiedler (1917–2003), among the first champions of literary post-modernism, connected it to the radicalism of the countercultures: "post-humanist, post-male, post-white, post-heroic . . . post-Jewish" (quoted in ibid.: 8). Ihab Hassan (1925–) came to regard it as expanding upon antirepre-sentational currents within European modernism – what he called a "litera-ture of silence" – and as emblematic of broader cultural shifts. For Hassan, two principal characteristics defined this new era: "immanence," meaning consciousness of the discontinuity between language and the world that it described, and "indeterminacy," which he defined as "heterodoxy, pluralism, eclecticism, randomness, revolt, deformation" (quoted in Bertens 1995: 44). Similarly, Charles Jencks introduced the term in the 1970s to describe a stylis-tic revolt against the dominant modernist ideology in architecture. Postmodern architecture rejected the minimalism, abstractionism, and functionalism of the modern or international style in favor of an ironic, sometimes whimsical, eclectic, and hybrid mixing of different genres and codes – "less is a bore" rather than "less is more." Jencks conceived of "postmodern" architecture as a microcosm of broader artistic and philosophical trends (Jencks 1987).

From the onset then critics used "postmodern" to describe and to advocate qualitative changes in expression. What the postmodern meant varied ac-cording to what it was in rebellion against. As part of this rebellion, diverse tendencies within modernism were conflated. Yet critics' conception of the postmodern always had wider ramifications. This is apparent from my brief discussion of Fiedler and Hassan. It is also true of Jencks, who regarded the postmodern as part of a rapidly spreading pluralism, made possible by an emerging information society, spreading world communications systems, and the growth of a consumer culture. Yet if these critics had an inkling of the broader significance of postmodern literature and architecture, others were in the forefront of conceiving of the postmodern more broadly. In this context the French philosopher Lyotard's *The Postmodern Condition: A Report on Knowledge* (1984) played a central role. It seems likely that Lyotard's point of departure was the characterization of the postmodern sensibility as found in Hassan and other American critics.[1] He helped shift the axis of the debate from one about artistic style to one about our contemporary condition and its philosophical underpinnings. The result was a discussion that was both wider in its geographical reach – it in fact became international – and reson-ated throughout the humanities and the social sciences.

In *The Postmodern Condition* Lyotard focused on the transformations in consciousness brought about by changes in the organization of knowledge. He attributed this to the shift from an industrial to a postindustrial economy.

By this transition, Lyotard seems to have several intertwined developments in mind – including new technologies (especially computerization), multinational corporations, declining state power, and the commodification of knowledge. The growth of the knowledge economy, in his view, spelled the decline of traditional intellectuals. Lyotard traced the postmodern sensibility to the late nineteenth century. It constituted an attack on deeply held modernist assumptions or "metadiscourses," notably Marxism. Modern thought designates "any science that legitimates itself with reference to a metadiscourse . . . making an explicit appeal to some grand narrative, such as the dialectics of Spirit, the hermeneutics of meaning, the emancipation of the rational or working subject, or the creation of wealth" (Lyotard 1984: xxiii). In contrast, postmodern thought was its binary other: local, contextualized, decentered, and fragmented. Drawing on the ideas of the philosopher Ludwig Wittgenstein (1889–1951), Lyotard argued that truth and meaning in postmodern thought were not universal but produced through socially specific "language games." That is, meaning emerged through a complex network of linguistic relationships created in the context of social practices rather than being a reflection of the objective world.

Lyotard's portrayal of the modern/postmodern dichotomy situates transformations in thought in the context of broader changes. Thus, the development of a postmodern sensibility is inseparable from the large-scale changes that it seeks to understand and make it possible in the first place. Lyotard's grasp of this broad picture – what he calls postindustrialism – is connected to an extensive literature that grapples with recent economic, political, social, and cultural transformations. In seeking to comprehend these transformations, a contingent of social and cultural theorists has questioned the adequacy of established modes of understanding, particularly Marxism.

A fond farewell to Marx

The understanding of society as postindustrial called the classical picture of class society into question. The neoconservative critic Daniel Bell in *The Coming of Post-Industrial Society* (1973) sketched out an influential version of the emerging social formation. Bell highlighted several characteristics: the emergence of a service economy, the centrality of knowledge production, the importance of rapidly developing information technologies (notably computerization), and a new emphasis on consumption. While this society had not rid itself of structural inequalities, it was founded on a new class structure, one where the most prominent group was professionals, whose position emanated from the ownership and control of knowledge rather than of property. There were three other classes: technicians and semi-professionals, clerical workers and sales people, and semi-skilled and craft workers. The industrial working class, hitherto the anchor of class analysis, was conspicuously absent.

An equally influential interpretation of the emerging new world came from the Marxist literary critic Fredric Jameson (1934–), who understood postmodernism in terms of the base–superstructure model (Bertens 1995: 160–84; Jameson 1984). For Jameson, the emergent postmodern sensibility – depthlessness, pastiche, simulations, an eternal present bereft of history, and nostalgia – signified a crisis of representation. It was the ideological expression of a new phase in the history of capitalism, where representation itself had been transformed into a commodity. This view was reminiscent of cultural studies scholars (see above). Drawing on the Belgian Trotskyist economist Ernest Mandel (1923–1995), Jameson divided the trajectory of industrial capitalism into three historical phases: an initial period of market capitalism which bred "realism," a second era of imperialist capitalism whose ideological expression was "modernism," and a third global capitalist stage in which postmodernism emerged as the dominant sensibility. Jameson described the last of these phases as eliminating "the enclaves of precapitalist organization it had hitherto tolerated and exploited in a tributary way: one is tempted to speak in this connection of a new and historically original penetration and colonization of Nature and the Unconscious: that is, the destruction of precapitalist third world agriculture by the Green Revolution, and the rise of the media and the advertising industry" (Jameson 1984: 78).

In Jameson's schema the relationship between the working class and Marxism fell victim to the postmodern crisis of representation, a divide between theory and practice, but he retained a residual faith in the Marxist class narrative as a historical explanation. Other left-wing intellectuals, however, were losing confidence in the Marxist worldview as a whole. In France intellectuals were turning away from Marxism in droves: the combined effect of disappointments over the 1968 May events, disillusionment with the traditional left (particularly orthodox Communism), and a growing awareness of the importance of new social movements. André Gorz (1924–), who in his provocatively titled book, *Farewell to the Working Class: An Essay on Post-Industrial Socialism* (1982), relentlessly attacked classical Marxism, capturing the new mood among French intellectuals. According to Gorz, the new technologies of postindustrial society were transforming the traditional employment structure. A postindustrial working class – both a secure and privileged labor elite and a permanent underclass – was supplanting the industrial proletariat. The emergence of this new class spelled the demise of the established labor movement, for working-class experience no longer produced solidarity and collective consciousness or the aspiration to control the labor process:

> The only certainty, as far as they are concerned, is that they do not feel they belong to the working class, *or to any other class*. They do not recognise themselves in the term "worker" or in its symmetrical opposite, "unemployed." Whether they work in a bank, the civil service, a cleaning agency or a factory, neo-proletarians are basically non-workers temporarily doing something that means nothing to them (Gorz 1982: 70–71).

In contrast to France, left-wing intellectuals in Britain might have found the classical Marxist paradigm problematic but were more reluctant to abandon it. An influential instance of this tendency is found in *New Times: The Changing Face of Politics in the 1990s* (Hall and Jacques 1990), whose point of departure was Gramsci's analysis of Fordist civilization in his *Prison Notebooks*. The *New Times* project was produced by a group of intellectuals who gravitated around the journal *Marxism Today*, an autonomous organ of the British Communist Party. Communist and non-Communist writers, representing a wide swathe of left-wing perspectives, contributed to it. The *New Times* initiative constituted one of the few instances of a self-consciously postmodern politics, sponsored by an established political party, that contributed to a national political debate whose consequences went beyond the confines of the academy. Indeed, it arguably had an impact on "New Labour," or at least the latter was cognizant of the former when it constructed its language.

New Times writers argued that the standardization, mass production, scientific management, economies of scale, and centralized and hierarchical structures of Fordism were being supplanted by a post-Fordist economy. This emerging formation consisted of flexible manufacturing systems, decentralization, sophisticated forms of stock control and marketing, diverse patterns of consumer demand, a rapidly growing retail and service sector, and increasing wage discrepancies between skilled and unskilled workers. Just as mass socialist politics developed in the early twentieth century in response to Fordist imperatives, the present moment called for its post-Fordist equivalent: a politics acknowledging new conditions, new forms of inequality, new pressure points, and new forms of struggle. Here, *New Times*'s response was not so much to break with its labor and socialist past as to decenter it. The old-style universalism of the class struggle was displaced by a "politics of difference" acknowledging a diversity of identities, constituencies, and social movements as well as a widening of what counted as politics itself. For *New Times*, class was still relevant, but its political role was not preordained. It was one identity among many. That held for individuals as well as for groups.

The *New Times* project positioned itself in relationship to a Marxist tradition of understanding modernity. Yet its own analysis left little of the classical Marxist edifice actually standing. The distinction between base and superstructure was all but obliterated. There was no presumed link between the structural location of classes and their identity and consciousness. While in some ways its analysis of post-Fordism constituted a contemporary rewriting of the Marxist grand narrative, *New Times* took pains to distance itself from Marxism's totalizing ambitions and indeed owed much to the spirit of Lyotard's critique of them (Mulhern 2000: 115). The post-Fordist thesis was "not committed to any prior determining position for the economy" (Hall and Jacques 1990: 119). Rather than seeing politics as a binary conflict between labor and capital, it identified multiple "points of power and conflict." It rejected the idea that there was one "power game," arguing for the idea of "a network of strategies and powers and their articulations – and thus a politics which is always positional" (ibid.: 130).

New Times's commitment to identity and new movement politics arguably constituted a form of radical pluralism that had little to do with Marxism at all. Its understanding of identity was grounded in a discursive notion of the subject drawn from postmodern and poststructuralist thought, particularly as conceived within cultural studies. The link to cultural studies was, among other things, through Hall's leading role in articulating the *New Times* position. *New Times* supplanted the centered, rational, stable, and unified self, underpinning Marx's class theory with, as Hall wrote, a conception that was "more fragmented and incomplete, composed of multiple 'selves' or identities in relation to the different social worlds we inhabit, something with a history, 'produced,' in process. The 'subject' is differently placed or *positioned* by different discourses and practices" (ibid.: 120). We are entering post-Marxist terrain.

Not contributors to *New Times* (but connected to the *Marxism Today* milieu) Ernesto Laclau and Chantal Mouffe, in *Hegemony and Socialist Strategy: Towards a Radical Democratic Politics* (1985) and other related writings, produced a sweeping and systematic critique of classical Marxist theory from a post-Marxist point of view. Laclau and Mouffe's critique of Marxism focused on its structural analysis of the mode of production, which viewed class consciousness and struggle as being determined by structurally determined interests. In their words: "It is not the case that the field of the economy is a self-regulated space subject to endogenous laws; nor does there exist a constitutive principle for social agents which can be fixed in an ultimate class core; nor are class positions the necessary location of historical interests"

(Laclau and Mouffe 1985: 85). Their critique was not new. It had been fired at "orthodox" Marxism so frequently that little of it was left standing long before Laclau and Mouffe took aim. Indeed, as discussed in Chapter 2, there was a wide array of scholarly work, founded on loose allegiances to the Marxist tradition, which distinguished itself from the orthodox version. Laclau and Mouffe extended their critique to this work as well. They argued that Gramscian hegemony had temporarily salvaged classical Marxism by stressing the pluralist, open-ended, and autonomous nature of political and ideological struggle, while shoving economic determination further and further into the background. Ultimately, the logic of hegemony (according to them) was to leave behind economic determination and preoccupation with class structure altogether. Drawing on poststructuralist theories of the subject, Laclau and Mouffe argued that the social world consisted of multiple sites of antagonisms created by the interaction of numerous discourses. These discourses constructed any number of subject positions and, indeed, individual and collective identities could themselves be crosscut by multiple discourses. Social movements were purely contingent, ultimately deriving their identity through practice. Laclau and Mouffe continued to advocate socialism: not because it was historically necessary (a claim rooted in a modernist metanarrative), but because it was a defensible ethical position and could widen the scope of participatory democracy.

Laclau and Mouffe's work represents a bold attempt at rethinking social and political theory in light of new social movements and the growing importance of identity politics. They might distance themselves from class theory, but they also raise important questions relevant to rethinking it. An important question that their work raises is the role of determination in society and politics, important for class theory since it is founded on a presumed relationship between structural location and consciousness. It is one thing to suggest that economic relationships do not necessitate particular forms of interest, that class position does not guarantee class consciousness, or that political movements tended to be loose, precarious coalitions created by the actions of diverse identities and groups. It is another thing to say (as Laclau and Mouffe sometimes seemed to) that economic life, however broadly conceived, could not play a prominent role in creating forms of politics and ideology. As Stuart Hall (broadly sympathetic to Laclau and Mouffe's position) observes of their argument: "there is no reason why anything is or isn't potentially articulatable with anything. The critique of reductionism has apparently resulted in the notion of society as a totally open discursive field" (Hall [1986] 1996: 146). In other words, the conception of an entirely contingent social world raises as many problems as one where contingencies are explained away.

The death of class?

Critiques of class theory did not only take place in the context of postmodern thought. They also developed within mainstream sociology, where there was a dialogue between theoretical models and quantitative empirical research. It is now tempting to look back at the 1960s and 1970s as a golden age of class studies. It should be recalled that sociological class analysis developed in an inhospitable climate (see Chapter 2). The economic downturn of the 1970s, renewed labor militancy, and an expanding left-wing intellectual culture (in part because 1960s student radicals had become prominent academics and scholars) were all factors in creating a more friendly environment for accepting class's significance. But class continued to be an idiom associated with the left. Its position in the academic world was always problematic. And it has a history of being pronounced dead, something that should be kept in mind when considering its current obituaries.

The crisis in sociological class analysis was precipitated by efforts to understand developments already cited: postindustrialism and post-Fordism, consumerism, postmodern culture, the end of Communism, declining working-class militancy, new identities and social movements, and the triumph of the new right. For some sociologists, these "new times" necessitated rethinking their core ideas. The result was numerous critiques of class theory, although upon closer examination they have predominantly targeted its "strong" version, that is, Marxism (Holton [1989] 1996). Critics rejected Marxist approaches on several grounds, most importantly its economic determinism, which in this context tended to mean positing a casual link between structured forms of economic inequality, antagonistic social interests, and specific forms of consciousness, group affiliation, and politics. Perhaps politics in the industrial age was divided along class lines. It was no longer true in the postmodern world.

Attacks on "strong" versions of class theory have been frequently accompanied by efforts at defending – or at least exploring the viability of – "weak" ones. In practice this has meant a growing interest in Weberian class analysis, for which there was no necessary connection between class position and class action. A class was an aggregate of individuals. Its likelihood of acting collectively was purely contingent. And members of classes may be distributed along other axes of power, in the Weberian tradition status and political-party affiliation being the two most central. John Hall (Hall 1997), John Scott (Scott [1994] 1996) and Jan Pakulski (Pakulski [1993] 1996) were among the sociologists advocating this alternative. Though he would later reject the concept of class altogether, Pakulski, at this juncture, advocated seeing "the social fabric as always combining a warp of class with a weft of status and a rich embroidery of associative-party relations" (Pakulski [1993] 1996: 70). Similarly, Hall regarded the Weberian approach as centered on "meaning-ful action" rather than "materialist causality." It attempted to understand the "historical interplays" of class and other modes of inequality (gender and ethnicity among them). It investigated "how these processes occur within complex, differentiated organizational and extraorganizational fields, power complexes, and state formations, on the basis of culturally available embed-ded and emergent patterns of meaning" (Hall 1997: 17).

John Goldthorpe, who played such a prominent role in neo-Weberian class analysis (although he himself came to repudiate the label), was arguably responsible for the most vigorous defense of the "weak" class idiom, notably in "The Promising Future of Class Analysis" ([1992] 1996), written with Gordon Marshall. Goldthorpe and Marshall welcomed the demolition of Marxist class analysis, which they had never advocated in the first place, while continuing to maintain that class was critical to understanding advanced industrial societies. They had never claimed that class was the only – or even the main force – underpinning collective consciousness and political action. Following Mancur Olson (Olson 1965), they were acutely aware of the ob-stacles that individual calculation posed to collective projects and saw their actualization as being produced only under special conditions. In fact, they did not advocate class theory at all: they supported a research program ex-ploring "the interconnections between positions defined by employment rela-tions in labour markets and production units in different sectors of national economies; the processes through which individuals and their families are distributed and redistributed among these positions over time; and the conse-quences thereof for their life chances and for the social identities that they adopt and the social values and interests that they pursue" (Goldthorpe and Marshall [1992] 1996: 99). For Goldthorpe and Marshall, the salience of class was purely an empirical question, and the evidence pointed in one direction. Rather than declining or withering away there was "a remarkable persistence of class-linked inequalities and of class-differentiated patterns of social action, even within periods of rapid change at the level of economic structure, social institutions, and political conjunctures" (ibid.: 109).

Goldthorpe's (and Marshall's) defense of the class idiom confronted many of the most formidable objections to it, but it produced its own set of prob-lems. First, as Rosemary Crompton argued, Goldthorpe's understanding of class might have yielded important results, but it suffered from his (and his associates') blindness towards the role of gender in class formation (Crompton 1996). Equating class position with the male breadwinner of the family, Goldthorpe's occupational-aggregate approach simultaneously ignored women's unpaid domestic work and the growing number of married women in the workforce. As a consequence, women were reduced to "male appendages." Second, Goldthorpe's classification of classes into groupings of occupations might be measurable and might be a useful variable for predicting certain elements in people's life chances. But in excluding broader questions pertaining to consciousness, action, power, and culture, "class" became a shadow of its former self. Indeed, there was a real question of whether anything significant remained. As Bryan Turner asked: "why would *class* continue to feature so significantly in the sociological repertoire and vocabulary? Why not refer instead to occupation, economic organisation, labour markets and social attitudes?" (Turner 1996: 258). It's a good question.

Jan Pakulski and Malcolm Waters, in *The Death of Class* (1996a) and elsewhere, have their own answer to this question. They found the concept of class to be so vitiated that it was no longer defensible. They acknowledged that class played an important historical role. They had no wish to deny, for instance, the "bounded lifestyles and political solidarities" of the early nineteenth century or the "large-scale, sub-national quasi-communities" that replaced them at the turn of the next century (Pakulski and Waters 1996b: 680). However, Pakulski and Waters believed that class had become increasingly marginal by the late twentieth century, and (though both of them only a few years earlier had defended the "weak" idiom) they now regarded their work as pronouncing "the last rites on the demise of a faithful theoretical and conceptual servant" (Pakulski and Waters 1996a: vii). This position by no means entailed abandoning the "moral and ideological commitments" that class theories, especially their strong version, often implied. If anything, it was the opposite. They regarded "the causes of emancipation and equality" as being "better served by recognizing their actual sources rather than reducing them to an old comforting theoretical touchstone" (ibid.: 26).

How did they imagine the postclass world? First, class inequalities were being supplanted by a culturally based "status-conventional" system rooted in "consumption patterns, information flows, cognitive agreements, aesthetic preferences, and value commitments." Second, social groupings in contemporary society increasingly consisted "of a virtually infinite overlap of associations and identifications that are shifting and unstable." These identifications and connections were unstable and in flux. Third, there were increasingly no central divisions along which group preferences could be organized, while life chances were "self-referential" rather than "externally constrained." Fourth, the active process of class consciousness and collective action was being replaced by a "constant respecification and invention of preferences and symbolic dimensions that provide for continuous regeneration" (ibid.: 155).

Their prose is far from elegant, yet Pakulski and Water's message is crystal clear. Class and class conflict were yielding to multiple divisions along status lines. They were producing

> a complex mosaic of taste subcultures, "new associations," civic initiatives, ethnic and religious revolutionary groups, generational cohorts, community action groups, new social movements, gangs, alternative lifestyle colonies, alternative production organizations, educational alumni, racial brotherhoods, gender sisterhoods, tax rebels, fundamentalist and revivalist religious movements, internet discussion groups, purchasing co-ops, professional associations, and so on (ibid.: 157).

Clearly many of the groups and associations that they cite either are unique to the contemporary world or are playing more central roles than they had previously. It is also true that these new identities lack the solidity once associated with belonging to a class culture. And there is no doubt that numerous individuals have multiple affiliations, although membership in some groups certainly precludes belonging to others. Yet it is an open question whether this spells the death of class. As critics have pointed out, Pakulski and Waters might have shown that the class structure was neither the primary form of determination in society nor a strong indicator of political affiliation. But this does not mean that class should be thrown out altogether. For Erik Olin Wright, Pakulski and Waters mistake "the increasing 'complexity' of class relations for their 'dissolution'" (Wright 1996: 711). For Jeff Manza and Clem Brooks, class cannot explain everything, but it could still explain some things (Manza and Brooks 1996: 722). And for Szonja Szelényi and Jacqueline Olvera, Pakulski and Waters's understanding of class minimizes the "massive entry" of women into the labor force. Szelényi and Olvera argue that in addition to the "direct" class position of social agents discussed in *The Death of Class*, there are also "affiliative ties to various significant others, including not merely the spouse but also parents, friends, co-workers and children" (Szelényi and Olvera 1996: 728). The result is that there are conceivably three kinds of class decomposition, conflated by Pakulski and Waters into one.

Finally, for Pakulski and Waters, class might no longer be a meaningful category of analysis, but they believe that at one time – notably during the early phase of industrialization – this was otherwise. However, it is not just recently that class has been articulated with gender, race, nationality, ethnicity, religion, region, and so forth, although the particular form of that articulation is specific to the historical context. Pakulski and Waters argue that the classical class models once captured an earlier phase of modernity but do so no longer.

Others have come to question whether the class model holds for this earlier phase as well.

The end of the social?

Pakulski and Waters asked questions about the role of class, which had implications for the way that we understand the dynamics of the contemporary world, but they remained within the paradigm of mainstream sociology. However, a movement was afoot that cast doubt on the very theoretical assumptions that we use to apprehend the social world in the first place. Sociology and classical social theory more generally are deeply intertwined with the advent of modernity. Not only is modernity the object that it apprehended, but also the major sociological paradigms that developed to conceptualize the modern helped shape social, cultural, and political practices. As previously discussed, the idea of civil society from the beginning was constructed (see Chapter 1). If in fact we are living through a transition that spells the end of modernity as traditionally understood, are the basic tenets of sociology and classical social theory still viable? And, if not, how should they be reconceived?

It does not take much of an imaginative leap to see that the understanding of class is affected here, as the classical model, derived from the writings of Marx and Weber, depends on the fact that there are objective social relationships. At stake are modes of understanding that have bestowed upon class its power and meaning: the structure–action dichotomy, the privileged role accorded to society in shaping human life, indeed the very ideas of society and the social. In the most sweeping, polemical, and outlandish challenge to social theory's foundations, Jean Baudrillard (1929–), in an expression of postmodern pluralism, has entertained several scenarios regarding the "death of the social." Among these, he has declared that the social might have corresponded to a transitory stage of historical development, but it has lost its explanatory power, becoming mere cant in sociological discourse. As he stated it:

> Our "society" is perhaps in the process of putting an end to the social, of burying the social beneath a simulation of the social. There are many ways for it to die – as many as there are definitions. Perhaps the social will have only an ephemeral existence, in the narrow gap between the symbolic formations and our "society" where it is dying. Before, there is not yet any social; after, there is no longer any. Only "sociology" can seem to testify to its agelessness, and the supreme gibberish of the "social sciences" will still echo it long after its disappearance (Joyce 1995a: 91).

Less dramatically but more thoughtfully, Zygmunt Bauman (1925–), the author of *Intimations of Postmodernity* (1992) and related writings, undertook rethinking sociology's and social theory's categories in light of postmodernity, the revision of which had decisive implications for conceptualizing class. For Bauman, ever since the breakdown of the orthodox consensus of the 1950s, sociology had been in the process of redefining itself, as it confronted changes that eventually came to be known as postmodern society. A postmodern sociology was coming into existence, but it remained stuck within the same epistemological rut that governed its modernist predecessor. Continuing to claim that its assumptions and procedures were universal in their reach, it was oblivious to the historical and cultural ground of its own existence. Thus there was a "postmodern sociology" but not a "sociology of the postmodern."

Bauman's point of departure was to deconstruct modernist sociology: a construct that he freely admitted he produced from a postmodern vantage point. Sociology had not just developed in conjunction with, or as a response to, modernity. It had produced modernity, in the sense that it created the discursive apparatus that fixed our understanding of it: its systemic character, cohesiveness, homogenization, totalizing tendencies, structural conflicts, equilibrium-producing mechanisms, and functional relationships. In the process it produced the concept of society itself. Bauman's thinking echoed that of the French sociologist Alain Touraine, who he evoked as a kindred spirit (Touraine 1992). For Touraine, sociology and social theory produced a conception of the social that domesticated modernization's destructive and destabilizing urges by finding underlying principles of social integration. Sociology's claims to universalism notwithstanding, its mental horizons were the nation-state, which reinforced the idea that social structures were cohesive and self-reproducing totalities.

For Bauman, most in need of the wrecking ball was the idea that the social world was a cohesive totality, founded on a preexisting structure that provided the ground for individual and social action. He advocated, in effect, the collapsing of "structure" into "agency":

> a new concern with the process in which ostensibly "solid" realities are construed and reconstrued in the course of interaction; simultaneously, the ascribed potency of agency is considerably expanded, the limits of its freedom and of its reality-generating potential pushed much further than the orthodox imagery would ever allow. The overall outcome of such revisions is a vision of a fluid, changeable social setting, kept in motion by the interaction of the plurality of autonomous and unco-ordinated agents (Bauman 1992: 54–55).

The privileged position accorded by Bauman to process and agency decentered the entire sociological enterprise. The modernist vocabulary of systemic order and change was displaced by a new dynamic mode of apprehension, one that stressed contingency, fluidity, under-determination, randomness, and local and autonomous practices. The totality was envisioned as a "kaleidoscopic – momentary and contingent – outcome of interaction"; and society was supplanted by the terrain of "sociality," habitat, self-constitution, and self-assembly. Bauman's efforts at displacing the binary opposition of structure and agency had clear affinities with those of Anthony Giddens, who in *The Class Structure of the Advanced Societies* (1975) and elsewhere, sought to overcome the opposition by arguing that structure itself was a process – what he called "structuration" – simultaneously constituted by human agents yet the medium of this constitution. Similarly, Pierre Bourdieu observed: "Any theory of the social universe must include the representation that agents have of the social world and, more precisely, the contribution they make to the construction of the vision of that world, and consequently, to the very construction of that world" (Bourdieu 1987: 10). Bourdieu defined this more process-oriented realm as *habitus* or habitat. Drawing on this idea, Bauman wrote, "habitat neither determines the conduct of the agents nor defines its meaning; it is no more (but no less either) than the setting in which both action and meaning-assignment are *possible*. Its own identity is as under-determined and motile, as emergent and transitory, as those of the actions and meanings that form it" (Bauman 1992: 191).

Bauman's emphasis on sociality, agency, and self-assembly had consequences for reorienting our understanding of class. With the dissolution of the structure/ agency model, the distinction between "class in itself" and "class for itself" lost all meaning. The class structure was collapsed into class consciousness and action, a position that E. P. Thompson would have undoubtedly applauded. Yet in his historical writings on the early working class, Thompson acknowledged that working-class agency, however culturally inflected, was a response shaped by exploitative relations of production, a position that Bauman abandoned. And he would have undoubtedly opposed Bauman's rejection of "the identity between the working class and the problem of injustice, and inequality" (ibid.: 206). What remained, for Bauman, was a multitude of social antagonisms and potential political movements reminiscent of Laclau and Mouffe's post-Marxism. Bauman aligned himself with Touraine, who jettisoned the language of class politics for that of social movement, which (as Bauman wrote) "is fully its own creation; it generates its own subject, it constitutes itself as a social agent" (ibid.: 55).

Conclusion

Whatever we might ultimately think of Bauman's work, it represents a thought-provoking attempt to rethink the "social," to imagine the dynamic process of social interaction beyond the binary models – social being/consciousness and structure/action – on which postwar sociology and class theory had been founded. In this, Bauman stands beside the *New Times* project, the political reflections of Laclau and Mouffe, and the post-class theory of Pakulski and Waters as different versions of poststructuralist- and postmodern-inflected social theory and politics that grapple with the major transformations of our time. If championing different positions, they share a common goal of moving beyond the terms set by the classical tradition of social theory and class analysis.

Sociologists such as Goldthorpe and Wright have continued to defend class theory, a reminder that prominent scholars believe that recent changes are often overblown or that overhauling major categories of social thought, especially class, is unnecessary. It was still possible for writers inspired by postmodernism and poststructuralism (as in the *New Times* project) to argue that the language of class mattered – or at least potentially mattered – while defenders of sociological class analysis (such as Goldthorpe and Wright) could say the same for class position. Putting these two positions together proved difficult if not impossible. Yet clearly advocates of social approaches to class theory had been put on the defensive. That scholars who edited an early 1990s collection of essays engaged in class analysis titled it *Bringing Class Back in: Contemporary and Historical Perspectives* (McNall *et al.* 1991) speaks volumes. Clearly there would be no reason to bring class "back in" unless the perception existed that it had been marginalized in the first place.

One of the ambiguities emerging from Bauman's ideas is their relationship to understanding the past. Given his claim that the sociology of the postmodern must be aware of its own historical contingency and avoid universalistic aspirations, does postmodern social theory have consequences for interpreting the past? It would be foolish to impose the postmodern world on what came before it. It would be equally foolish to act as if transformations in social theory have no consequences for historical understanding. In the words of Patrick Joyce: "A general perspective on the *processual* nature of social reality suggests itself as of as much use in interpreting the past as the present, especially when it so successfully reveals the tendency of traditional accounts to privilege structure over process in interpreting the very past these accounts purported to describe" (Joyce 1995a: 72). Thus, postmodern and poststructuralist ideas, if part of the present, have implications for the past as well.

When they filtered into social history, the results were explosive, not least for the understanding of social class.

Notes

1. Lyotard's interest in the postmodern seems to have stemmed from – or at least was stimulated by – attending an American conference in 1976, "The International Symposium on Post-Modern Performance." Ihab Hassan delivered the keynote address. Hans Bertens finds it "tempting" that listening to this address "did actually make him [Lyotard] aware of the term's potential right then and there" (Bertens 1995: 112). This view gains plausibility, given that the published version of Lyotard's 1976 conference paper acknowledged "the theatrical, critical, artistic, and perhaps political inquiries which make up what Ihab Hassan call 'post-modernism'" (quoted in ibid.: 112).

From social to cultural history

Historians, by and large, do not focus on deciphering contemporary trends. Yet their view of the past is informed by engaging with, and living in, the present, and many (although how many is not entirely clear) have been accordingly drawn to postmodern, poststructuralist, linguistic, and cultural approaches sweeping through sections of the humanities and the social sciences. As in other disciplines, these currents have unsettled received opinion in history. Nowhere was this truer than in social history, where cultural approaches challenged the aspiration to write "total history," based on the material understanding of society, and resulted in historical work emphasizing the discursive underpinnings of individual and groups practices. The growth and expansion of this "new" cultural history had important implications for how historians viewed class, frequently the organizing category of social-history narratives. Rather than class consciousness being conceived as ultimately rooted in an objectively verifiable structure, the new cultural history, where it privileged class at all, saw it as a form of representation. In Chapters 4 and 5 I examine the cultural turn in history as it played itself out in two national historiographical traditions. In this chapter I look at changes in French historiography; in Chapter 5 I examine analogous shifts in Britain.

Is all the world a text?

A symbolic moment in the changing of the guard was the publication of a collection of essays, edited by Lynn Hunt, *The New Cultural History* (1989a). The "new" in the title alluded to the adjective used to describe the social history of the 1960s and 1970s: its implicit suggestion was that cultural history was now the cutting edge of historical scholarship. The book's first section consisted of essays on an eclectic mix of scholars – the historians Natalie Davis, Dominick LaCapra, E. P. Thompson, and Hayden White, the philosopher-historian Michel Foucault, and the anthropologist Clifford Geertz. Their diverse views suggested the multiple directions that cultural history might take as well as the editor's embrace of alternative disciplines to those that usually interested social historian. Where social historians sought inspiration from the fields of sociology, demography, and economics, those attracted to cultural approaches were drawn to anthropology, literary criticism, and philosophy. Significantly, *The New Cultural History* gave little warning of just how important poststructuralism and postmodernism would become in a very short time, an indication perhaps of the fluidity of the intellectual situation.

One way of charting the challenge that cultural approaches posed for social history is through the historiographical essays of Geoff Eley (1949–) (Eley 1979; 1996; 2005; Eley and Nield 1980; 1995; 2000; 2007). Part of the generational cohort who began to make their mark in the 1970s, Eley is English (rooted in the intellectual and political traditions of the British new left), is a social historian of modern Germany and European socialism, and has primarily spent his academic career at the University of Michigan. His effort-less ability to move between these three intellectual environments – Britain, Germany, and the United States – gives him a rare vantage point. His historio-graphical essays, written over more than a 20-year period (some with his colleague Keith Nield, editor of *Social History*), provide an entry point into social history's shifting intellectual currents, and, given the enormous influence of this field on the direction of history as a whole, some insight into recent trends in the historical profession more broadly.

Eley's key contribution to analyzing these trends is "Is All the World a Text? From Social History to the History of Society Two Decades Later" (1996). The essay is a reprise of Eric Hobsbawm's classic article from the 1970s (see Chapter 2) as well as a revision and update of Eley's own earlier reflections on the state of social history and the historical profession. Writing in 1979, Eley simultaneously expressed confidence and disquiet regarding social history's direction: "Thus although the possible scope of social history has expanded out of all recognition and its *potential* ability to recast the discipline as a whole has grown accordingly, the actual realization of any new totalizing ambition has remained comparatively rare" (Eley 1979: 64). By the time of "Is All the World a Text?" he detected a breakdown of consensus among social historians' regarding the very meaning of their enterprise. "A rough division," he wrote, "seems to have opened within this 'broad church' between those who have been rethinking their assumptions to the point of radically subverting the determinative coherence of the category of the social and those who continue defending the particular social-historical materialism that formed them" (Eley 1996: 194).

In a sense, Eley charted the unraveling of Hobsbawm's original conceptualization of the field, calling into question, rather than adding to, the six clusters of scholarly work that the earlier writer included under the social-history umbrella. Eley did not produce an alternative categorization: in the current situation it seemed more appropriate to "mention certain aspects of the surrounding flux." He cited the impact of feminism and gender theory (a pervasive thread in the essay), the influence of Foucault, critiques of the history of *mentalitiés* (underwritten by the movement from a materialist to a discursive notion of culture), the challenge of contemporary cultural studies, and a declining faith in producing total history (although he also noted a direction in more global approaches as well). I have discussed some of these already. I will analyze the rest in due course.

Of paramount importance for Eley was the first signs of historians' interest in the linguistic turn. At one level he had in mind historians' growing tendency to see language and culture as constitutive forces in their own right, rather than within a base–superstructure framework that situated them in relationship to material social relations. This trend grew out of the exploration of nonreductionist versions of Marxist theory – from the Gramscian understanding of hegemony to the Althusserian insistence on the relative autonomy of ideology and politics (see Chapter 2). It was manifested in a sustained engagement with work in fields far removed from social history's original dependence on sociology: anthropology, literary theory, linguistics, and semiotics, among others. At another level Eley was referring to the radical challenge that discursive and cultural models of understanding posed to social history's objectivist, empiricist, and materialist foundations. If this critique was taken seriously, society could no longer be understood as a unitary object; history could no longer be regarded as a totality; and social structures were deprived of having determinate effects. Eley conceived of the social formation in Stuart Hall's terms: as "a complex, overdetermined and contradictory nexus of discursive practices," a formulation emphasizing the complex interplay between the various modes in which people represented their world(s). Eley endorsed a historical practice bereft of its role in delineating the march of history (a nod in the direction of Lyotard). In Eley's words: "The grand ideals that allowed us to read history in a particular direction, as a story of progress and emancipation, from the Industrial Revolution and the triumph of science over nature, to the emancipation of the working class, the victory of socialism, and the equality of women, no longer persuade. All bets are off" (ibid.: 213).

Eley located himself amidst these changes. He was somewhere between historians who acted as if nothing has changed and those who "have taken the train to the end of the line, through the terrain of textuality to the land of discourse and deconstruction" (ibid.: 214). That Eley titled a section of his essay "All the World is a Text" – devoid of the question mark found in the essay's title – is revealing. He was not about to give up on writing social history, but he clearly believed that it must be reconceived. He argued for abandoning constructionist assumptions, the belief that carefully conceived methodologies and research strategies were sufficient to recreate historical experience, for deconstructive ones (see Chapter 2). "History's value is not as an archive or a court of 'real experience,' " he wrote. Rather, it was a site of difference and contestation, a theoretically formulated space "in which the ever seductive unities of contemporary social and political discourse, the naturalizing of hegemonies, can be upset" (ibid.: 216).

It is at this juncture that Eley advocated that social historians pay close attention to the work of Foucault, who though by no means a professional historian, thought philosophically and critically about the nature of historiography, historical narrative, and the archives, while grounding his own understanding of discursive formations through archival research. One of the most influential writers in the humanities and the social sciences since the 1950s, Foucault is important in the present context for two reasons. First, rather than study texts as expressing the subjective intention of their producers, Foucault proposed to study them as objects in their own right: their meaning was produced in relationship to other texts. He was not so much interested in textual meaning as how that meaning was produced, that is, the underlying discourses governing it. For Foucault, discourse shaped our understanding of the world and produced objects of knowledge, simultaneously creating potentialities and setting limits to what it was possible to know. Second, Foucault charted the historical trajectories of discursive formations, the interrelated connection between disciplinary formations, institutional power, and the construction of identities. Reversing the Enlightenment maxim, Foucault argued that power is knowledge (Hutton 1991: 87). He saw power as being wielded not only by the state or other centralized bodies (as traditionally held): it was omnipresent, functioning "outside, below and alongside the State apparatus, on a much more minute and everyday level" (Foucault 1980: 60).

Foucault did not make it easy for historians to take kindly to him. He once remarked that he was not a professional historian but that nobody was perfect (O'Brien 1989: 28). His work challenged historians' assumptions at several levels. It called into question the epistemological foundations of their work, arguing that the discourse of history itself set the parameters and limits to what was knowable. It refused to take for granted historical archives, seeing them as constructed material events rather than as the raw material for generalization. It challenged historians' taken-for-granted categories, whether pertaining to the economy, society, or class. The history of society was inseparable from the history of the discursive formations that produced the idea of the social in the first place. How it came to be fixed at particular moments had itself to be understood historically. And Foucault lacked an interest in causality, which he saw as intrinsically teleological. For Foucault, history lurched from one episteme (or discursively based worldview) to the next, but he resisted giving a causal explanation as to why the shift took place.

Reflecting on the implications of Foucault's thought for working-class history, Eley suggested that historians must rethink the process whereby workers developed forms of class consciousness. Instead of beginning with the working class as an established social fact, he advocated asking the question: how did the "ideology of class" emerge as an "organizing reality" at a particular moment in the development of industrial capitalism? Viewing class formation from this perspective involved rethinking the relationship between structure and interests, the ground on which the class model was based:

> Rather than asking which working-class interests were reflected in which organizations and forms of action (so that working-class consciousness becomes expressively derived), we should start asking how the prevailing understandings of working-class interest were produced, how particular practices and institutions encouraged or hindered particular constructions of working-class interest, and how one specific set of images of what the working class was came to be entrenched. From this perspective, "interest" is far more an effect than a cause (Eley 1996: 218–19).

For Eley, the working class's identity was thus discursively produced. It was contingent, fluid, changeable, and potentially unstable. It could be made, unmade, and remade.

The French Revolution after the linguistic turn

Ely's exploration of the ramifications of ideas privileging language and culture for the practice of social history and the class narrative represented a schematic articulation of what, in effect, was already showing up in historical work. In this section I look at the revisionist critique of the social interpretation of the French Revolution and the impact of the cultural and linguistic turn in reframing the revolutionary decades. Before I do that I want to briefly consider the implications of cultural approaches for *Annales* history (see Chapter 2).

Annales historians' advocacy of unifying the social sciences through total history and their commitment to recovering the *mentalitiés* of historical groups inspired social historians throughout the world. Traian Stoianovich stated that "for the last three decades (since 1946–1949) there has been no more prestigious and important school of history" (Stoianovich 1976: 19). Yet ten years later Lynn Hunt subtitled an essay on the current state of French history "The Rise and Fall of the *Annales* Paradigm" (Hunt 1986: 210), an acknowledgment of both the *Annales'* centrality and the changes that were afoot. Hunt gave several reasons for *Annales'* decline. Most important was the shift from viewing *mentalitiés* as emerging out of social and economic relations to acknowledging their independent impact on society and history. Or as the cultural historian Roger Chartier put it: "The entire realm of imagined social reality (*l'imaginaire*) of a given period thus forms a basic mental structure, a system of representations, the genealogy of which must be worked out, and a reality as real as the specific relations within a society" (Chartier 1988: 45). Ironically, the *Annales* school had positioned itself as a materialist alternative to Marxism's economic determinism but was now being attacked alongside it. As Marxism shed its orthodox baggage, perceptions of the distance between them began to shrink. They might represent different variants of materialism, but they were materialist nonetheless.

Like the *Annales* approach, the Marxist or social interpretation of the French Revolution was one of the great achievements of modern historiography. Its dominance in the two decades following World War II represented an accomplishment that few (if any) left-wing interpretations within Western historiography could boast. It was a source of pride for radical historians and played a critical role in the growth of history from below. We can glean just how much the intellectual atmosphere in French revolutionary historiography had changed in the past 40 years by considering essays by Michel Vovelle (a product of the historiographical tradition of Lefebvre and Soboul) and William Doyle (a leading "revisionist" critic), both written to commemorate the Revolution's bicentennial anniversary. When the English historian Alfred Cobban, the founding father of modern revisionism, attacked Lefebvre's work in the 1950s, the latter dismissed his arguments because they robbed the Revolution of its historical significance (Doyle 1988: 12). In contrast, Vovelle (who held the same academic post at the Sorbonne as Lefebvre and Soboul) acknowledged the widespread perception that the revisionist position had triumphed, advocated the abolition of the "revisionist" and "Jacobin" labels altogether, and argued that a consensus in revolutionary historiography no longer existed (Vovelle 1990). Doyle, striking a triumphant chord, portrayed the "classic" interpretation as being in ruins and noted that "over the last thirty-five years we have been watching it fall apart," with only "ruined remnants" left intact (Doyle 1990: 744). The tables indeed had turned.

Revisionists were unified in their opposition to Marxists' contention that the Revolution (1) originated from the class struggle between the bourgeoisie and the nobility and (2) ushered in a bourgeois capitalist order. Briefly, they believed that the revolutionary bourgeoisie was not a capitalist class that owned or controlled the means of production. The prerevolutionary era was no longer feudal, although feudal remnants might still exist. And the nobility was more oriented towards capitalism than allowed for in the orthodox interpretation. Indeed, the nobility and the bourgeoisie were part of a single bloc, which had undergone internal divisions and fissures. Rather than facilitating the growth of capitalism, the Revolution had retarded it for more than a generation. Only in the middle of the nineteenth century did anything approximating the capitalist world envisioned by Marxists begin to appear. Looking back on the historiographical controversy, Doyle argued that class conflict had been the principal casualty.

As Gary Kates suggests, historians' sympathy (or lack of) for the Revolution is linked to their politics, Marxists being supportive of its most radical stages, neoliberals backing its initial, less violent phases, and conservatives condemning it altogether (Kates 1998: 1–20; Schechter 2001: 5). More specifically, a shift in the overall political climate facilitated transformations in historiographical perspectives on the revolutionary decades. The appeal of revisionism is intertwined with the decline of the left, the collapse of orthodox Communism, the crisis in Marxist thought, and the triumph of neoliberalism and the new right.

However, efforts to explain historiographical positions in terms of politics have limited value. Not only is it overly deterministic: it does not capture the complexity of intellectual debates, which have their own internal dynamic. Doyle and Vovelle may be on different sides of the controversy from one vantage point, but they both assume that the Revolution's origins are socio-economic. For Lynn Hunt, the absent presence in their exchange is François Furet (1927–1997), who "brings the revisionist and the classical interpreter together in defense of the traditional and not-so-traditional social history against the threat of politico-linguistic determinism" (Lucas *et al.* 1990: 763).

A former member of the French Communist Party, trained in the *Annales* tradition, Furet took aim at the orthodox interpretation – what he called the "revolutionary catechism" – and shook the world of French history in ways that were impossible for revisionist historians based in Britain or the United States. Furet endorsed the revisionist attack on Marxist orthodoxy, yet his own critique dug deeper, deconstructing the historical discourse of the Revolution as a whole. Generations of historians, he argued, had so closely identified with the revolutionary actors – whether in sympathy or in opposition – that they ended up reproducing the revolutionaries' version of the events. One of the distortions that resulted from historians' identification with the revolutionaries was that they ignored the continuities between the revolutionary era and the Old Regime. Returning to Alexis de Tocqueville's classic but neglected text, *The Old Regime and the French Revolution* ([1856] 1987), Furet found that, despite its revolutionary rhetoric, the French Revolution expanded an egalitarian ideology begun under the old regime rather than completely breaking with it. According to Ronald Schechter: "By depriving the old corporate structures of society of their power . . . the crown induced its subjects to grant moral authority to 'men of letters,' who necessarily lacked political experience and instead propagated abstract ideas about equality and the sovereignty of the people" (Schechter 2001: 3).

Furthermore, Furet shifted the focus of historical investigation from the nexus between socio-economic determinations and politics, pivotal to the social-history paradigm (shared by Marxists and revisionists alike), to a more culturally oriented perspective stressing the causal impact of political language and discourse. Originating in eighteenth-century "centres of democratic sociability" – the emerging public sphere of cafés, salons, Masonic lodges, and philosophical societies – the Revolution "ushered in a world where mental representations of power governed all action, and where a network of signs completely dominated political life" (ibid.: 4). Furet's deconstruction of the discourse of French revolutionary historiography and his stress on the enabling of new linguistic codes in French political culture was analogous to, if not explicitly influenced by, Foucault's vision of a new cultural history (Hutton 1991: 96). Furet's vision of the Revolution represented the historian's equivalent of proclaiming "the death of class" (see Chapter 3).

Furet was certainly no more successful than his predecessors or contemporaries in transcending the partisan politics of French revolutionary historiography. Nor did he escape the discursive field of revolutionary historical writing. His critique of revolutionary excess was itself a type of commemoration, a commemoration of a revolution that might have been. Yet he undeniably played an enormously important and creative role in expanding the scope of historical scholarship on the Revolution and shifting its focal point. Lynn Hunt represents an example of a historian who critically adapted Furet's privileging of political language, notably in her study of French revolutionary culture, *Politics, Culture, and Class in the French Revolution* (1984). Hunt strove to free the study of the revolutionary milieu from two related tendencies within historical writing: the tendency (1) to see it as a reproduction at the political level of conflicts originating in the social structure and (2) to reduce it to a vehicle effecting long-term structural change, robbing it in the process of its own concreteness and specificity. Like Zygmunt Bauman and other sociologists discussed in Chapter 3, she sought to displace the structure/action dichotomy, emphasizing the autonomous and active role that historical agents played in constructing their world. She wanted to restore to revolutionary culture its own distinctive dynamic:

> Through their language, images, and daily political activities, revolutionaries worked to reconstitute society and social relations. They consciously sought to break with the French past and to establish the basis for a new national community. In the process, they created new social and political relations and new kinds of social and political divisions. Their experience of political and social struggle forced them to see the world in new ways (Hunt 1984: 12).

Elsewhere, Hunt explicitly aligned herself with poststructuralist perspectives, portraying her goal as examining "the ways in which linguistic practice, rather than simply reflecting social reality, could actively be an instrument of (or constitute) power" (Hunt 1989b: 17).

Hunt sought to achieve her goals through an enlarged understanding of the political: she analyzed the cultural politics of costumes, carnival masks, oaths, festivals, statuary, and coins. Here, she was influenced by Maurice Agulhon, who "showed how images of the Republic on seals and statues shaped French political perceptions," and Mona Ozouf, who "demonstrated how revolutionary festivals were used to forge a new national consensus." Taken together, they showed "that cultural manifestations were part and parcel of revolutionary politics" (Hunt 1984: 15). Suggestive of Hunt's approach was her analysis of the revolutionaries' deployment of the figure of Hercules. Following the execution of Louis XVI, the new regime was faced with a crisis of representation. It did not want simply to replace the representation of one authority figure with another. It challenged the notion that the sovereign people could be represented at all. From this point of view, the choice of Hercules for the seal of the Republic confirmed the necessity of the act of representation as well as the contradictions that this act produced. Hercules embodied the heroic struggle and supremacy of the people, but it was the revolutionaries (rather than the people) who proclaimed it.

Hunt's examination of the symbolic dimension of politics in *Politics, Culture, and Class in the French Revolution* clearly aligned her with the aims and goals of the new cultural history, which, as we have seen, she played an important role in championing. But the book also clearly suggested her roots and training in social history. It was caught between two worlds. In her treatment of the social composition of the revolutionary class, she deployed new-social-history methodologies, basing her generalizations on a detailed and rigorous quantitative analysis of local and regional sources. Her conclusions regarding the class composition of revolutionary officials in big cities, for instance, were founded on archival evidence from geographically dispersed locations: Amiens, Bordeaux, Nancy, and Toulouse.

In a sense, Hunt's picture of the Revolution's political class vindicated Marxist class theory. The revolutionary class was bourgeois: it owned and controlled the means of production (mostly merchants, professionals, and artisans with shops), and it had a shared class consciousness, founded on opposition to the Old Regime. Yet Marxist class analysis did not explain what delineated militant republicans from their moderate and royalist opposition, since they could all come from the same bourgeois background. It did not help account for why some of the most advanced capitalist regions were the most reactionary, some of the most republican the least. And the antiabsolutist and antifeudal values of the whole class did "not mark off the militant republicans from their predecessors of 1790–91 or separate the Jacobins of Amiens, for instance, from their wealthy merchant opponents" (ibid.: 178). The bourgeoisie, she argued, were, in fact, too diverse – their economic, social, and political interests too divergent – to be assigned a political ideology. However, if the revolutionary political culture could not be explained via Marxist class analysis, the revolutionaries still had ties: "The members of the new political class shared certain values that were shaped in large measure by common cultural positions." At the level of ideas, they shared an allegiance to secularism, rationalism, the nation and (in the case of republicans) popular participation. The ties likewise resulted from "family networks, organizational relationships, and common cultural relationships" (ibid.: 178–79). In short, the Marxist explanation was not so much mistaken as simply unhelpful.

Rethinking labor history

Marxist class theory was likewise under challenge in French labor history. The study of the nineteenth-century working class was pivotal to social history's growth, expansion, and achievement. It consisted of a "bottom-up" recovery of working people's lives in the context of social and economic relationships, emphasizing the radicalization of artisans in the face of proletarianization. Yet by the 1980s historians of the French working class were having their doubts. William Reddy accepted that class could be usefully conceived as an abstract relationship but did not believe that it helped explain the political actions of historically specific actors: their practices could not be read off, as it were, from their structurally defined class interests (Reddy 1992). Reddy, accordingly, rejected a vocabulary – what he described as a "subsidiary terminology" – which produced the impression that social classes roamed the historical stage. Terms such as "proletariat, working class, *petite bourgeoisie*, peasantry, bourgeoisie, aristocracy, gentry, Junker class" should not "appear as subjects of action verbs like perceive, resist, seek, struggle, think, rule, demand and so on" (ibid.: 24). Acknowledging that sociologists, social and cultural historians, literary scholars, and unorthodox Marxist theorists had produced a rich body of scholarship renewing class theory, Reddy found that ultimately their work rested "on metaphorical extensions or inversions of received Marxist categories that are thereby revealed to be no more than metaphors themselves" (Reddy 1987: 32).

Reddy's own preference was to jettison the language of class altogether in favor of new metaphors that could better capture economic, social, political, and cultural relationships. This shift in emphasis is evident in Reddy's attempt to rethink the basis of market society and monetary exchange, a discourse created by liberal economists but (despite their critique of it) acquiesced to by Marxists as well. For Reddy, the language of political economy notwithstanding, exchanges between buyers and sellers of labor tended to be unequal, the result of their different social and economic standing. Employers frequently worked under the assumption that labor was abundant; impoverished workers were not in a position to be choosy. The conflict between the two groups could not be reduced to differential interests: it was rooted in power. "Wealth allows the rich to discipline the poor through their bodies and through their sense of familial or other social duty. Everyone does not want money and power, but everyone does have a body susceptible to that discipline which follows in the wake of propertylessness in all money-based action societies" (ibid.: 199–200). For Reddy, "asymmetrical monetary exchange" enabled a wide range of intertwined social and political relationships – including deference, subordination, discipline, resistance, and violence. It could help explain instability, crisis, and historical transformation across a broad spectrum of practices, although it did not inevitably produce them.

As critiques such as Reddy's began to infiltrate scholarly discussions, the idea that French labor history was in crisis began to be openly discussed. Such sentiments could be found in a collection of essays by a group of mostly

American historians of French social history: *Rethinking Labor History: Essays on Discourse and Class Analysis* (Berlanstein 1993b). In the book's introduction its editor, Lenard Berlanstein, wrote that "the new labor history has entered the 1990s uncertain about the authority of earlier achievements and divided about basic methods and concepts." He spoke of "a widespread sense among an expanding circle of scholars that the shades have fallen from their eyes and that labor history will not be the same and should not be the same" (Berlanstein 1993a: 8). As the book's title suggested, the need to rethink labor history was provoked by the challenge of discourse theory, that is, the linguistic turn, which, as Berlanstein stated, represented a "radical new 'agenda'." It involved (1) paying attention to the discursive formations that produce workers as a group and constituted working-class experience and (2) deconstructing social history's own discourse, notably terms such as "class, work, wages, markets, and skill." These ideas posed a threat to social history as it had been conceived, for it suggested that the categories employed by social historians were themselves discursively pro-duced. Contributors' responses varied: from Donald Reid (Reid 1993), who believed that linguistically informed history opened up material reality to a multiplicity of meanings and an understanding of history as involving con-testations over these meanings, to the sociologist Ronald Aminzade (Aminzade 1993), for whom institutions and ideologies neither were independent of material conditions and class forces nor were capable of simply creating inter-ests out of discourses, unconstrained by material realities.

Christopher Johnson, whose work on working-class culture helped form the narrative of the new French labor history, neither held on to conventional Marxist explanations nor dismissed the linguistic turn (Johnson 1993). But he was leery of the wholesale dismissal of the Marxist tradition, as he was of uncrit-ical appropriations of poststructuralism. Relying on the ideas of the German neo-Marxist theorist Jürgen Habermas (1929–), he advocated bringing together the "lifeworlds" of workers – "symbolic representations expressed in discourses" – with the systemic constraints acting on them. Johnson only alluded to the practical consequences of what this meant for concrete histor-ical research, but he did suggest that it might help us understand how an unruly and often militant working class, through the actions of its parties and unions, came to be relatively integrated into a system of state administration.

In his essay for *Rethinking Labor History*, William Sewell Jr. contrasted the "intellectual doldrums" of labor history with the vitality of feminist theory and scholarship (Sewell 1993: 15–16). The feminist historian Gay Gullickson endorsed this view, portraying French labor history as "neither dead nor in crisis" but "moving into an exciting new era of broadly inclusive narratives" that combined a new understanding of the process of proletarianization and "a new awareness of the role gender conceptions of language have played in the past and in our histories" (Gullickson 1993: 211).

Leora Auslander's "Perceptions of Beauty and the Problem of Consciousness: Parisian Furniture Makers" (1993) exemplifies this trend. It is not an essay on women workers, the subject often associated with feminist historical work. Rather Auslander, following the lead of Joan Scott (see Chapters 5 and 6), used a feminist and linguistic perspective to challenge the idea that working-class experience was homogeneous, that working-class identity was equivalent to its representation by organized labor, and that class could be conceived in isolation from gender. She considered the trajectory of furniture makers in nineteenth-century France, drawing on her own experience as a cabinetmaker prior to graduate school. Her argument was that furniture makers were just as interested in the beauty of the products that they made as the material benefits they received from belonging to unions. She demonstrated that "beauty" was silenced by the discourse of organized labor as well as becoming increasingly coded as feminine. Artisans, she concluded, were now "part of a society that distinguished among men who labored to produce exchange value, women who consumed aesthetic value, and the men – neither fully men nor members of the artisanal class – who produced and assessed aesthetic form" (Auslander 1993: 170–71). Those that continued to desire control over the aesthetic quality of the objects that they produced were in danger of crossing the boundaries of both their gender and their class. I will be discussing the contribution of feminist scholars to our understanding of class in greater detail in Chapter 6.

One of the most provocative contributions to *Rethinking Labor History* was Sewell's challenge to the materialist assumptions governing this field of historical inquiry (Sewell 1993). Like Johnson, Sewell was an important voice in the new labor history. His early work, derived from his Ph.D. dissertation, was produced within a sociologically informed paradigm (Sewell 1974). It leaned heavily on quantitative evidence gleaned from marriage registers and other archival sources. It focused on a single local case – the radicalization of nineteenth-century Marseilles artisans. Sewell had a multidimensional conception of the transformations in working people's lives, stressing economic, demographic, social structural, and political change. But it ultimately relied on the base–superstructure model, whereby working-class culture was analyzed within the framework of the social structure.

In his early work Sewell had shown that workers from unskilled trades, and from skilled trades where members were recruited locally, remained politically conservative. Skilled workers who experienced competition from workers who moved to the Marseilles area were more likely to become politically radical. Yet, as he himself admitted, what he had failed to accomplish was an explanation for why this transformation in workers' consciousness took place. This is the question that Sewell tackled in his influential book *Work and Revolution in France: The Language of Labor from the Old Regime to 1848* (Sewell 1980). Tracing artisanal culture back to the eighteenth century, he found continuity between the corporate mentality of Marseilles workers in the 1840s and in the Old Regime, and he showed how that mentality was radicalized through a discursive reworking of its core assumptions under the pressure of the revolutionary upheavals of the 1830s and 1840s. The advent of working-class consciousness resulted from the universalizing of the traditional loyalties that workers manifested in particular trades. This wider solidarity came about when workers' corporations came to see themselves (as Sewell explained it in a related text) "as free associations of productive laboring citizens, rather than as distinct corporations devoted to the perfections of a particular craft" (Sewell 1986: 63).

Rather than taking his lead from the social-history project that originally informed his training, Sewell – like the historians Natalie Davis and E. P. Thompson – found his inspiration from cultural anthropology; in Sewell's case a notable influence was Clifford Geertz (1926–), who studied the systems of meaning that people used to frame their experience of the everyday world. Sewell's move from working in a dialog with sociology to drawing liberally from anthropology took place during the years that he spent at the Institute for Advanced Study, Princeton University, in the second half of the 1970s. "What the discussions with anthropology offered was, above all, a means of restoring to social history the dimension of meaningful human action, which had been largely eliminated by the new social history's pervasive objectivism" (Sewell 2001: 212). We can see this at work in *Work and Revolution in France*, when Sewell stated:

> If we can discover the symbolic content and conceptual coherence of *all* kinds of working-class experiences, then the workers' adoption of explicit political ideologies will no longer appear as a sudden intrusion of "ideas" from the outside but as the introduction or elaboration of yet another symbolic framework into lives that – like all ours – were already animated by conceptual issues and problems (Sewell 1980: 11).

From this point of view, class consciousness was not imposed on intellectually passive working people. It was collectively produced by countless workers intent on framing their experience in a meaningful way. Such a position had affinities with E. P. Thompson, which Sewell readily acknowledged.

He, however, was ultimately moving in a different direction than charted by Thompson. He thought that Thompson's view of class formation, which privileged the cultural and experiential handling of productive relations, paid insufficient attention to shifts internal to working people's discourse, the linguistic ground of class consciousness. He argued that "understanding the emergence of class discourse in England and France in the early 1830s requires abstracting both the structure of class discourse and the structures of pre-existing discourses out of the experiences and the temporal sequences in which they exist" (Sewell 1990: 72).

Sewell's attraction to the linguistic turn was apparent in his contribution to *Rethinking Labor History*, "Toward a Post-Materialist Rhetoric for Labor History" (1993). He sought, in effect, to achieve for labor history what Laclau and Mouffe had accomplished for political theory, a labor-history practice that challenged the materialist assumptions of the field, while simultaneously acknowledging the creative legacy of the tradition that produced those assumptions. Labor historians' understanding of society and history, he argued, arbitrarily privileged material over cultural, political, or ideological causes as well as ignoring the cultural dimension of material processes. Thus, money, though a symbolic medium of exchange, was uncritically assigned to the economic and thus the material sphere. Moreover, labor historians privileged the manufacturing over the service sector, for it was deemed the site of "material" production and the realm of the proletariat. This viewpoint was increasingly problematic at a time when service, administration, and the professions – often involving more mental rather than physical labor – were becoming so prominent in advanced capitalist economies.

For Sewell, such categorical confusions were themselves historically produced. He attributed the equation of the material, the physical, and the economic to Enlightenment thought, which inverted the medieval privileging of the ideal over the material. Marx reproduced this inversion (through his encounter with Hegel) without critically examining it. As a post-materialist, Sewell advocated going beyond this binary opposition. Social relations, he suggested, were shaped by meaning, scarcity, and power; that is, they were always discursive, but also constituted by other determinations. He believed that "the discursive features of the social relationship are themselves always constitutively shaped by power relations and conditions of choice under scarcity." But he also maintained that "scarcity is always shaped by power and meaning, and power is always shaped by meaning and scarcity" (Sewell 1993: 33).

Like Eley, Sewell sought to adapt the linguistic turn to the project of social and labor history, displacing the binary opposition of idealism and materialism, social being and consciousness, and structure and action. The implication of such thinking for conceptualizing class formation was that it was viewed as being discursively produced within determinate historical conditions. Historians must pay as much attention to the internal shifts within class discourses as the context in which they operated and helped define. Yet despite Sewell's efforts at drawing on social and cultural approaches, he himself was moving in a decidedly cultural and linguistic direction. In *A Rhetoric of Bourgeois Revolution: The Abbé Sieyès and "What is the Third Estate?"* (1994), Sewell explored the rhetorical complexities of what was arguably the most influential pamphlet written during the French revolutionary period. Sewell was not oblivious to the pamphlet's social or class context, but he stressed that its discursive contradictions had important political ramifications.

Deconstructing labor history

Among the challenges to the conventional wisdom of social and labor history, the most unorthodox arguably came from a writer who did not start out as a historian at all. It originated from a philosopher, Jacques Rancière (1940–), who, like Foucault, fused a critique of existing historical practice with his own forays into the archives. Emerging from the Althusserian and Maoist milieu of May 1968 France, Rancière sought to recover the voices of nineteenth-century working-class people, liberated from the shaping influence of those who spoke for them – whether inside or outside the working class. His project recalled E. P. Thompson's efforts at rescuing working peoples' voices from the condescension of history. Yet it represented a critique of it as well, or at least the tradition of social history to which Thompson belonged. Rancière was a leading force in the intellectual collective that produced the social-history journal *Les révoltes logiques*, whose evaluation of France's most prestigious social history journal, *Le movement social*, on the occasion of its one-hundredth issue, was that it told us what we already knew. He regarded the discourse of social history as creating narratives of working-class life and socialist thought that masked their heterogeneity and contradictions (Reid 1989: xv). His own goal he described as "impossible": "knowledge that can be neither the science finally saying the truth about State and Revolution, the proletariat, socialism and the Gulag; nor the voice in person of the excluded and the voiceless; at the very least [a knowledge that is] the maintenance of an irony, of a distance of knowledge from itself that echoes that which does not come to be represented, [a knowledge that] at least prevents the smothering of all that is now insupportable" (quoted in ibid.: xxx). It seems as if Rancière's goal was to attain a self-consciousness and critical distance from taken-for-granted categories used in conventional labor history by deconstructing them. He wanted to enable the voices of those who had been smothered by such categorization. Yet he was aware that he could not speak for them.

Donald Reid, the historian responsible for introducing Rancière's historical work to English-speaking audiences (and to whom my own analysis is indebted), recalled that his initial encounter with *The Nights of Labor* (1989), Rancière's major contribution to labor history, was disorienting:

> Maurice Agulhon, Christopher Johnson, William Sewell, none had quite prepared me for Rancière's book . . . What bothered me was that Rancière did not introduce workers' writings to illuminate insights derived from studying their activities in the community or the workplace. On the contrary, it was precisely the distance between the workplace and the accounts of those who wrote of it that interested him. Nor did Rancière use workers' pronouncements to reproduce familiar narratives of class formation and class consciousness . . . What Rancière spoke about instead was a kind of suffering and longing among workers for the opportunity to do unproductive labor, such as writing poetry and philosophizing, which had little place in most studies of the working class (Reid 1993: 39).

What Reid was pointing to was Rancière's deconstruction of the category "working class" itself. Where Thompson had undoubtedly "listened" to his historical subjects, he portrayed their politics as predominantly rooted in their workplace and community. In *The Making of the English Working Class* (Thompson [1963] 1968), he regretted the failure of Romantic intellectuals and working-class radicals to make common cause. Yet the boundary between the world of workers and poets was never breeched – the dichotomy between mental and manual labor sustained. This is precisely the barrier that Rancière sought to breakdown. He foregrounded "migrants who move at the borders between classes, individuals and groups who develop capabilities within themselves which are useless for the improvement of their material lives and which in fact are liable to make them despise material concerns" (Rancière 1988: 50). He was less interested in the expressions of workers' corporate identity and emerging class consciousness than the poetic musings, philosophical speculations, and literary wanderings that challenged the very meaning of what it meant to be working class. As Rancière stated it:

> Such is their venture as they seek to appropriate for themselves the night of those who can stay awake, the language of those who do not have to beg, and the image of those who do not need to be flattered. We must take this detour

on the supposedly direct road from exploitation to class message, from worker identity to its collective expression. We must examine the mixed scene in which some workers, with the complicity of intellectuals who have gone out to meet them and perhaps wish to expropriate their role, replay and shift the old myth about who has the right to speak for others by trying their hand at words and theories from on high. Perhaps it is through a few singular passions, a few chance encounters, and a few discussions of the sex of God and the origin of the world that we may see the image of the great labor community take visible shape and hear its voice sound out (Rancière 1989: 22–23).

Challenging the borders between manual and intellectual labor is only one of the ways that Rancière problematized conventional notions of what constituted the working class. Just as important, he reconceived the proletariat. Marx had portrayed the proletariat as "the class to which the future belongs" and had charted its progress from acts of individual challenge and small-scale acts of militancy to a cohesive and disciplined political force. It is an image rooted in the common experience of exploitation, has universal implications, and is founded on a historical logic. Nothing could be farther from Rancière's understanding of the proletarian milieu in the years before 1848. He viewed it as a way of life marked by instability, volatility, and uncertainty:

> this aleatory population, in every sense of the word, represents less the army of the marginal or declassed than the proletariat in its very essence that is concealed under the wretched or glorious images of the factory damned or the pioneers of mechanics. They represent very accurately the aleatory history and geography that bring together those individuals who live, each and every one, in the absolute precariousness of having no trump to play but the availability of their arms and suffering from the day-to-day uncertainty of their employment more than from the exploitation of their project (ibid.: 147).

This passage suggests that Marx's distinction between the world of the proletariat and lumpenproletariat must itself be deconstructed.

Similarly, Rancière took on one of the bulwarks of the new social history, the contention that the nineteenth-century radical movement was spearheaded by disgruntled artisans rather than by the emerging factory proletariat. In "The Myth of the Artisan: Critical Reflections on a Category of Social History" (1983), Rancière rejected this idea, arguing for, in effect, an inverse relationship between the level of artisanal skill and the intensity of radical political action connected to it:

The highest level of militancy is to be found among the poor relations, those trades that are a crossroads or an outlet: for instance, among the tailors but not the hatters; among the shoemakers but not the curriers; among the woodworkers but not the carpenters; among the typographers who, in their relation to the intellectual world, are outcasts as well (Rancière 1983: 4).

Rancière based his position primarily on an examination of the tailors, shoemakers, and typographers. They were crafts held in low esteem by their fellow workers, frequently not the first choice of those practicing them, and in greater flux than those with higher status. Ironically, it was both because of the tenuous connections between such workers and the "forced leisure time" enjoyed by them – owing to their trade's role as a "refuge or outlet" – that these artisans were drawn to radical Saint-Simonian groups. There was nonetheless a disparity between how workers and radical groups perceived each other. Saint-Simonians regarded the workers as "robust" recruits to an "industrial army" undertaking a great "historical epic." The workers, however, felt otherwise: "The less sophisticated workers sought in Saint-Simonism a kind of mutual aid society which, for the poorest among them, would function as a welfare office, and for the others as a kind of social security system. The more enlightened workers were seeking intellectual growth, an escape from the worker's world" (ibid.: 5). As in *The Nights of Labor*, Rancière was drawn to workers whose acts of writing and politics represented "the fallout from an impossible effort to escape the 'culture' of their everyday working lives" (ibid.: 14). He was drawn to the multiple, heterogeneous, and contradictory forms of working-class existence.

In the same issue of *International Labor and Working-Class History* in which "The Myth of the Artisan" was published, Christopher Johnson (Johnson 1983) and William Sewell Jr. (Sewell 1983) provided thoughtful responses to Rancière's essay. Both were sympathetic to his efforts to problematize the relationship between working-class authors and the wider opinion they were often assumed to represent. Johnson and Sewell admired Rancière's critical reading of texts by such authors. And they were broadly supportive of his challenge to the dogmatic attachment to the link between skill and labor militancy. Yet neither Johnson nor Sewell believed that Rancière's account necessitated abandoning the link between them, and both found major flaws in his argument and the evidence that he marshaled for it. Sewell explicitly rejected Rancière's contention that there was an inverse relationship between skill and militancy. He pointed out that skill was not confined to technical competence. Shoemakers and tailors may have been relatively poor, been held in low esteem by other artisans, and possessed minimal skills. However, they had a status distinct from unskilled workers and fought frantically to maintain it at a time when their privileges were under attack. Moreover, Rancière incorrectly attributed to typographers a low-level status among artisans, and he ignored completely groups such as the Lyonnais *canuts* (silk workers), who were highly skilled, paid relatively well, and held in high esteem, and yet were known for their militancy. As Sewell hinted at, but Johnson emphasized, a major lacuna in Rancière's argument was that he willfully ignored the role of encroaching capitalism on trade solidarity and politics. In Johnson's words: "What Rancière leaves out of his entire discussion, amazingly, is the impact of capitalism. One has the impression that shoemakers and tailors had always been the maligned or casual, 'easy' crafts he describes. What made them become militant when they did? What else but the explosive consequences of emergent industrial capitalism?" (Johnson 1983: 23). It was one thing to distance himself from rigid deployments of Marxist determinism, but Rancière allowed himself to be blinded to a crucial context in the lives of nineteenth-century workers.

Conclusion

Taken together, the critiques and new directions in French revolutionary and labor historiography suggest the extent to which a crisis in social history was brewing. There were certainly social historians who continued as before and continued to produce valuable scholarship. But the ground was shifting beneath them and the field as a whole was in fragmentation and disarray. Here, the new cultural history simultaneously challenged social history's foundation, while suggesting multiple directions and alternatives. The turmoil in the historical profession – as in sociology – was informed by the sea change in economic, social, political, and cultural shifts simultaneously taking place. But the crisis in social history was relatively autonomous as well. It involved a confluence of ideas that had their own inner dynamic: whether framed in terms of cultural anthropology, a poststructuralist understanding of language, or an insistence on the autonomy and diversity of political practices.

For class, the handwriting was on the wall. It lost its dominance in French revolutionary historiography, as the consensus that had coalesced around the class interpretation was in disarray. Class was not dead for French labor historians, but the diversity of opinion in *Rethinking Labor History* and related scholarship suggested that it was being conceived in multiple ways. Certainly the most radical form was via the linguistic turn, which challenged the socioeconomic underpinnings of class theory, viewing class language as a cultural

construct. As it turned out, it was not a historian of the French labor movement whose deployment of these ideas proved to be the most contentious.
It was the British historian Gareth Stedman Jones. His reinterpretation of
Chartism turned British labor historiography on its head, and its impact was
felt widely. This is the subject of the next chapter.

Chapter 5

The languages of class

The new British social and labor history was by no means exclusively Marxist. However, E. P. Thompson – and other cultural Marxist historians – cast a long shadow on its growth and development. Thompson's emphasis on class consciousness in the making of history, his stress on the cultural dimension of political struggle, his Herculean labors in the cause of history from below, and his belief that English working people by the 1830s had made themselves into a class through their own political agency inspired more than a generation of historians. Since the 1980s Thompsonian social history has been the subject of widespread debate. Its portrayal of British historical development has been called into question. So also have its theoretical assumptions: the privileging of experience, materialist explanations of political practices, and the centrality of class struggle. In this context the title of James Thompson's essay, "After the Fall: Class and Political Language in Britain, 1780–1900" (1996), speaks volumes.

In this chapter I discuss the challenges to Thompsonian social history, the debates that have ensued, and the new directions that have resulted. I look at historiographical developments that have challenged Marxist-inspired interpretations of British history. Revisionist accounts have tended to stress the constitutive role of political developments and rethought the relationship between class relationships and class struggle, in some cases to the point where class has been rejected as a meaningful category altogether. As in French social and labor history, many of the revisionist critiques have been inspired by the linguistic and cultural turn, which calls into question the social-history approach adhered to by Thompson, his supporters, and his followers.

Ironically, while the status of Thompson's legacy pervades these critical appraisals, the historiographical debate that most directly confronted it focused on a subject that he himself did not analyze in any real depth – Chartism. The dispute was precipitated by Gareth Stedman Jones's path-breaking essay "Rethinking Chartism," published in *Languages of Class: Studies in English Working Class History, 1832–1982* (1983). To my knowledge no historiographical debate, in any national tradition, so dramatically captures either the challenge of the linguistic turn to the assumptions of social history and class analysis or social historians' passionate defense of their project. As the debate broadened in scope, it involved historians of varying specialties and time periods. Most important here is the social/cultural historian Patrick Joyce. His advocacy of a postmodern history, which saw class identities and the social realm as discursive categories requiring historical explanation, represents a significant challenge to the conventions of social history well beyond anything Stedman Jones proposed and proved equally, if not more, controversial. The title of this chapter, appropriately enough, is taken from the title of the book that played such a pivotal role in launching the debate.

Chartism and the historians

To better appreciate why Stedman Jones's reappraisal of Chartism was both so influential and so provocative, it is important to understand what Chartism was and how it has been understood by historians – in the context of new social history but earlier as well. The Chartist movement surfaced in the latter part of the 1830s, peaked and declined in the following decade, and had all but disappeared by the middle of the 1850s. It was the first national political movement to draw its principal support from working-class people and the laboring poor. The Charter, its principles now a given of modern democracies, consisted of several demands: universal male suffrage, the secret ballot, the end of property qualifications and the advent of salaries for members of Parliament, uniform electoral districts, and annual parliamentary elections. A major focal point of the Chartist campaign was the presentation of these demands to Parliament on three separate occasions. However, this parliamentary political focus does not do justice to Chartism's multidimensional nature: its outdoor demonstrations, its national organization (the National Charter Association), its network of local branches, its wide-ranging print culture, and the riots and attempted risings implicitly and explicitly associated with it. Over the course of Chartism's life span, many of its activists were arrested and prosecuted for seditious and subversive activities.

Historically, Chartism has had a special status among British left-wing social and labor historians. They tended to regard the Industrial Revolution (and the social and political movements that surfaced in response to it) not just as a pivotal moment in British historical development but also as central to defining the modern experience more generally. They believed this in part because Britain had undergone the Industrial Revolution first and hence defined the meaning of that experience. They also held to it because Marx based his understanding of capitalist development and evolving class consciousness on the British industrial case and hence it had general implications. Seen in these terms, Chartism was accorded a central position in the universal narrative of working-class struggle. In the words of Dorothy Thompson, one of the leading historians of Chartism:

> Chartism's claim to have been the first large-scale national movement to embody the demand for universal male citizen rights has lent it an especial interest as a movement which tackled at an early stage many of the complex questions which were later to face modern labour movements. Many of these were seen to have been presaged in the Chartist period, either explicitly in the political programme of the movement or in the many debates, discussions and activities which accompanied the main agitation (Thompson 1993: 20).

In short, Chartism was both a national and universal event.

Long before the new social history, and from both sides of the political divide, Chartism was portrayed as a product of socio-economic experience, the political expression of class consciousness. This was true of the romantic and conservative writer Thomas Carlyle (1795–1881), for whom, its stated political goals notwithstanding, Chartism expressed the social immiseration of "these wild inarticulate souls, struggling there, with inarticulate uproar, like dumb creatures in pain, unable to speak what is in them!" (quoted in ibid.: 22–23). Among socialists, Marx and Engels produced an indelible image of Chartism as a political movement expressing working-class consciousness. For Engels, it was "the compact form" of the proletariat's opposition to the bourgeoisie. Marx reiterated this viewpoint and expanded upon it:

> Universal Suffrage is the equivalent of political power for the working classes of England, where the proletariat forms the large majority of the population, where, in a long though underground civil war, it had gained a clear consciousness of its position as a class . . . The carrying of Universal Suffrage in England would, therefore, be a far more socialistic measure than anything which has been honoured with that name on the Continent. Its inevitable result, here, is the political supremacy of the working class (quoted in ibid.: 26).

Marx's powerful understanding of Chartism raised as many questions as it solved. If Chartism represented an expression of class consciousness, why did it not – as Marx's theoretical model (as opposed to his more nuanced political observations) implied (see Chapter 1) – lead to demands for a transformation of productive relationships or at least establish the foundation for doing so? Most important, given these expectations, why was the collapse of Chartism followed by the labor movement's greater willingness in the second half of the century to negotiate with capitalists and give its support to the Liberal Party, while socialism, let alone revolutionary socialism, never became more than a minority current?

A classic answer to this question attributed the accommodation of the labor movement to the mid-nineteenth-century appearance of a "labor aristocracy." The idea surfaced in the middle of the nineteenth century, was used by Marx and Engels to explain Chartism's split into two movements, was developed by Vladimir Lenin (1870–1924) as a general explanation of labor movement reformism, and entered modern historical scholarship with Eric Hobsbawm's empirical treatment of it (Hobsbawm 1964). Subsequently, John Foster restated it in orthodox Leninist terms (Foster 1974). Roughly speaking, the labor aristocracy thesis suggested that, following Chartism's decline and industrial capitalism's stabilization, the working class became divided between unskilled, marginalized workers and skilled, privileged, and influential labor aristocrats who accommodated themselves to, and fought for reforms within, a more stable, prosperous, and pliable capitalist order.

In general, Chartist historiography, informed by the new social and labor history project of the 1960s and 1970s, developed along two interrelated paths. First, Asa Briggs's edited collection, *Chartist Studies* (1959: 2), proclaimed that "a study of Chartism must begin with a proper appreciation of regional and local diversity." The book helped facilitate a wave of microhistorical investigations. Second, E. P. Thompson never analyzed Chartism in any depth, but his treatment of it in the closing pages of *The Making of the English Class* was immensely influential. The aspiration for the vote, he argued, symbolized "equality of citizenship, personal dignity, worth" as well as a "new way of reaching out by the working people for *social control* over their conditions of life and labour" (Thompson [1963] 1968: 910). More generally, Thompson's evocative recreation of working-class experience inspired historians to view Chartism as more than purely symbolic of economic grievances and more than just a precursor to the organized labor movement. He inspired them to take Chartist political goals and aims seriously, to see them as a political expression of working-class consciousness.

Yet if Edward Thompson never made specific contributions to Chartist historiography, his wife Dorothy most conspicuously did. Born to a family of artisans and musicians in London, Dorothy Thompson grew up in Kent, was educated at the local county school for girls, graduated from Girton College, Cambridge, and for many years taught in the History Department of the University of Birmingham (Thompson 1993; Walker 2000). Overshadowed by her charismatic and remarkably influential husband, she nonetheless participated in many of the intellectual and political ventures that he took part in, including (more than him) participation in the Communist Party's Historians' Group, the founding of the new left, and participation in various incarnations of the Campaign for Nuclear Disarmament. She balanced the frequently conflicting demands of motherhood, political activism, and an academic career. As she has recalled:

> This story explains why my output has been small for a career covering more than forty years. In a working partnership exact equality is seldom achieved, and I have had less time and space for my work than Edward has. However, I don't think that I resent this at all, since the quality of his work is its own justification. If I did not respect his work I might feel differently, since I don't suffer from undue modesty. If our work is set side by side there is no doubt which is more important and interesting (Thompson 1993: 9).

Dorothy Thompson might not have displayed the same theoretical flare or inspired literary style as her husband, but she made her own distinctive mark on historical scholarship. She was in the forefront of expanding the parameters of women's history in the 1970s, evidenced by "Women and Nineteenth-Century Radical Politics: A Lost Dimension" (Thompson 1976). She has written about Queen Victoria, in the context of gender relationships and popular politics (Thompson 1990; 1993: 164–86). Her most prominent scholarly achievement is a full-length study, *The Chartists* (1984), the culmination of decades of research and writing (Thompson 1971; Epstein and Thompson 1982).

Dorothy Thompson influenced Chartist historiography in multiple ways. In the late 1960s and early 1970s, she helped set a new research agenda for the field. Thompson called for a closer examination of the Chartist leadership, a more sustained analysis of the role of violence within the movement, and greater attention being paid to Chartism's origins. She advocated that researchers develop a better geographical understanding of Chartism, a more sophisticated grasp of the occupations of its adherents, and a greater comprehension of the movement's long-term impact. *The Chartists* itself was a product of this research agenda as well as providing a new and innovative political interpretation (Taylor 1996). Thompson drew on the findings of many of the local studies that followed in the wake of Briggs's *Chartist Studies*. Yet she argued that ultimately Chartism was a national political movement, understandable in light of its activists' goals, aspirations, and strategies. She acknowledged Chartism's economic and social roots, while distancing herself from the reductionism inherent in the "knife and fork" view, found in Briggs among others, which attributed the movement's militancy to the "'cyclical fluctuations' of the early nineteenth-century British economy" (Briggs 1959: 2).

Thompson traced the origins of Chartism to disappointments over the working-class's exclusion from the provisions of the 1832 Reform Bill, a milestone of parliamentary electoral reform that increased the electorate's size, while overwhelmingly benefiting the middle class. Working-class aspirations to achieve the political franchise were buttressed by (1) opposition to legislative initiatives enacted by the first parliament elected under the Reform Bill's provisions and (2) anger at governmental attempts to suppress workers' militancy. Adopting a posture suggestive of a long collaborative relationship with her husband, Thompson sympathetically recreated the aspirations of the Chartists from their own perspective. She conceived of Chartism as a rational, sophisticated, and lucid political response by working-class people, an advance from the more spontaneous outbursts of eighteenth-century plebian protests. Though the Chartists were undoubtedly unsuccessful in the short term, she argued, they left an indelible imprint on political culture, a creative and imaginative legacy that informed later working-class activism.

By the time that Thompson published *The Chartists*, the consensus among historians of Chartism (and social historians more generally) was beginning to disintegrate. Her book was overshadowed by Stedman Jones's revisionist critique of existing Chartist historiography (including implicitly her own approach) and his challenge to the theoretical assumptions of social history more generally. Stedman Jones challenged social historians' taken-for-granted understanding of class formation, arguing that its assumption of a causal connection between class position and class consciousness ignored the constitutive role of language.

Rethinking Chartism

Gareth Stedman Jones (1942–) holds a singular position among British social and cultural historians. He has been a long-time editor of the *History Workshop Journal*, a journal closely associated with the socialist and feminist project of history from below. His early work (as he acknowledged) was indebted to, as well as critical of, E. P. Thompson's account of working-class formation in *The Making of the English Working Class* (Stedman Jones 1983: 12). However, between 1964 and 1981 Stedman Jones was also on the editorial board of *New Left Review*, a Marxist journal, which, under the editorship of Perry Anderson, criticized Thompson's socialist-humanist politics and "populist" historical view. Stedman Jones's first book, *Outcast London* ([1971] 1984), was not a celebratory account of the London poor: it sought to understand the triumph of liberal ideology in Victorian Britain. Stedman Jones later recalled that the book was aligned with *New Left Review*'s efforts at understanding why England had failed to produced a revolutionary intelligentsia and focused on the triumph of liberal ideology among workers (Stedman Jones [1971] 1984: xiii–xiv). Where Thompson, probably speaking for many (if not most) social historians, famously declared "the poverty of theory" (Thompson 1978b), Stedman Jones believed in the importance of historians developing a theoretical dimension to their work. In an early essay, "History: The Poverty of Empiricism" (1972), he attacked the empiricism of the British historical profession, lamented its virtual obliviousness to modern European social thought, and defended the centrality of theory to the historian's enterprise. He aligned himself with the totalizing ambitions and social-scientific spirit of the *Annales* school. He was among the few British social historians to profit from a theoretical engagement with Althusser's thought (see Chapter 3).

As a socialist historian, Stedman Jones likewise aspired to confront the left's mythologies, the precondition (in his view) for conceiving of political advance of a meaningful kind. Consider, for example, the essay "Working-Class Culture and Working-Class Politics in London, 1870–1900: Notes on the Remaking of a Working Class" in *Languages of Class* (Stedman Jones 1983: 179–238), which simultaneously paid tribute to and was critical of Thompson's classic account of working-class formation. Stedman Jones sought to reconcile Thompson's portrayal of a heroic working class, which seemed primed to challenge the dominant order, with the tepid reformism that would come to characterize the dominant thrust of the labor movement. He found a "remaking" of the working class at the end of the nineteenth century, a period often represented by labor historians as a militant period, personified by the new unionism, mass strike actions, and the spread of socialist influence. For Stedman Jones, what in fact had been created was a deeply conservative, insular, and inward-looking working-class culture that accepted the capitalist order as "an immovable horizon," simultaneously embodied in the music hall and the Labour Party.

Stedman Jones's understanding of Chartism challenged taken-for-granted assumptions regarding the movement's "social" and "class" nature, found in the new social history as well as earlier interpretations. For Stedman Jones, the idea that Chartism was a political movement rooted in social or class grievances was founded on a problematic notion of the relationship between society and politics. This notion was derived from a conception of the link between social being and consciousness, originally formulated by Marx and powerfully developed by Thompson, that regarded class consciousness and action as resulting from the experience of objective class relations. Stedman Jones argued that this view was based on an "essentialist conception of class, in which all the different languages of class are measured against Marxist or socio-logical conceptions of class position." As a result, historians "have taken as their task the demonstration of concordance with, or the explanation of devi-ation from, positions which socio-economic logic ascribes" (ibid.: 21). For Stedman Jones, what this perspective failed to take into account was the role of language. Where the social-history paradigm assumed that it was a transpar-ent medium giving voice to experience, language in fact played a constitutive role in producing consciousness. Drawing on insights from what he described as "the broader significance of Saussure's work," Stedman Jones argued that language was material, the implication being that historians could not simply derive experience from language, because the latter in fact structured the former's expression. As he stated it:

> Language disrupts any simple notion of the determination of consciousness by social being because it is itself part of social being. We cannot therefore decode political language to reach a primal and material expression of inter-est since it is the discursive structure of political language which conceives and defines interest in the first place. What we must therefore do is to study the production of interest, identification, grievance and aspiration within political languages themselves (ibid.: 21–22).

Stedman Jones used this "non-referential conception of language" to deci-pher Chartist texts. His achievement was not so much to uncover new sources but to read those that were already known in a fresh light. In this, he accorded the language of Chartism its own autonomous weight, which meant lavishing attention on it as a political discourse. Stedman Jones argued that Chartist lan-guage was rooted in the tradition of political radicalism, which harked back to the seventeenth century but coalesced as a political program a century later. Radicalism was based on opposition to the political monopoly of the govern-ing classes. Its association with populist and democratic movements in Ireland, America, and, above all, revolutionary France gave it a subversive edge. Radical discourse was embraced by a string of disenfranchised groups that wanted parliamentary representation and electoral rights within the framework of the English constitution. When the Reform Bill of 1832 failed to produce the working-class vote, the language of radicalism became the vehicle for giving vent to workers' frustration at having been frozen out.

For Stedman Jones, two important consequences flowed from viewing Chartism in this way. First, rather than being understood as the "superficial encasement of proletarian class consciousness" or a "simple medium of translation between experience and programme," Chartist discourse played a constitutive role in shaping working-class grievances and indeed the contours of class consciousness itself (ibid.: 105). Second, when radicalism was placed at the center of the narrative, alternative ways of viewing Chartist consciousness surfaced. Chartism could now be seen as being founded on a division between the "represented" and the "unrepresented," not capitalists and workers. Hence, working-class antagonism to the middle class was often restricted to those who participated in, or benefited from, the state's tyrannical practices. It "was not ascribed to their role in production, but to their participation in a corrupt and unrepresentative political system, and it was through this political system that the producers of wealth were conceived to be deprived of the fruits of their labour" (ibid.: 106–07).

Third, viewing Chartism in political terms had an impact on the interpretation of its demise. Given that Chartism was framed as a radical discourse calling for the reform of the political system, its appeal was bound to wane when those demands began to be met – or at least when there were signs that they would be met. If the fall of Chartism could be attributed to the fragmentation of its political discourse, "there is then little need to introduce ambitious sociological explanations, such as the emergence of a labour aristocracy, co-option by the middle class or the invention of new and subtle means of social control, in order to explain the disappearance of Chartism" (ibid.: 107). In short, Stedman Jones dispensed with modes of understanding that had long since been ingrained within Chartist historiography. It is not that he denied the role of class. However, he saw it as language that was defined by political practices.

In "Rethinking Chartism" (ibid.: 90–178) Stedman Jones was challenging the foundation of social history, based on the primacy of socio-economic determinations – whether in terms of the base–superstructure model, social being and consciousness, class structure and class consciousness, or a combination of these. Stedman Jones, in fact, was in the first stages of articulating a cultural-history approach emphasizing language and discourse and the constitutive role of politics.

The rethinking of the relationship between the political and social, language and experience, found in "Rethinking Chartism" was likewise evident in Stedman Jones's analysis of the contemporary crisis of the left. Following the triumph of Thatcherism in the 1979 parliamentary election, the labor movement entered into a period of soul searching. Discussions regarding its condition and future prospects took place in journals such as *Marxism Today* and *New Socialist*. Among the most influential and discussed interventions (cited in Stedman Jones's own analysis of Labour's crisis) was Eric Hobsbawm's "The Forward March of Labour Halted?" (published with responses as *The Forward March of Labour Halted?*) (Hobsbawm *et al.* 1981), which analyzed the movement's predicament from a base–superstructure historical perspective. Hobsbawm attributed Labour's decline to the combined impact of larger economic units, the growth of monopoly capital, a greatly enlarged public sector, and a greater number of female workers. The net result was increased sectional divisions, the fragmentation of the common working-class way of life, and an atmosphere that hindered unified class action and threatened the solidarity of the labor movement as a whole.

Stedman Jones's essay, "Why is the Labour Party in Such a Mess?" (Stedman Jones 1983: 239–256), was by no means only a response to Hobsbawm's argument, but it certainly challenged the latter's theoretical assumptions. Posing the same theoretical questions as in "Rethinking Chartism," Stedman Jones was skeptical of the supposition that the Labour Party could be understood historically from the perspective of either a transformation in its material conditions or changes in the pattern of class relationships. He believed that that it was "more fruitful to treat the Labour Party as a vacant centre – as a space traversed or tenanted by groups possessing different and sometimes incompatible political languages of widely varying provenance, a changing balance of forces and their discursive self-definitions, defined primarily from without" (ibid.: 22).

Similarly, Stedman Jones objected to the portrayal of the labor movement as having made continuous evolutionary progress only to reach an impasse in the 1970s and 1980s. The Labour Party, and the labor movement more generally, was "better understood in terms of a succession of discontinuous conjunctures which enabled it to achieve specific forms of success at rather widely separated points in time" (ibid.: 23). Just as Chartism represented the last moment of English radicalism and the labor movement redefined itself in the latter part of the century, Labour's 1945 electoral triumph could be viewed as the final cohesive expression of that late nineteenth-century political remaking (discussed earlier in this chapter) and the discourses that held it together. For Stedman Jones, twentieth-century Labour discourse was produced by an alliance of trade-union activists and progressively minded middle-class professionals who demanded deference from their working-class allies. This coalition was crumbling under the weight of social, political, and cultural contradictions, but the political language that helped produce it continued to be the "common sense" of the left and hence an obstacle to genuine rethinking. In effect, Stedman Jones was advocating the need for a new political language, one capable of addressing those excluded from Labour's target audience of white male organized workers and professionals: notably immigrants, women, single-parent families, and the unemployed. Given that Stedman Jones believed in the necessity of a new political language, it is not surprising that he later contributed to the *New Times* project (see Chapter 3).

Debating Languages of Class

The debates precipitated by *Languages of Class* provide a focal point for discussing the consequences of the cultural and linguistic turn for British social history as well as recent historical work made possible by it. The debate is divisible into two phases. The first, which I discuss in this section, primarily consists of immediate rejoinders – many in the form of extended book reviews – to Stedman Jones's revisionist project. The second phase, the subject of the next section, begins roughly in the early 1990s and extends well into the decade. It is intertwined with wider discussions over the relevance of postmodern ideas for historical work, especially as espoused by Patrick Joyce.

Stedman Jones was certainly not the only historian to explore the implications of a nonreferential theory of language. As we have seen, historians such as Geoff Eley and William Sewell were moving in parallel directions. Yet no historian adopting such a posture (with the possible exception of Joan Scott, who will be discussed below and in Chapter 6) evoked the same intensity of response as Stedman Jones. Despite the fact that *Languages of Class* consisted of mostly published work, even though "Rethinking Chartism" was barely more than 100 pages and its argument had already been made in an earlier though less provocative version (Stedman Jones 1982), the book – and particularly the essay – provoked an astounding level of critical response among social and labor historians and other scholars as well. Rereading the book after many years, I am struck by its tentativeness. Stedman Jones wrote, for instance, that his intent was not "to imply that the analysis of language can provide an exhaustive account of Chartism, or that the social conditions of existence of this language were arbitrary" (Stedman Jones 1983: 95). Of the more general state of the linguistic turn, he observed that "it would be foolish to pretend that the harnessing of elementary insights derived from theories of language to problems of substantive historical interpretation is in anything other than an extremely primitive state" (ibid.: 24). If E. P. Thompson had undertaken such a venture it would have been fiercely polemical. In contrast, Stedman Jones adopted a cautious and measured tone throughout.

So how do we account for the response? First, Stedman Jones was not free from lecturing his colleagues. He implored historians to "confront the implications of landmarks in twentieth century linguistics for the study of the social" and suggested that "if history is to renew itself, and in particular, in this context, social and labour history, it cannot be by the defensive reiteration of well tried and by now well worn formulae" (ibid.: 24). It hardly takes a leap of the imagination to envision scholars, who never imagined that there was a crisis in the first place, seeing this as a form of attack. Moreover, the timing of the essays – written at a time of right-wing triumph in Britain and the United States – was certainly a factor in eliciting heart-felt responses from historians, many of whom found themselves politically on the defensive. Stedman Jones himself recalled three intellectual and political developments that shaped his interests: feminist challenges to the class narrative, the historian Hayden White's work on the tropes of historical narratives, and local social histories that contradicted the overarching story told by the left (Stedman Jones 2001: 118).

Second, Stedman Jones's understanding of Chartism, and the labor movement more generally, was replete with political implications. Britain was the site of the first Industrial Revolution and proletariat. It was pivotal to the creation of socialism as a mode of thought. It was the inspiration for Marx's understanding of the historical dynamic of capitalism. Chartism stood at the crossroads, looking backwards to a long-standing tradition of protest over lost rights – artisans and peasants who were being stripped of their means of production – and forward to the march of organized labor. This vision gained ground as a result of the pervasive influence of E. P. Thompson and other British historians – notably Dorothy Thompson – who had developed it in the context of participation in the Communist movement. Stedman Jones's understanding of Chartism, and the labor movement more broadly, challenged these deeply held beliefs. If Chartism could be framed as the end of the radical tradition, what remained of the idea that it was the fruit of "the making of the English working class"?

Third, *Languages of Class*'s juxtaposition of caution and provocation helps account for the extraordinary debate that followed. Defenders of the new social history could accuse Stedman Jones of betrayal; those who rejected what they deemed as the old pieties, wished that he had gone farther. Stedman Jones himself never responded to his critics until well after the most heated exchanges in the debate had subsided, meaning that he himself became a "vacant center" whereby critics freely read him for their own purposes (although given the passions enflamed by his essay it is not clear how much difference his active participation would have made) (Stedman Jones 1996). The book, in sum, provided a focal point to discuss the crumbling consensus among social historians as well as an occasion to highlight new historiographical directions. The debate started out to be about Stedman Jones: it was soon apparent that the stakes were much higher.

The debate should be seen in the context of earlier discussions among Marxist scholars, both centrally involving E. P. Thompson. In the 1960s Thompson and Perry Anderson crossed swords over the trajectory of modern British history, the political potential of the labor movement, the nature of historical practice, and what it meant to be a socialist intellectual (Anderson 1992; Thompson [1965] 1978). Their exchange represented a confrontation between two intellectual traditions within Marxism. Thompson defended socialist humanism and the English empirical idiom. Anderson located himself within a more philosophically rooted, Western Marxist theoretical tradition (see Chapter 2). This debate was simultaneously renewed and expanded as a result of the growing influence of Althusserian theoretical practice in Britain in the 1970s. Thompson's powerful, yet ultimately ill-conceived, polemical assault on Althusser's Marxism, "The Poverty of Theory" (1978c) provided the lightening rod. In failing to distinguish between those who had critically engaged with Althusser's ideas – for instance, Stuart Hall and Stedman Jones – from card-carrying Althusserians, he produced false polarities that hindered genuine intellectual exchange. In the debate that ensued, the relationship between theory and evidence in historical inquiry, the connection between structure and agency in human history, the link between class structure and class consciousness, and the relation between ideology and experience were all intensely discussed (Dworkin 1997: 219–45).

The debate on Stedman Jones's work had echoes of these earlier debates. It renewed the debate over whether continental modes of philosophical thought – predominantly French – were compatible with English norms of historical practice. (I think of these exchanges as the theoretical equivalent of arguments in mainstream British political culture regarding Britain's relationship to the European Union. Some view it as an assault on sovereignty; others an opportunity for a more cosmopolitan identity.) Yet the discussions stimulated by Stedman Jones's book were also conspicuously different from the Marxist theoretical discussions that preceded them. They involved scholars outside of Britain, particularly North America. Most importantly, Marxism no longer represented the unassailable, taken-for-granted theoretical ground that it had once enjoyed.

Initial responses to *Languages of Class* ran the full gamut: wholehearted enthusiasm (Meacham 1985), respectful yet critical (Gray 1986; Cronin 1986), orthodox Marxist refusal (Foster 1985), varying degrees of cultural Marxist critique (Epstein 1986; Kirk 1987; D. Thompson 1987), and rejection of class analysis altogether (McCord 1985). There were three recurrent criticisms. First, generally admitting that he had been right to call attention to the centrality of language, critics nonetheless found Stedman Jones's understanding of it to be of limited value. The most important objection was that *Languages of Class* deployed a theory of language that did not sufficiently attend to the changing historical context. Nor did it leave room for the conflict over meaning itself: what might be described in Marxist terms as the "class struggle over language." Second, Stedman Jones claimed to be deploying a nonreferential theory of language to understand Chartist politics, but he was in fact engaging in an old-fashioned intellectual history of political ideas, which by definition excluded less formal manifestations of working-class expression from its purview. Third, Stedman Jones misrepresented Thompson's understanding of class. The latter specifically rejected teleological understandings of working-class politics that knew in advance what form it should assume and described it as "false consciousness" when it did not conform to such expectations. Stedman Jones's political portrayal of Chartism might refute orthodox Marxism, but not Thompson's view of it, since he had no such expectations in the first place. In fact, Thompson had an ambiguous relationship to Marxism. He was neither completely free of nor ruled by a teleological understanding of class consciousness.

James Epstein – an American historian of the early English working class and coeditor of the volume in which Stedman Jones's first version of "Rethinking Chartism" appeared (Epstein and Thompson 1982) – blended these critiques. For Epstein, Stedman Jones failed to acknowledge that political language was contested and unstable. He privileged political writings, while ignoring "symbolic action and contest." Epstein contended that:

> The public language of Chartism was preeminently the language of the mass platform. It was through the great "monster" demonstrations at Kersal Moore outside of Manchester or Peep Green in Yorkshire that hundreds of thousands of working-class men, women, and children came to feel an identity of interests, and were able to sense the scale and power of their movement. Chartist language cannot be fully understood outside the rituals and collective solidarities of this context (Epstein 1986: 199).

Epstein's insight into the public language of Chartism is an important correction to Stedman Jones's emphasis on political writings. He does not, however, define what constitutes "preeminence"; nor does he explore the relationship between the two forms of expression to the movement as a whole.

Epstein subsequently elaborated on his understanding of language in, among other places, "Understanding the Cap of Liberty: Symbolic Practice and Social Conflict in Early Nineteenth-Century England" (1989), an essay that, as its title implies, traced the shifting meanings of the radical symbol, the cap of liberty, in relationship to a volatile and swiftly changing historical context. Epstein saw the cap as a symbol mediating the tensions between constitutionalism and republicanism. He situated it in the context of radicals' efforts to redefine the English constitution, to offer an alternative to the version espoused by the governing classes. The importance that Epstein attributed to symbolic gestures in political movements recalled Lynn Hunt's analogous exploration in *Politics, Culture, and Class in the French Revolution* (1984) (see Chapter 4). But where Hunt, writing in a French context, seemed intent on distancing herself from Marxism altogether, Epstein wrote from a cultural-Marxist perspective, challenging Stedman Jones's understanding of the relationship between language and class. Epstein argued that there were links between class position and the construction of symbolic meaning: the meaning of the cap of liberty was embedded in plebian and working-class experience. Where Stedman Jones privileged the role of political discourse in constructing class experience, Epstein argued that it was through the struggle over meaning "that classes define themselves in oppositional relationship to each other" (Epstein 1989: 117).

Among the earlier responses to *Languages of Class*, the most important arguably was a "scholarly controversy" published in *International Labor and Working Class History*. It consisted of Joan Scott's poststructuralist and feminist critique as well as responses to her essay by Bryan Palmer, Christine Stansell, and Anson Rabinbach (Scott 1987; Palmer 1987; Stansell 1987; Rabinbach 1987). Scott's intervention is noteworthy because, first, she pushed Stedman Jones's theoretical insights beyond what he himself proposed. Second, her essay produced responses that were often more about her position than his (a harbinger of later developments whereby Stedman Jones's work became a lightening rod for debating wider issues in social and cultural history). In the next chapter I will focus on Scott's contribution to understanding the relationship between class and gender. In the present context I highlight what she has to say about the relationship between language and class.

Scott found Stedman Jones's rereading of Chartism to be theoretically innovative, while suggesting that he did not fully pursue the logic of his own argument. In practice he adopted a method of reading, derived from intellectual history, which traced the trajectory of a cluster of political ideas rather than (as his own argument dictated) the underlying system of meaning that produced them. "To say, as Stedman Jones does," wrote Scott, "that for

Chartists class was about politics (meaning participation in government), is to miss the opportunity to see how class constructed (and contained) a large social vision through which people established, interpreted, and acted on their place in society (acted not only in dramatic political movements, but also in the practical matters of everyday life)" (Scott 1987: 6). An important part of the problem, in Scott's view, was Stedman Jones's understanding of language, which too often restricted it to "words people say to one another, rather than conveying the idea of meaning as the patterns and relationships that constitute understanding as a 'cultural system'" (ibid.: 6). In Scott's view, despite claiming to deploy a nonreferential theory of language, he never fully explored one of its central insights, the contention that stitching together binary oppositions across the cultural field produced meaning. What it meant to be working class was not only built on the opposition of what it meant to be a capitalist or an aristocrat. It was founded simultaneously on the difference between being a wage laborer or politically unrepresented, on the one hand, and a propertyless woman or child, on the other. For Scott, "the meaning of class extended far beyond the topic of work and workers, because it built on and offered a way of thinking about the relational and differentiated structure of all social life." She advocated an interpretation of Chartism that did not "reduce it neatly to a formal political struggle or a particular strategy offered by an organized group, but to examine the process through which class was conceived" (ibid.: 6–7).

Of the historians to respond to Scott's essay, the most defiant was Bryan Palmer, a Canadian labor historian and a devoted admirer of E. P. Thompson's cultural Marxism, as evidenced in multiple defenses of his historical, theoretical, and political practice (Palmer 1981; 1994). In "Response to Joan Scott" (1987), Palmer accepted Scott's view that Stedman Jones's reading of Chartism was an exercise in the history of political ideas, hence underplaying the class dimension. Yet if Scott regarded this as evidence that Stedman Jones was not poststructuralist enough, Palmer perceived it as an occasion to reaffirm his commitment to cultural Marxism, condemn Stedman Jones's (and Scott's) preoccupation with theory, and denounce the idea that language was all that mattered. Not that he believed that Scott or Stedman Jones actually asserted the last of these, but he believed that they came "dangerously close to it."

Palmer's unease with such trends developed into a full-scale polemical assault against scholars who subscribed to the linguistic turn, particularly social historians. In a book whose title speaks volumes – *Descent into Discourse: The Reification of Language and the Writing of Social History* (1990) – he adopted a strategy reminiscent of Thompson's "The Poverty of Theory." Palmer entered into the belly of the beast, fully engaging with its philosophical sources – Barthes, Derrida, Foucault, and Gayatri Chakravorty Spivak (1942–), among others – as well as historians who in one way or another felt an affinity with them – for example, Rancière, Reddy, Scott, Sewell, and Stedman Jones. Christopher Johnson observed that "it is a great romp, marvelous polemic, and certainly reminds us of some of the dangers of deconstruction gone berserk" (Johnson 1993: 55). Palmer's book likewise produced a Manichean universe of theoretical right and wrong that, in all likelihood, confirmed the views of social historians who disliked the linguistic turn in the first place, was summarily dismissed by committed poststructuralists, and left those interested in bringing together the insights of linguistic and social approaches with no place whatsoever. Palmer did not reject historians' attempts to play closer attention to language out of hand, and in some cases he approved of them. Yet ultimately he argued that such efforts required an explicitly cultural Marxist framework, hence eliminating any possibility for a middle ground.

Descent into Discourse is like "The Poverty Theory" in another way. It was as much about politics as theory. Palmer attributed the descent – and the rejection of class that went with it – to the triumph of the new right in the 1980s and left-wing intellectuals' abandonment of working-class politics. In Stedman Jones's case, Palmer believed that a dogmatic Marxist position espoused earlier in his career was supplanted by "a reformist popular frontism in which class consciousness is immaterial" (Palmer 1990: 142). Summing up his feelings, Palmer wrote: "History read wrongly and politics conceived poorly are but two sides of the same coin" (ibid.: 143). In the first decade of the twenty-first century, whether Stedman Jones did or did not abandon socialism does not seem of any real consequence. It does, however, demonstrate what was simmering beneath the surface in discussions over Stedman Jones's work: for a contingent of social historians, *Languages of Class* simultaneously signified theoretical *and* political betrayal.

Social history wars

The second phase of the debate was more sweeping in its implications and went well beyond the original discussions prompted by Stedman Jones's effort at reformulating social history. It roughly began in the early 1990s, a time when the political landscape was rapidly changing. The end of Communism signified a momentous shift in global political relationships. For Hobsbawm, it symbolically constituted the end of the century itself – the "short twentieth century" as he called it (Hobsbawm 1994). Most left-wing social historians had roundly rejected Soviet Communism, but they could hardly deny the aftershocks of its collapse. Socialism's feasibility on the world stage appeared to vanish into thin air. If a radical impulse could still be mustered, it would have to develop within a triumphant capitalist order dominated by multinational corporations, a single superpower, and rampant globalization.

The intellectual landscape was changing as well. As discussed in Chapter 3, postmodernism in its various guises – the linguistic turn being one component part – was spreading through some (but by no means all) sectors of the humanities and the social sciences. It came to history relatively late, but its impact was no less important. Historians were divided over whether it was an opportunity to rethink their assumptions and practice or whether it had to be contested at all costs (Jenkins 1997: 239–386).

The nucleus of the second burst of discussions of *Languages of Class* was *Social History*, a journal whose origins coincided with the high tide of that field of historical investigation. The "*Social History* wars" were precipitated by David Mayfield and Susan Thorne's critical appraisal of Stedman Jones's essays (Mayfield and Thorne 1992; 1993). They rejected the view (implicit, they believed, in *Languages of Class*) that a clear choice existed between the new social history and the cultural and political history of the linguistic turn. Quite surprisingly, they found that Thompson's view of class formation, with its emphasis on agency, was closer in spirit to the deconstructive perspective of Derrida and Paul de Man (1919–1983) than was Stedman Jones's. Their argument was rejected by Jon Lawrence and Miles Taylor, who found that Mayfield and Thorne had not only misconstrued the theoretical trajectory of Stedman Jones's development: they had also failed to understand its real importance – which was not theoretical as all (Lawrence and Taylor 1993). It was at the center of creating a new vision of nineteenth-century popular politics that stressed continuity (rather than rupture) with eighteenth-century antecedents, a perspective in tune with recent, gradualist perspectives on the Industrial Revolution. Stedman Jones's efforts at detaching popular radicalism from an assumed social foundation made it possible to study hitherto neglected dimensions of political movements ("religion and atheism, constitutional and commercial theory") and to emphasize the role of the state, political parties, and trade unions in providing the "terrain and context" of popular politics.

Just as the earlier debate involving Scott and Palmer moved well beyond what was being proposed in *Languages of Class*, the same happened in the later one. In the exchange between Mayfield and Thorne and Lawrence and Taylor, a major bone of contention was the connection between Stedman Jones and the social-turned-cultural historian Patrick Joyce. For Mayfield and Thorne, Stedman Jones and Joyce signified different expressions of the same impulse of linguistic determinism; for Lawrence and Taylor, despite a common interest in language, they represented dramatically different historiographical directions. In their responses, Joyce, and subsequently James Vernon, rejected Mayfield and Thorne's argument as representing "the received wisdom of social history's elders" and Lawrence and Taylor's as a "complacent faith in empirical research" (Joyce 1993: 82). Joyce and Vernon advocated a cultural history of the social rooted in postmodern and poststructuralist thought (Vernon 1994).

Patrick Joyce was from an Irish Catholic working-class background: one foot in the Gaelic culture of rural western Ireland from where his father's family originated, the other in London where he grew up. He portrayed himself as "twice removed" from the English establishment. His background was personified by his Catholic education. Joyce attributed his keen interest in the relationship between knowledge and power (to his mind embedded in all historical work) as resulting from his marginal yet insider status as an Irish Londoner (Joyce 2001).

Like so many social historians, Joyce was drawn to the linguistic and cultural turn as a consequence of his disenchantment with Marxism. The transition from a Marxist-influenced to a postmodern historian is found in two major historical works: *Visions of the People: Industrial England and the Question of Class, 1848–1914* (1991) and *Democratic Subjects: The Self and the Social in Nineteenth-Century England* (1994). In the earlier text Joyce vacillated between overthrowing and rehabilitating class as a viable category for analyzing nineteenth-century popular politics. On the one hand, he believed that now that historians were less inclined to view the Industrial Revolution as a convulsive event, the timing of the proletariat's emergence as a class and the class culture that it produced must, at the very least, be delayed. Joyce's own inclination was to put off the emergence of this class culture until after World War I, a sharp contrast with either E. P. Thompson (the 1830s) or Hobsbawm (Hobsbawm 1984: 194–213) and Stedman Jones (the late 1800s).

On the other hand, if Joyce did not reject class altogether, he certainly found it a problematic and overblown category. He accepted that there was a unity to working-class experience. However, he characterized it as primarily the "consciousness of *a* class," rather than the "consciousness of class" itself; that is, it did not conform to the classic Marxist notion of "class for itself." This consciousness was most prominently manifested through "a family of populist discourses," which transcended class divisions, were universalistic in their aspiration, and embraced a moral vision of the world built on a division between a wronged and disenfranchised people and an oppressive ruling class (Joyce 1991: 329). Reminiscent of Stedman Jones, Joyce argued that these populist discourses were prominent in producing working-class identities. Yet Joyce cast his web wider than Stedman Jones. Beginning with the study of relatively formal political expressions, he extended his purview to what he called the "symbolic structure of 'everyday' community life" (dress, gesture, and the built environment) and ended up analyzing the languages of the popular arts (the music hall, broadside ballads, dialect literature, and so forth).

Joyce described *Visions of the People* as a work in progress. Once long-held assumptions regarding class fell by the wayside, the familiar appeared strange. Any picture of popular consciousness could only be regarded as provisional. James Epstein, for one, welcomed the exploratory nature of the book, while questioning whether Joyce had fully come to terms with the full import of the postmodern impulse. Joyce, in effect, replaced the category of class with that of populism. "However ambiguous (and non-social)" this may be, observed Epstein, it "is arguably at odds with postmodernist questioning of the privileged status of all categories – the reading of texts being universally subversive of stable meaning and structures" (Epstein 2003: 36). Furthermore, Joyce adopted a "socially determinate theory of language and meaning," only to explain the rise of "socially ambiguous discourses" in terms of the piecemeal and uneven nature of industrial development. He was not nearly as liberated from the base–superstructure model as he imagined.

Indeed, Joyce reached similar conclusions himself in his subsequent book, *Democratic Subjects*. Referring to *Visions of the People*, he wrote:

> This earlier work was marked by a nostalgia for collective social subjects and bedrock "experiences," upon which values and culture could be based. Collective subjects like "the people" and "the working class" still haunt the book, subjects that are taken as pre-constituted and which then function as the source of discourse, so that "populism" is too easily given coherence by virtue of its origin in a supposedly coherent collective subject. Subjects are seen as constructing meanings, whereas meanings construct subjects (Joyce 1994: 11).

In *Democratic Subjects* Joyce crossed the postmodern divide. He had originally given the book the title "The Death of Class." Although the idea was abandoned in favor of the more playful and less provocative one ultimately chosen, the original intent (as well as the decision to share it with readers) clearly signified his determination to make a final break with Thompsonian social history. Indeed, the book's introduction is tantamount to a postmodern manifesto for social historians, with all the boldness and originality, arrogance and idealism that such an enterprise entails.

I will return to Joyce's theoretical reflections in connection to social history, but first I want to say something about his historical practice. For those familiar (and comfortable) with the genre of social-history writing, *Democratic*

Subjects can be something of a surprise. Joyce refrained from the typical organization of the social-history narrative. Each of the first two parts constituted a study of a single individual – the working-class writer Edwin Waugh and the middle-class reformer John Bright. For Joyce, despite their different class positions, they shared a common sense of self, rooted in a religious view of the world, which emphasized the centrality of the moral life and pictured society in terms of a shared humanity, "humanity" playing an analogous role to what "populism" had in *Visions of the People*. Taking its lead arguably from feminist interest in the relationship between the public and private (see Chapter 6), the section on Waugh is the most unconventional: it is dominated by the analysis of his unpublished diary.

Historians are rarely absorbed by a single text, a practice that is, of course, routine in philosophy and literary criticism. But as Epstein pointed out (Epstein 2003: 42–43), Joyce's interpretation of that text continued the conventional practice of focusing on its meaning (content) as opposed to how that meaning was produced (form). Joyce's exploration of the autodidact Waugh was indebted to Rancière, who challenged stereotypes of working-class artisans, exploring the lives of worker-intellectuals who dreamt of transcending their uncertain and unstable existence through acts of poetic imagination (see Chapter 4). For Joyce, Waugh was "a classically liminal figure who is forever half leaving what he came from in order to discover and to demonstrate that he wholly belongs to it" (Joyce 1994: 37). Waugh mythologized work and class identity to combat assaults on workers' integrity but, ultimately, saw labor as the vehicle to achieve an all-inclusive humanity rooted in the heart, not the intellect.

Joyce's *Democratic Subjects* was part of a broader project of reframing social history – and indeed history more generally – along postmodern lines. Joyce argued for this in multiple places (Joyce 1995a: 3–16; Joyce 1998), but "The End of Social History?" (Joyce 1995b) most directly challenged social historians' assumptions. For Joyce, social history was the legacy of a now antiquated modernism, founded on "essentialist" notions of society and class: "The social was the vast, neutral background in which everything was registered and everything connected. If society was the system, or the machine, class was the motive force, and historical principle, which drove the machine" (Joyce 1995b: 75). In contrast, Joyce championed an antifoundational postmodernism, in his view, a way of thinking in step with the momentous transformations of the late twentieth century.

What does this mean for society and class? Borrowing from poststructuralist feminist thought, particularly Joan Scott, Joyce suggested that if gender was culturally produced, that is, gendered identities were not derived from stable, already-known referents, the same could be said for class. In short, Joyce advocated a historical practice that traced the way in which discourses pertaining to "class" and the "social" were produced:

> The search now is how meanings have been produced by relations of power, rather than for "external" or "objective" class "structures," or other "social" referents. It also follows that if identity is composed through the relations of systems of difference, then it is marked by conflict, and is plural, diverse and volatile. The view of identity is one in which many "identities" press in and react with one another (we are men and women, parents and children, members of classes and nations, modernists and post modernists, and so on) (Joyce 1995b: 82).

The history of the social, as championed by Joyce, took its cue from Foucault (see Chapter 4). Joyce likewise drew from poststructuralist feminist theory, itself indebted to Foucault; Zygmunt Bauman's sociology of the postmodern (see Chapter 3); and Dipesh Chakrabarty of the Subaltern Studies group, who sought to write a postcolonial history liberated from the intrinsic Eurocentricism of modernist historical narratives (see Chapter 8).

An example of the alternative to social history and the class narrative advocated by Joyce is found in James Vernon's *Politics and the People: A Study in English Political Culture, c.1815–1867* (1993). Vernon regarded "reading politics as an attempt to put the decentered Humpty Dumpty back together again by making identity fixed, stable, and coherent (however provisionally) through the narrative forms of its languages"; and he saw the political sphere as involving "a discursive struggle to empower people by imagining them as legitimately acting subjects around specific fixed identities" (Vernon 1993: 5). Vernon's reading of nineteenth-century political history reversed the common sense of liberal and Marxist interpretations. Rather than seeing political developments as constituting a steady march towards democratization, he conceived of them as closing off spaces for participatory politics. Drawing on a wide variety of oral, visual, and printed sources, not usually looked at by political historians, Vernon portrayed the "unreformed" political system prior to 1832 as containing numerous participatory forms. He especially emphasized various expressions of melodrama, which belonged "to all political groups and to none, although they were, of course, used and appropriated in different ways" (ibid.: 332). As a form of expression, melodrama developed in the wake of the French Revolution as part of an effort to give new meaning to a world whose understanding of society, politics, and religion were in flux. It dealt in a world of moral absolutes, representing the social in terms of a Manichean struggle between good and evil. Vernon traced the closing down of these spaces, reform being defined predominantly in terms of propertied men, a raucous visual and oral culture being supplanted by one that was more restrained, formal, and print-dominated.

Another historian worth citing in this context is Dror Wahrman, who in *Imagining the Middle Class: The Political Representation of Class in Britain, c.1780–1840* (1995) and other writings inverted the terms in which class and the social were conventionally understood (Wahrman 1992a; 1992b). Social reality, in his view, did not determine social representation nor was it determined by it. Politics, the realm of agency and contingency, linked them together. Class was a political construct that produced an understanding of social relationships. Writing of the emergence of the middle class, with clear ramifications for class theory generally, Wahrman wrote: "It was politics, investing social concepts and language with importance and relevance . . . that determined when and where notions of 'middle class' appeared, and thus the purported 'emergence' of this social class" (Wahrman 1992b: 112). Wahrman traced the category "middle class" in Britain to the French revolutionary wars, when the Friends of Peace founded their moderate opposition to British policy on the basis of a social rather than a political identity. They proclaimed themselves to be the propertied middle classes, the bedrock on which the nation was founded. At the time there was no room for such a group in the Whig/Tory discourse of English politics. It became possible during the Reform Bill agitation, when a new social group was needed to defend the constitutional principle of virtual representation as a bulwark against working-class demands for the franchise. A history of the middle class – its emergence imagined as early as the English Revolution and Reformation – was produced after the fact in order to give the group political legitimacy.

Joyce's postmodern call to arms was by no means greeted with universal enthusiasm. Neville Kirk rejected postmodern historical approaches altogether, ultimately seeing Joyce and Stedman Jones as being linguistic determinists. Kirk's contribution to the *Social History* wars was just one instance of a principled, determined, and resolute assault on post-Marxism, postmodernism, and the linguistic turn in book reviews (Kirk 1987), essays (Kirk 1994; 1995), edited volumes (Kirk 1996; Belchem and Kirk 1997), and full-length historical studies (Kirk 1998). Just as important, Kirk eloquently defended the continuing relevance of the new social history and a materialist understanding of class:

> As a result of many years of hard theoretical and empirical labour, historians and others have clearly *demonstrated* that socio-economic, political and cultural systems and processes have emerged and changed over time.

People have been observed to move up and down social ladders, populations to rise and decline, social classes to coalesce and fragment, and economies to "move" and "work" in patterned, if far from "lawed" ways. It has furthermore been demonstrated that social forces and changes often take place "behind people's backs" and in unintended and partly unrecognized ways . . . Language can be present in the construction and comprehension of social life. But, as brilliantly argued by social anthropologist Maurice Bloch, language is not necessarily present, and exists alongside a variety of nonlinguistic influences. Scholars have convincingly shown that the presence of class structures, demographic trends and even concepts in society is ultimately not dependent upon their registration in language (Kirk 1994: 238).

Kirk spoke for a group of social historians who were determined to defend the continued relevance of the tradition to which they belonged and who believed that postmodernism in its various forms spelled the death of intellectual and political work as they understood it.

Geoff Eley and Keith Nield (the editor of *Social History*) were likewise critical of Joyce, as suggested by their response to the latter's "The End of Social History?" in their jointly authored "Starting Over: The Present, the Post-Modern and the Moment of Social History" (1995). Given Eley's enthusiasm for the linguistic and culture turn (see Chapter 4), we might expect that he and Joyce might find a common ground. Indeed, in "The End of Social History?," Joyce had enthusiastically cited an unpublished paper that Eley and Nield had jointly given in 1994 (Joyce 1995b: 75-76). Yet where Joyce had burned his bridges with his historical materialist past, Eley and Nield sought a dialogue between the "old" new social history and cultural Marxism on the one hand, and new cultural and linguistic approaches on the other. They believed that Joyce's position obliterated the differences between orthodox Marxism and the various strands of creative Marxist thought characteristic of new left scholarship. Most important, they argued that he failed to take into account the role that capitalism played in shaping and reshaping peoples' subjectivities, the recognition of which entailed retaining a notion of class, however reformulated. As they stated it:

The licence for the blanket repudiation of class is insecure, itself resting on a perhaps surprising and causally imperious totalizing move, an under-specified assertion of the consequences of how the "world has changed." Yet, we would argue, especially in the latest transnational and globalized forms, capitalism continues to entail necessary logics of inequality and exploitation, of who gets what, and through what mechanisms. In the world

of these logics, class is more than the master category of a now allegedly dis-
credited marxist analytical "realism," and remains at the very least a useful
descriptive term for the conjunctural outcomes of capitalism's distributive
logics . . . Capitalism continues to make people poor. This, too, is a dimension
– part of the "means and manner" – of "the continual recreation of society"
(Eley and Nield 1995: 359).

Joyce matched Eley's and Nield's stridency in his reply, rejecting their
characterization of him as caricature (Joyce 1996: 98). Yet his own position
here is unclear. It certainly does seem that he has abandoned a materialist
understanding of the impact of capitalism on peoples' consciousness, as Eley
and Nield suggest. It seems unlikely, however, that he is denying that realities
such as unemployment, income disparities, forms of labor exploitation, and
the inequities of the global market have no impact on people's lives. More
likely, he regards capitalism as a discursive formation, which itself is part of the
history of the social. Yet in the present context the importance of the exchange
between Joyce, on the one hand, and Eley and Nield, on the other, is that it
captures the passions aroused by postmodernist approaches, even among
those who might be thought of being in sympathy with them, and suggests the
simplifications that can result when scholars are lumped together.

Beyond binaries

Debates precipitated by Stedman Jones's *Languages of Class* have been polemical. Polemics make it possible, of course, for disagreements to be sharply
posed, ideally leading to the rethinking and reframing of positions. They are
also responsible for caricatures, simplifications, and misrepresentations of what
others have to say and exacerbate differences. Of course, not all the participants in the debate under discussion have embraced polemics as a mode of
argumentation. Indeed, as the dust begins to settle, it just might be that such
voices are helping change the tone of the discussion, making contributions
that go beyond the social/cultural binary.

Within Chartist historiography Miles Taylor has suggested that, despite
continuing sharp disagreements in the approaches advocated by Dorothy
Thompson and Stedman Jones, there might after all be the basis for a new
consensus (Taylor 1996). He cited four reasons. First, both Thompson and
Stedman Jones treated Chartism as an "articulate popular movement" that put
forward rational demands and arguments. Second, rather than simply place

Chartism within the "hungry forties," they saw it within a longer timeframe, stretching back to the Reform Bill crisis of the early 1830s. Third, local and regional variation notwithstanding, both viewed Chartism as a national movement, with a recognizable leadership, program, and publishing network. And fourth, neither explained either the rise or fall of Chartism using models of economic or sociological determinism.

The effort to create a position that is neither in the social or cultural history camp is found in David Cannadine's *Class in Britain* (2000), an overview of the British social-history debate as well as a contribution to it. Cannadine situated himself in relationship to both the Marxism of the new social history and the postmodern and cultural approaches that sought to replace it. He aligned himself with those who critiqued the Marxist notion of class for its socio-economic reductionism, although his analysis of Marxism beyond the writings of Marx himself was virtually nonexistent. He thus gave the impression that debates within the Marxist tradition on the limits of the classical model have never taken place. Cannadine likewise distanced himself from the post-modern rejection of class. He argued that Britain, at least at the level of cultural and political self-description, has been saturated with class sentiment, although what he had in mind by such sentiment was closer to Weber's understanding of status than either Marx's or Weber's understanding of class (see Chapter 1). Cannadine saw British understandings of class as having assumed three distinct forms: a finely graded pyramid; a three-tiered model of upper, middle, and lower; and a binary opposition of "us" versus "them," the people against the powerful.

Cannadine's book describes these three forms as they have developed since the eighteenth century. If he defended class as a central form of social description, he by no means vindicated Marxists' privileging of class struggle. He found the most compelling social description of British society to be a stable hierarchy. Regarding nineteenth-century Britain, Cannadine wrote: "When, in the pages of *Pride and Prejudice*, Lady Catherine de Burgh opines that she liked to have 'the distinctions of rank preserved,' she spoke not only for her order and her generation, but for the majority of Britons during the first three quarters of the nineteenth century" (Cannadine 2000: 104). The book is populated by many (mostly English) figures who would concur. They represented the nineteenth-century equivalent of our "talking heads": literary figures, politicians, and religious leaders dominate. In the chapter in which she is quoted, the fictional Lady Catherine is, ironically, among the very few women cited. In short, Cannadine does not provide sufficient evidence to assert that Lady Catherine's perspective represents those of most Britons.

A third effort to create an intermediate position is found in James Epstein's *In Practice* (2003). Epstein had roots in the cultural Marxist tradition. However, he took seriously the challenges provided by postmodern, postcolonial, feminist, and cultural-studies scholarship. "Historians," he observed, "might do well to lower their disciplinary defenses, worry a bit less about postmodernism's threat to social history and seize on the very real openings available for writing new kinds of social and cultural history" (Epstein 2003: 56). Epstein retained a qualified support for class as a framing device for historical work, while advocating a view of culture that might well be accepted by both cultural and social historians. Culture was "performative": a "practical activity, subject to appropriations, conflict, change, and fragmentation, as activity embedded within a network of relational fields or positions, including the social and the political" (ibid.: 9).

This view, according to Epstein, allowed the restoration of power and politics to cultural investigations. It had four ramifications. First, culture could never be divorced from unequal power relations. Second, political culture was not autonomous: it was a site of struggle – whether in terms of class, race, gender, and so forth. Third, reading texts involved understanding not only how they produced meaning but also the context in which they were fashioned and received. Fourth, the situated nature of expression was both constraining and enabling, making possible expressive forms of agency and repertoires of meaningful action.

One of the essays in *In Practice*, a coauthored essay with John Belchem, "The Nineteenth-Century Gentleman Leader Revisited" (ibid.: 126–45), gives us some idea of what Epstein had in mind. They acknowledged the "gentleman leader" as a fixture of nineteenth-century politics, who spoke to the "people" rather than the working class, but they likewise believed that the meanings attached to him varied according to the context, changed over time, and had a class dimension. They showed this by contrasting the cluster of meanings that coalesced around leaders in Chartist open-air meetings as opposed to more sober indoor ones presided over by Bright and Gladstone. In short, Belchem and Epstein sought to create a bridge between social and cultural history, displacing the idea that they were incompatible.

Conclusion

Taken together, the contributions of Taylor, Cannadine, and Epstein provide evidence that the passions aroused by Stedman Jones's *Languages of Class*,

Patrick Joyce's work, and the broader debates over social and cultural history may indeed be subsiding. There is no returning to the "halcyon" days of the 1960s and 1970s: the conceptual and political terrain in which "class" thrived has been transformed. Yet the concept is by no means dead. What many of the scholars that I discussed in this chapter have come to realize is that, if class is to remain a viable category, it must be articulated with other determinations and identities. Eley, Epstein, and Scott have acknowledged this. Kirk (Kirk 1995: 2) and Dorothy Thompson have as well. In Thompson's words: "If earlier definitions of class can now be seen to have been over-simplified and inadequate to describe all kinds of social tension, then we need different definitions. Gender, regional and national loyalties, religious and ethnic divisions have been neglected as divisive factors, just as monarchism, an overarching 'British' form of patriotism and a generalized adhesion to Christian principles have been under-estimated as forces of national cohesion" (Thompson 1993: 17). The articulation of class with these and other forms of division and cohesion is the subject of the next three chapters.

Foregrounding others

Foregrounding gender

Writing in the introduction to *Sex and Class in Women's History* (1983), the three American editors – Judith Newton, Mary Ryan, and Judith Walkowitz – noted differences between feminist scholarship in Britain and the United States:

> If as feminist historians we have all viewed sex-based divisions as central to processes of social transformation, British historians have tended to place more emphasis on class than their American counterparts . . . Many feminist historians in Britain, moreover, have emerged from a socialist and labor-oriented tradition which assigns a key place to the study of class relationships . . . (Newton *et al.* 1983: 2).

British feminist historians have been in the forefront of producing a gendered understanding of class, while being part of a transatlantic discussion with feminist historians in North America and elsewhere. Their work developed in the context of the "second-wave" feminist movement that surfaced in the late 1960s and the 1970s.

For our purposes, it is perhaps possible to distinguish between two phases of British feminist history. In the first phase, roughly corresponding to the decade of the 1970s, feminists sought to recover the lives of women who had been "hidden from history" – housewives and textile workers, Chartist activists and militant suffragettes. Feminist historians were inspired by history from below, while critiquing its blindness to the role of women in the making of history. Such work played a critical role in restoring historical balance, but it ultimately reinforced women's marginal status, as it often supplemented existing historical accounts, rather than resulting in a new synthesis.

The second phase began in the late 1970s overlapping and intertwined with the first, and continued arguably to the present. Feminists sought to deconstruct the assumptions on which dominant historical accounts were based by placing gender at the center of historical writing. Those historians highlighted in this chapter explored the interwoven relationship of gender and class. Their endeavor overlapped with work inspired by the linguistic turn. Here, gender and class were seen as systems of difference, the products of language and culture and the power relations governing them. Fields such as labor history were viewed as being based on gendered assumptions, oblivious to how class, an ostensibly gender-neutral category, was inflected with masculine assumptions. This perspective – its most influential articulation being Joan Scott's – proved controversial, even among feminist historians interested in recovering the meaning systems of historical actors. Feminist historians – such as Anna Clark, Leonore Davidoff, Catherine Hall, Sonya Rose, and Carolyn Steedman – retained a class dimension in their work and often combined cultural and social approaches rather than seeing them as polar opposites.

Hidden from history

In this section I situate the emergence of "second-wave" British feminist history in relationship to the emerging women's liberation movement and the class perspective of history from below. Contemporary British feminist history grew out of the emergence of second wave feminism, which first surfaced in the late 1960s and the 1970s (Dworkin 1997: 192–94). As in the United States, British feminism grew out of the student and civil rights movement, the counterculture, and opposition to the Vietnam War. Like blacks and other minorities, women who were political activists regarded themselves as an oppressed group – the "longest revolution," as the title to Juliet Mitchell's influential feminist text stated it (Mitchell [1966] 1984). Feminist historians frequently had roots in the labor movement, were often adult education teachers, and were energized by a growing network of informal "consciousness raising" groups. Indeed, it was within the framework of the History Workshop initiative (see Chapter 2) that the first nationwide women's movement was launched.

Although there was feminist history in Britain before the 1970s, it only existed intermittently. Texts such as Alice Clark's *Working Life of Women in the Seventeenth Century* ([1919] 1982) and Ivy Pinchbeck's *Women Workers and the Industrial Revolution, 1750–1850* ([1930] 1981) were isolated instances and were largely forgotten until second-wave feminist historians rediscovered them. Feminist historiography during the 1970s signified a new phase: it marked the founding of a scholarly network and instituted the first glimmers of an institutional presence. Feminism began to be a force to be reckoned with in intellectual and political debates.

Socialist feminist historians were rooted in the socialist and Marxist traditions, but they argued that these political ideologies were only a point of departure, that women's social and political position must be rethought from the point of view of feminist theory and politics. Socialist feminists advocated that historians not just fill in the gaps of existing historical accounts with sections on women, but situate women, even as housewives, at the center of labor history. As Sally Alexander and Anna Davin wrote in *History Workshop Journal*:

> Feminism not only demands a history of the family but also seeks to explain why women's work as the reproducers of labour power, and their servicing of labour power in the home, has remained invisible for so long. By bringing women into the foreground of historical enquiry our knowledge of production, of working-class politics and culture, of class struggles, of the welfare state, will be transformed (Alexander and Davin 1976: 5).

Socialist feminist historiography was rooted in the cultural and political milieu of the 1960s and 1970s, but it was influenced by the older generation of Marxist historians, especially E. P. Thompson, while cognizant that these historians had been mostly oblivious to women's experiences and aspirations. Socialist feminists sought to bring to light the lives of women who had been historically marginalized, oppressed as much by their gender as by their class.

In this early phase of feminist history, there were several notable achievements. Jill Liddington and Jill Norris's *One Hand Tied Behind Us: The Rise of the Women's Suffrage Movement* (1978) explored the hidden story of turn-of-the-century female textile workers in Lancashire, who campaigned simultaneously for the vote and for a feminist and working-class agenda. Liddington and Norris's account was based on local archival sources and interviews with daughters and granddaughters of the protagonists. Barbara Taylor's *Eve and New Jerusalem: Socialism and Feminism in the Nineteenth Century* (1983) recovered the centrality of women's issues in the early socialist movement. She focused on the Owenite socialists of the 1820s to the 1840s, who, she demonstrated, were interested in liberating both women from their enslavement to men and the working class from economic oppression under capitalism. Like Liddington and Norris, Taylor hoped that the fusion of socialism and feminism in the past could provide an inspiration for a renewed connection between them in the present and the future.

Of the feminist historians writing at this time, Sheila Rowbotham (1943–) was arguably the most influential (Dworkin 1997: 195–98). Rowbotham was a product of the counterculture and the new left. She was greatly influenced by the organizing strategies of the civil rights movement. She was active in the Vietnam Solidarity Campaign and in the Trotskyist International Socialists. And she served on the editorial board of *Black Dwarf*, a radical journal infused with the cultural politics of the time. Most importantly, she became immersed in the emerging feminist movement, to which she was drawn because it brought together personal, familial, and conventional political issues.

Rowbotham's historical work grew out of her participation in the women's movement. Her books were sweeping in their scope, often written with a non-academic audience in mind. Her first book, *Women, Resistance, and Revolution* (1972), was perhaps the first historical analysis of feminism to come out of second-wave feminism. It traced the historical connection between feminism and revolutionary socialism in various countries, including Britain, France, the United States, Russia, and China. Rowbotham shortly afterwards published *Hidden from History: 300 Years of Women's Oppression and the Fight Against It* (1973). A pioneering survey of women in Britain from the seventeenth century until the 1930s, the book provided a kind of roadmap for future research. It sought to achieve for women what history from below had accomplished for the working class. Yet Rowbotham was acutely aware that "patriarchy, the power of men as a sex to dispose of women's capacity to labour, especially in the family, has not had a direct and simple relationship to class exploitation" (Rowbotham 1973: ix).

In Rowbotham's long career as an activist and historian, *A Century of Women: The History of Women in Britain and the United States in the Twentieth Century* (1997) was her *magnum opus*. This ambitious history of women on both sides of the Atlantic Ocean traced the interwoven relationships between their two cultures. Not theoretically grounded, the work skillfully captured the aspirations and lives of a multitude of female voices – the famous and the obscure, the poor and the rich, radical and conservative, white and non-white. These included Alice Wheeldon, the English suffragette who in World War I became part of an underground network that helped conscientious objectors elude the authorities and was imprisoned for her efforts; Theodosia Goodman, the daughter of a Jewish tailor from Cincinnati, remade by Hollywood as Theda Bara, who for a brief four years was perhaps the very first Hollywood sex symbol from an immigrant background; and Jayaben Desai, the political activist who led a strike at Grunwick's photographic processing laboratories in 1976–1977, critical to the Asian workforce's drive to unionize and emblematic of a rapidly changing British labor movement.

In comparison with her writings in the 1970s, Rowbotham viewed the political future with less certainty and confidence. Her exploration of popular culture, attention to gender, and sensitivity to its complex relationship with class, race, and ethnicity suggested the impact of the political and intellectual developments of the intervening years. There was also significant continuity with her earlier work. In the book's conclusion Rowbotham wrote: "My own search over the years has certainly been based on an effort to reveal suppressed possibilities – those understandings that time rushes past which can also be a means of releasing aspiration" (Rowbotham 1997: 590). The spirit of the original socialist-feminist project was still perceptible.

Separate spheres

However important the work of Rowbotham and other feminist scholars might have been to recovering women's presence in history, eventually such a project rubbed up against its limits. It made inroads into fields such as labor history, where new scholarship on women workers forced male historians to take note. Yet in the historical profession as a whole, women's history could be relegated to a subdiscipline, ignored by, say, political historians for whom the principal actors were still men. A *History Workshop Journal* editorial noted that it was important to recover "the worlds that women have inhabited" but it could also "lead to a ghettoization of women's history, and to its presentation in forms which historians working in different fields find easy to ignore" (*History Workshop Journal* 1985: 1–2).

Undoubtedly the most important development in feminist historiography in the late 1970s and the 1980s was a shift of intellectual energy from the study of women to the examination of gender relationships, which did not, by any means, imply that women were featured less prominently. This scholarship on the historical construction of gender relationships has permanently changed the landscape of the social sciences and the humanities, transforming the study of men as well as women, and leading to whole new fields, the history of masculinities being an example. Historians first used the term "gender" in the late 1960s in order to define the social relations between men and women. They used it to differentiate the "social meanings" from the biological data of sexual difference (Newman 1991: 61). Privileging gender relationships challenged traditional ways of conceptualizing history, for it linked, rather than separated, the public world of civil society and the state with the private and domestic world of the household and family. For the purposes of this study, I look at the importance of such thinking for conceptualizing class, by focusing on Leonore Davidoff and Catherine Hall's highly influential and path-breaking book, *Family Fortunes: Men and Women of the English Middle Class, 1780–1850* (Davidoff and Hall [1987] 2002).

Catherine Hall's (1956–) development as a historian exemplifies this shift in focus. Hall's intellectual and political trajectory was shaped by the tradition of Marxist historiography, participation in new-left politics, and political activism in the women's movement (Dworkin 1997: 202–05). While an undergraduate at the University of Birmingham, she studied with the Marxist medievalist Rodney Hilton. She was part of the final phase of the new left of the early 1960s, meeting her husband Stuart on a protest march against nuclear weapons. She joined the first women's liberation group in Birmingham in 1970, an experience she recalled as being devoted to numerous conversations with other women, mostly mothers, about "the things that felt wrong with our lives, especially our isolation" (C. Hall 1992a: 4). Hall's decision to become a nineteenth-century historian grew out of her immersion in feminist politics. She is currently a professor of social and cultural history at University College, London. But like many feminist historians in Britain, the earlier part of her academic career was spent outside of a history department. The margins can be a "very productive terrain" she once observed (ibid.: 34).

Hall's main research focus has been on the nineteenth-century English middle class. Her interests took shape in the second half of the 1970s, the end of the "utopian moment" of the women's movement and the beginning of the "long haul" (ibid.: 11). Hall wanted to grasp her own middle-class origins, an aspiration in tune with the women's movement's emphasis on self-knowledge. She had also begun to question the dominance of history from below, which celebrated the resistance of the oppressed, while "ignoring material which documents the continuing power, albeit often challenged, of the bourgeoisie" (ibid.: 94). When Hall began to do research on nineteenth-century social and cultural life, it was a wide-open field: most scholarship done under the rubric of the new social history focused on the working class. She spent three months reading through *Aris's Birmingham Gazette* from the 1780s to the 1840s. At first she was frustrated, for women were absent from the newspaper's pages. However, she reached an important realization:

> The newspaper was contributing to the construction of a new middle-class male public sphere by the very items that were chosen to be reported, whether philanthropic meetings, civic processions or significant funerals.

Men moved to the centre of the story – not to displace women, but in order to be able to make sense of the particular articulations of masculinity within the middle class (ibid.: 17).

Hall pursued this line of inquiry in conjunction with Leonore Davidoff (1932–). Currently a research professor in the Department of Sociology at the University of Essex and a founder of the influential journal *Gender and History*, Davidoff was born in New York City, was educated in both the United States and Britain, and has lived most of her adult life in Britain. She is a trained socio-logist but with the propensities of a historian, strengthened by association with the History Workshop initiative of the 1970s. Of her work, Davidoff has written: "Ever since my post-graduate thesis on married women's work, I have been interested in the way gender and class have framed the way the home, family, and economy have been perceived and experienced in the modern period" (Contemporary Authors Online 2001). Like other feminist scholars of the burgeoning women's movement, Davidoff's early work – initiated prior to when second-wave feminism took off – focused on a dimension of historical experience largely ignored by male historians. Important here was her research on domestic servants, who, though considered by Marxists to be "unproduc-tive" laborers (because they did not contribute to making commodities), were the largest contingent of nineteenth-century women workers, more than a mil-lion strong by the late 1800s. Davidoff's scholarship was deeply enriched by listening to her mother-in-law, Edith Annie Lockwood, who, born in Yorkshire in the late 1800s, held her first of several positions in domestic service when she was eleven. As Davidoff recalled: "Her vivid and detailed recollections of work patterns, emotional reactions and concepts of hierarchy, refracted through a female servant's encounters with the provincial upper-middle class world while living under the same roof, kindled my determination to give voice to servants as human beings in their own right as well as historical subject" (Davidoff 1995: 4). Such work included "Mastered for Life: Servant and Wife in Victorian and Edwardian England" ([1974] 1995), which portrayed women domestic servants as caught in a web of submission to varying forms of patri-archal authority – whether wielded by fathers, employers, or husbands. Their subservience took place in the household, and thus they were excluded from the "great drama of market forces." "In theory they either did not exist or at most were residual categories. In reality they had to struggle for survival in what ever way they could, for in such a society 'he who pays the piper calls the tune'" (Davidoff [1974] 1995: 34).

Among Davidoff's most compelling early essays was "Class and Gender in Victorian England: The Case of Hannah Cullwick and A. J. Munby" ([1979]

1995) (briefly cited in Chapter 1). The essay charted the out-of-the-ordinary (although by no mean unique), maybe nonsexual relationship of the upper-middle-class Munby, obsessed with the strength, naturalness, and baseness of domestic servants, and the working-class servant Cullwick, who was strongly independent but apparently subservient to Munby's will. In the course of knowing each other, they acted out fantasies and rituals of dominance and submission, including Cullwick's licking of Munby's boots. Munby photographed Cullwick playing numerous roles, including a domestic servant, an angel, a middle-class lady, a man, and a slave. Davidoff's essay used diaries written by both Munby and Cullwick and the photos that he had taken of her and others. The essay told a story of two people who, at times, seemed to subvert the class and gender positions assigned to them as well as overturn the class/gender ideologies of Victorian society as a whole. They achieved against all odds a kind of intimacy that (at least for a time and up to a point) was mutually satisfying, even to the point of marriage. Yet their liaison simultaneously acted to reinforce these same positions and ideologies, as their relationship was circumscribed by Munby's fantasies and desires and the unequal distribution of social and economic power between them.

Originally published in 1987, Davidoff and Hall's *Family Fortunes*, the fruit of nearly ten years of research, was one of the most influential works of social/cultural history in the past 25 years. Meticulously and exhaustively researched – drawing on diaries, wills, newspapers, novels, letters, and prescriptive manuals – the book was assembled like a finely woven tapestry to convey the structure of feeling of English provincial middle-class life in the first half of the nineteenth century. *Family Fortunes* was based on detailed case studies drawn from the urban setting of Birmingham and from rural Suffolk and Essex. Hall and Davidoff charted the emergence of a distinctive middle-class consciousness. They linked the increasing economic dependence of middle-class women on their husbands and their intensified marginalization in public affairs to the creation of clearly delineated realms appropriate to men and women. This process was facilitated by the ideological vision of evangelical Christianity, for which the masculine, grubby, and public world of capitalism was to be offset by the female, spiritually grounded domain of home and family. This ideology found its material expression in the separation of home from work, the growth of the suburbs, the attention lavished on gardens, the creation of numerous male-dominated associations and societies, and the "shadowy but vital role of women in public."

If Davidoff and Hall believed that the remapping of gender via the ideology of separate spheres powerfully defined English society – both the world of the middle class and beyond – they did not regard those spheres as mutally exclusive. In the introduction to the 2002 edition, they explained that their original intention "was always to move beyond the public/private divide." In their words:

> We fleshed out these arguments, demonstrating in numerous instances the crossing of the boundaries, both in their imagined and material forms: the energetic women who claimed the right to vote in church meetings or speak in public; the armies of women who as domestic servants were employed in the so-called private sphere of the home; the independent women who utilized the language of their distinctive sphere to make claims for themselves (Davidoff and Hall [1987] 2002: xvi).

The relationship between public and private, male and female, was contradictory, fluid, historically contingent, and negotiable within circumscribed limits.

Their perspective, as Hall acknowledged, had affinities with American feminist historians, who focused more on individual rights and women's solidarity than scholars in the class-oriented, British feminist tradition. For American feminists, separate spheres, manifest in the emerging nineteenth-century middle classes, were oppressive and restrictive, but, as Nancy Hewitt suggested, "the counterpart of subordination in or exclusion from male-dominated domains was inclusion in all-female enclave" (Hewitt 1985: 299). Carol Smith-Rosenberg stated that women's separate cultures frequently acted as self-enclosed islands of camaraderie, in her words, "a world of love and ritual" (Rosenberg 1975). For Nancy Cott, the "doctrine of woman's sphere opened to women (reserved for them) the avenues of domestic influence, religious morality, and child nurture. It articulated a social power based on their special female qualities rather than on human rights" (Cott [1977] 1997: 200). Mary Ryan's *Cradle of the Middle Class: The Family in Oneida County, New York, 1790–1865* (1981) argued that American middle-class identity was shaped around "domestic values and family practices," while allowing that women could still exert power and influence in the public realm. A case in point was Utica's Female Reform Society, prominent in the 1830s and 1840s, which employed forms of "moral surveillance" usually assumed by church and state. "The performance of these functions by women, within their own self-created association . . . constituted a remarkable transmutation in the relationship of family and society" (Ryan 1981: 121).

Family Fortunes was likewise responding to discussions more explicitly pertinent to class going on in British socialist-feminist circles. Davidoff and Hall's conception of the class experience was rooted in the tradition of Thompsonian social history. They aspired to write history from the perspective of ordinary people, although their subject was the privileged (rather than the oppressed) class. "In this study," they wrote, "we have attempted to reconstitute the world as provincial middle-class people saw it, experienced it and made sense of it; to accurately reconstruct an emerging culture" (Davidoff and Hall [1987] 2002: 28). However, Davidoff and Hall departed from Thompsonian history in several respects, one being the role of ideology in the class experience. Where Thompson saw class culture as a manifestation of class experience, Davidoff and Hall regarded the ideological construction of experience as relatively autonomous.

Consider, for instance, a related essay by Hall, "The Early Formation of Victorian Domestic Ideology" (C. Hall 1992a: 75–93). She showed how the evangelicals of the Clapham Sect – crusaders for the abolition of slavery, the renewal of Christianity, the sanctity of the family, and female domesticity – helped shape an emerging middle-class consciousness. Yet given their social connections to the aristocracy and the old mercantile bourgeoisie, the group was not middle class in composition, especially if its core was defined by the growing contingent of manufacturers and industrialists. As Hall stated: "It is not that the Clapham Sect simply represented and reflected the interests of the new capitalist class: at a particular historical moment a particular class fraction or group can represent the interests of other factions or classes and can embody ideas and practices which have repercussions far beyond them" (ibid.: 82). Her thinking reflected the convergence of several strands of thought current in the 1970s stressing the relative autonomy of ideological formations, Gramsci and Althusser being notable influences (see Chapter 2).

Just as E. P. Thompson regarded the working class as defining itself in an antagonistic relationship to the aristocracy and middle class, so Davidoff and Hall saw the middle class's emerging consciousness as part of an effort to differentiate itself from the other two classes. Yet they accorded the process a gendered dimension. Regarding the middle class's efforts to define itself in contradistinction to aristocratic values, they made the following observation: "The valuation of actions and materials in monetary terms was regarded as a quintessentially masculine skill and prerogative. Such expertise was an essential part of the middle-class challenge to the aristocratic male whose skills lay with gambling, dueling, sporting and sexual prowess" (Davidoff and Hall [1987] 2002: 205). In effect, Davidoff and Hall sought an alternative to Thompson's implicit understanding of the class experience as being gender neutral, while broadly accepting his nonreductionist view of how classes formed.

In this regard they faced a challenge confronted by socialist feminists more generally. Class in the Marxist tradition was seen as being rooted in industrial production and the public sphere and thus by definition relegated the great majority of women to a supporting role. Indeed, Marx's thought itself was steeped in Victorian gender ideologies built on a male/public and female/ private distinction (Benenson 1983). Socialist feminists in the 1970s sought to create a Marxist analysis that incorporated the private domain of biological and social reproduction. However, as Sonya Rose observed: "Yet even in these discussions conducted at the level of abstract theory, the 'motor of history' remained in the public sphere. While domestic labor was seen to be functional for capitalism, productive relations and the politics generated as a consequence of them remained the stuff of historical transformation" (Rose 1997: 141).

Seen in this light, *Family Fortunes* might be regarded as providing last-ditch counseling for what Heidi Hartmann described as "the unhappy marriage of Marxism and feminism," a necessary but stressful union in which capitalism and patriarchy were distinct but interacting systems of oppression (Hartmann [1979] 1981). The book shared common ground with Joan Kelly's advocacy of a double vision of feminist theory that brought together socialist feminists' emphasis on social structure and radical feminists' insights into sexuality and socialization (Kelly 1983). It was theoretically connected to Michèle Barrett's position in *Women's Oppression Today* ([1980] 1988), which conceived of gender ideologies as predating capitalism but nonetheless historically vari- able, neither static nor unified, and embedded in specific historical and class contexts. For Barrett, under capitalism the family was the crucial ideological site for securing the sexual division of labor governing women's position at work and home. In the revised edition, published in 1988, Barrett was less sanguine about the potential for integrating Marxist and feminist insights, acknowledging that "the two world views" had "continued to go their separate ways in spite of our efforts at marriage guidance" (Barrett [1980] 1988: v). In effect, Davidoff and Hall sought to overcome the dichotomy of "dual system" theory, asserting that the class experience was saturated by gender. "Through the stories of individuals and families, *Family Fortunes*," they wrote, "argues that the men and women of the provincial middle class adopted distinctively different class identities, that the language of class formation was gendered" (Davidoff and Hall [1987] 2002: 450). The argument was framed in relation- ship to a specific historical case, but it had wider implications, posing a for- mative challenge to mainstream Marxist class theory.

Laura Lee Downs has written of *Family Fortunes* that it "marked a decisive moment in the turn to gender history in England, and in gender's diffusion out- ward into historical practice more broadly." It "became something of a classic overnight" and was "widely taught in university courses from the late 1980s, and not only in women's studies but in general history courses as well" (Downs 2004: 68–69). The book has also evoked critical responses. Downs, for one, aligned herself with feminist critics, for whom the book's very success in sympathetically recovering the middle class's worldview had the unintended effect of legitimizing it. Downs approvingly cited Carolyn Steedman's likening of *Family Fortunes* to the literary genre known as the *Bildungsroman*, "which, in its many forms, typically symbolizes the process of socialization, and makes its characters and its readers really want to do what it is that they have to do anyway (be married, have children, clean the stairs . . .)" (quoted in ibid.: 69).

Armanda Vickery wrote what was arguably the most wide-ranging critique of *Family Fortunes*. Here, two points stand out. First, she suggested that Davidoff and Hall's linkage of the middle class's formation to the destabilizing impact of the Industrial Revolution failed to take into account a body of scholarship that emphasized continuities between eighteenth- and nineteenth-century economic and social life (see Chapter 5). Second, Vickery argued that Davidoff and Hall's use of prescriptive literature to make the case for separate spheres was suspect because these sources could not reveal how their audiences received them. Rather than seeing a disappearance of women from public life, Vickery maintained the opposite:

Indeed, one might go further and argue that the stress on the proper female sphere in Victorian discourse signaled a growing concern that more women were seen to be active *outside* the home rather than proof that they were so confined. In short, the broadcasting of the language of separate spheres looks like a conservative response to an unprecedented *expansion* in the opportunities, ambitions and experience of the late Georgian and Victorian women (Vickery 1993: 400).

While provocative, such a critique did not put forward the kind of evidence that would provide a genuine alternative to Davidoff and Hall's argument.

However important *Family Fortunes* may be as a contribution to understanding the relationship between class and gender, it critiqued Thompson's understanding of class formation, but did not overthrow his crucial assumptions. Thus, Patrick Joyce portrays Davidoff and Hall's understanding of class formation as adding gender to a "conventional" Marxist understanding. As he describes it: "It is taken as a given, a pre-constituted structural entity, operating as a collective actor, which evinces collective traits of a class sort. To use a by now familiar formulation: in this account the bourgeoisie very decidedly makes the public sphere, the public sphere does not make the bourgeoisie" (Joyce 1995a: 288). Joyce seriously underestimates just how innovative integrating gender and class in fact is, but he aptly points out that *Family Fortunes* does not position itself in reference to debates over language and class going on within British social history at the time of the book's writing (see Chapter 5).

The point of departure for Hall's own subsequent work grew out of grappling with feminist critiques of white middle-class women's colonization of feminist history (see Chapter 7) and postcolonial theory's deconstruction of the relationship between center and periphery, metropole and colony (see Chapter 8). Her new direction was first articulated in the essays comprising Part III of *White, Male and Middle Class* (C. Hall 1992a). It was expanded upon and fleshed out in greater detail in the highly influential *Civilising Subjects: Colony and Metropole in the English Imagination, 1830–1867* (C. Hall 2002). Hall explored the relationship between class, gender, race, ethnicity, and national identity by focusing on a group of Protestant missionaries and their followers in Birmingham, England and Jamaica. The guiding thread of Hall's argument was "that colony and metropole are terms which can be understood only in relation to each other, and that the identity of coloniser is a constitutive part of Englishness" (ibid.: 12). Hall's insistence that the binary opposition of the two terms was constructed and that they mutually defined each other reflected her embrace of poststructuralism. Yet it was an American historian of France, Joan Scott, who was primarily responsible for introducing poststructuralist ideas into feminist historiographical discussions, ideas that turned out to be highly contentious.

A useful category of historical analysis

Joan Scott's collection of 1980s essays, *Gender and the Politics of History* (1988), has played a crucial role in shaping historians' discussions on gender. Scott's conceptualization of gender and class is as important as Gareth Stedman Jones's related argument concerning the language of class (see Chapter 5) – perhaps more so. Both historians challenged the common sense of social and labor history, but Scott's writing in this vein had immediate ramifications for women's and gender history. She carved out a position more epistemologically radical than Stedman Jones's. She challenged the materialist assumptions held by an important segment of feminist historians, arguing that gender was a linguistic and cultural construct varying according to historical circumstances. She was thus on a collision course with the practice of the new social history, including the women's history that grew out of it.

Writing in 1997, Theodore Koditschek observed that "there is no gainsaying the fact that Scott's anti-determinist, poststructuralist approach to the history of class and gender is admirably suited to the intellectual temper of our day." Her ideas captured the prevailing political and intellectual mood of the time: a moment of conservative triumph and left-wing collapse, when "familiar road maps for understanding no longer seem to work" (Koditschek 1997: 339). They were all the more potent, since – as in the case of William Sewell (see Chapter 4) and Stedman Jones – Scott had been an important contributor to the new social and labor history as well as the first wave of 1970s women's history.

Her first book, *The Glassworkers of Carmaux: French Craftsmen and Political Action in a Nineteenth-Century City* (1974), was inspired by Thompson's conception of history from below and scholarship situating class consciousness in relationship to transformations in the structure of work, particularly the historical sociology of Charles Tilley. She used quantitative evidence, heavily based on historical demographic methods, to understand the lives of workers who often left behind little in the way of written records. Scott's account situated a well-known 1895 glassworkers' strike in the context of long-term changes in the relations of production. Facing an erosion of their status owing to mechanization, glassmakers unionized, appropriating the language of class struggle to assert claims specific to their craft.

Scott's second book, *Women, Work, and Family* (Tilly and Scott [1978] 1989), coauthored with the sociologist Louise Tilly, was written in the early days of the women's movement as a text for newly created women's-studies courses. The book was a comparative study of the English and French working class over a nearly 300-year period. It was materialist to its core, situating women's job opportunities and their family position in relationship to economic and demographic changes. Scott and Tilly distinguished three historical phases: the preindustrial household economy, the family-wage economy of the early Industrial Revolution, and the family-consumer economy coinciding with industrial capitalism's maturation. They found "that the interplay between a society's productive and reproductive systems within the household influences the *supply* of women available for work. The characteristics of the economy and its mode of production, scale of organization, and technology influence the *demand* for women as workers" (ibid.: 230). However, they believed that women's lives were neither improved nor their position in the family transformed when the demand for their labor intensified.

The transition from Scott's early socio-economic, demographic, and quantitative work, grounded in history from below, to her championing of the linguistic and cultural turn in the 1980s, is found in *Gender and the Politics of History* (1988). In the book's most influential essay, "Gender: A Useful Concept of Historical Analysis," originally published in 1986, Scott argued that – unlike class, which had an established, if by no means agreed upon, theoretical grounding – gender, a concept only recently deployed in the human sciences, still had not been placed on firm foundations. The obstacles to its development, in her view, were both internal and external. On the one hand, the leading schools of feminist thought had reached a theoretical impasse. In the case of socialist feminists, intensive efforts and wide-ranging debates had failed to harmonize feminist theories of patriarchy and Marxist ones of capitalism. On the other hand, this impasse was not only attributable to their theoretical incompatibility: it was rooted in the problematic nature of the materialist assumptions on which the entire enterprise had been founded, assumptions that were being questioned throughout the humanities and social sciences.

Scott implied that the emergence of gender as a category was not accidental, that it was part of this broader intellectual turbulence. In her words:

> It seems to me significant that the use of the word "gender" has emerged at a moment of great epistemological turmoil that takes the form, in some cases, of a shift from scientific to literary paradigms among social scientists (from an emphasis on cause to one on meaning, blurring genres of inquiry, in anthropologist Clifford Geertz's phrase) and, in other cases, the form of the debates about theory between those who assert the transparency of facts and those who insist that all reality is construed or constructed, between those who defend and those who question the idea that "man" is the rational master of his own destiny (Scott 1988: 41).

Scott sided with those believing that reality was a construct. She discarded the goal of unearthing "real" history in favor of elucidating how cultural meaning – conceived (following Foucault) as the relationship between knowledge and power (see Chapter 4) – shaped the lineaments of economic, social, and political practices.

Scott defined gender as a constitutive dimension of social relationships, based on perceptions of sexual difference, and a primary means of signifying power relationships. For her, these perceptions were inscribed in symbolic representations based on normative concepts, helped define numerous social and cultural practices, and played a critical role in the construction of subjectivity and identity. "These concepts," she wrote, "are expressed in religious, educational, scientific, legal, and political doctrines and typically take the form of a fixed binary opposition, categorically and unequivocally asserting the meaning of male and female, masculine and feminine" (ibid.: 43). They suppressed competing ones, while simultaneously producing an air of fixity and inevitability about themselves. Historians' task was to recover the process whereby symbolic representations of gender came into existence, shaped people's consciousness, and ultimately took on the "appearance of timeless permanence."

In part one of *Gender and the Politics of History*, Scott established her understanding of gender, while in part two she came to terms with the legacy of social and labor history (discussed in Chapter 5 and below). In part three she offered a glimpse of how theory worked in practice, focusing on the entangled relationship of gender and class. An example is " 'L'ouvrière! Mot impie, sordide . . .': Women Workers in the Discourse of French Political Economy, 1840–1860" (ibid.: 113–63). This essay explored efforts within the discourse of nineteenth-century French political economy to understand the disruptive and troubling presence of working women, who served as both an "object of study" and a vehicle for signifying ideas regarding social order and social organization. Within this discourse, female workers were represented as inhabiting a "world of turbulent sexuality, subversive independence, and dangerous insubordination," underscored by their designation as *femmes isolées*, a term that could refer to either "clandestine prostitutes" or women wage laborers living on their own (ibid.: 147). Female workers destabilized political economy's vision of a harmonious relationship between work and family based on innate sexual differences. The resolutions put forward to solve this problem were diverse: the repression of women's desires, the call for the return of the mother to the family, and the advocacy of equal pay for women workers as compensation for giving up their family role. They all shared, however, political economy's discursive underpinnings, which deployed contrasts produce meaning. Scott acknowledged that this discourse did not disclose the worldview of the workers who were its object: it was profoundly ideological. However, she argued that it "did not take place in a realm apart from the material, economic, or political." It "provided the terms by which relations of production and sexual divisions of labor were established and contested" (ibid.: 163).

Scott's essay analyzed debates in the realm of political economy because they furnished a window into how discourse contributed to women's marginalization as workers. Labor historians, who never questioned these discursive assumptions, became agents in this very process of marginalization. Scott confronted social- and labor-history practices more explicitly in analyses of two of its major practitioners. I've already discussed her reflections on Stedman Jones's rethinking of Chartism (see Chapter 5). I now consider her analysis of E. P. Thompson's *The Making of the English Working Class* ([1963] 1968), the embodiment of history from below.

Thompson had been influential on socialist-feminist historians seeking to recover the lives of women "hidden from history." Yet Scott believed that there were problems with his legacy. It was not that Thompson's narrative only included men, as his memorable portrayal of the religious visionary Joanna Southcott amply demonstrated. Yet, as Scott argued, feminist historians could not simply supplement Thompson's account with a fuller treatment of women workers in the hope that a more comprehensive understanding of class formation might eventually emerge. These efforts were doomed to rein-force women's marginalized role in working-class history, for they never ques-tioned the book's conceptual underpinnings. For Scott, Thompson's account of evolving class consciousness was founded on an unstated duality. Class formation took place in the realm of production; it found expression in the political rationalist philosophy of writers such as Thomas Paine; and it used gender-neutral language that was nonetheless implicitly male. By definition women were relegated to the domestic sphere or, as in the case of Southcott, associated with religion and emotion, the scourge of progressive class politics. There might be female wage laborers, but there was no room for women's class experience, except as helpmates to fathers and husbands or as bit players in the labor movement. As Scott explained it:

> Work, in the sense of productive activity, determined class consciousness, whose politics were rationalist; domesticity was outside production, and it compromised or subverted class consciousness often in alliance with (religious) movements whose mode was "expressive." The antitheses were clearly coded as masculine and feminine; class, in other words, was a gen-dered construction (Scott 1988: 79).

If such unconscious gender assumptions explained women's secondary status, how could an alternative narrative be conceived? Scott advocated jettisoning the idea that working-class consciousness was an expression of objective interests in favor of a conception that stressed the making of political allegiances. In her words: "It refuses its [Thompson's book's] teleology and retells it as a story of the creation of political identity through representations of sexual difference. Class and gender become inextricably linked in this telling – as representation, as identity, as social and political practice" (ibid.: 88). This attention to discourse had three dimensions. First, it involved analyzing how class categories were produced at specific historical moments. Second, it entailed delineating "how appeals to sexual difference figured in the process: how did the exclusion or marginalization of that which was constructed as feminine, for example, work to ensure acceptance of masculine codings for particular ideas of class? How did gender 'naturalize' particular meanings of class" (ibid.: 88)? Third, it explored the consequences of notions of class for organizing social experience.

Scott's contention that gender, class, and (in a later essay) "experience" were cultural and linguistic categories proved contentious (Scott 1992). Scott's work produced acrimonious debates among feminists, in part because it seemed to minimize women's experience, such an important dimension of the new feminist history (Downs 1993a, 1993b). Scott's own spirited defense of her position only added fuel to the fire (Scott 1993). Yet, as Kathleen Canning has pointed out, Scott and her feminist critics shared a common ground: "Thus, those feminist historians who came to reject biological essentialism as an explanation of the inequalities between the sexes were among the first historians to discover the power of discourses to construct socially sexual difference and to anchor difference in social practices and institutions" (Canning 1994: 370).

Indeed, Scott took a different route, but her understanding of the relationship between gender and class had clear affinities with what Davidoff and Hall espoused in *Family Fortunes*. All three writers believed that class and gender functioned together, that class consciousness assumed a gendered form, and that the meaning of both categories – class and gender – was fluid, ever changing, subject to contestation and reworking. Like other feminist historians, Hall was uneasy about what seemed to her the determinist implications of Scott's thought – "its potential for a loss of agency"; and she feared that the deconstruction of the autonomous subject "when driven to the limits" would "result in a curious loss of feeling in historical writing" (Hall 1991: 210). Yet, as a historian and a feminist, Hall identified with Scott's intellectual and political trajectory. In later work she explored poststructuralist ideas about language and identity first introduced into feminist historical writing by Scott, while placing her own distinctive stamp on them as well (see above). Scott, likewise, acknowledged the influence that British feminist historians had on her critique of Thompson. She cited Barbara Taylor's work on Owenite socialism (see above) and Sally Alexander's influential discussion of the discontinuities between feminist theory and Marxist labor history (Alexander 1984). In sum, the gendering of class was taking place on multiple fronts. The reimagining of the working class was just beginning.

Gendering the working class

An important achievement of British feminist historians in the 1990s has been integrating women into the working-class narrative – the "gendering of the British working class," as Theodore Koditschek appropriately titled an important article that surveys this historical work (Koditschek 1997). I discuss the contributions of three historians who have been important to this endeavor – Anna Clark (1957–), Sonya Rose (1935–), and Carolyn Steedman (1947–).

Taken together, Clark's *The Struggle for the Breeches: Gender and the Making of the British Working Class* (1995) and Rose's *Limited Livelihoods: Gender and Class in Nineteenth-Century England* (1992) help establish a reinterpretation of nineteenth-century working-class history. Their accounts emphasized the working class's adaptation of the separate-spheres ideology – the goal of attaining a "family wage" sufficient for women to remain in the domestic sphere and the aspiration of achieving the franchise for the male breadwinner of the household. Rejecting the notion that this process was fore-ordained, they charted its complexities, highlighting the gender conflicts within working-class life and their implications for class consciousness and struggle.

Of the two books, *The Struggle for the Breeches* most directly engaged with Thompson's *The Making of the English Working Class*, in part because it roughly covered the same period, though Clark's narrative reached the 1840s. The additional inclusion of the Chartist era turned out to be vital for Clark's argument. Ending his book in the 1830s made it easier for Thompson to privilege the role of male artisans in creating class consciousness and finish on an upbeat political note. As Clark suggested: "By incorporating gender and extending our examination of the making of the working class from the 1820s forward into the 1840s, a more open-ended view of class formation can be obtained" (Clark 1995: 177). Clark's book constituted a virtual "remaking" of the *Making*: her understanding of working-class formation was framed as much by a "struggle for the breeches" – gender antagonisms within the family, workplace, and politics – as Thompson's had been by workers handling productive relations in cultural terms. In fact, productive relations were themselves reformulated by Clark to have a gendered dimension. Clark's fusion of the gender and class dimension of working-class experience together undermined Thompson's "melodramatic" and "heroic" tale: it cast "a more sorrowful light" on working-class formation, replacing it with an ultimately tragic narrative: "Although artisan culture transformed itself from drunken misogyny to respectable patriarchy, its exclusivism persisted. The fatal flaws of misogyny and patriarchy ultimately muted the radicalism of the British working class" (ibid.: 271).

As part of her open-ended approach, Clark took seriously the "variety of ideologies and discourses" used by working-class people to define themselves. This was a nod in the direction of poststructuralism and the linguistic turn, but it was not a wholehearted nod. The choices of working people, according to Clark, were shaped not by discourse alone, "but by the realities of power: their own lack of political clout, and working men's desires to retain control over women in home and at work" (ibid.: 9). Such statements suggested, as James Vernon (Vernon 1997) argued, that Clark aligned herself more with Thompson's cultural-Marxist point of view (see Chapter 2) than Stedman Jones's linguistically informed one (see Chapter 5). However, Clark also stated that by "combining the study of working people's experience with the analysis of radical rhetoric," she hoped to go "beyond the sterile debate about whether it's economics or language that determines class consciousness" (Clark 1995: 4). Vernon saw her defense of "experience" as a confused claim, given that an important part of her argument was that dominant ideologies and discourses helped define the working class as a group. His criticism was consistent with his postmodern predilections emphasizing the discursive construction of categories such as "working class" (see Chapter 5) (Vernon 1997: 1003). Clark (like other feminist historians) found the epistemological choices of the *Social History* wars off-putting. She drew from both social and cultural approaches.

Briefly, Clark framed her narrative as a conflict between two formations that emerged beginning in the late eighteenth century (Koditschek 1997: 343). The first was principally consigned to skilled trades and was rooted in a narrow idea of masculine privilege. It was connected to male artisans' crumbling status – a consequence, in part, of the use of cheaper female labor. It was a homosocial and misogynist culture, rooted as much in the pub as in the workshop, and it frequently expressed itself through heavy drinking and wife beating. The second formation was more typically the product of the textile industry, where there was a tradition of a family labor system, where even under the pressure of proletariaization men accepted female labor as supplemental, and where strikes were regarded as community responses requiring women's support and participation. The result was a politics that was more inclusive, giving greater weight to the aspirations of women as well as men.

For Clark, an important expression of this latter formation was found during the Queen Caroline Affair of 1820. A scandal precipitated by George IV's successful effort to stop his estranged wife from becoming queen, it gave rise to widespread popular protests. By this time plebian radicals had produced a political discourse that appealed to women, linking their exclusion from the constitution to unemployment, poverty, and wartime affliction. "In defending Queen Caroline's rights as an abused wife," Clark wrote, "radicals were admitting that the rights of women were a political issue. In speaking to women's sense of victimization and holding up a manly ideal of chivalry rather than libertinism, the propaganda for Caroline promised a new harmony between working men and women, a resolution of the sexual antagonism that plagued them" (Clark 1995: 174). Clark also acknowledged that radical discourse's success hinged on "displacing" sexual antagonism onto the royal scandal rather than confronting it in the daily lives of working people.

The push and pull between the two formations – the one male-centered and exclusionary, the other more populist and inclusive – took on a new guise in the Chartist agitation of the 1830s and 1840s. Clark regarded Chartism as an expression of class consciousness, but she did not regard it as an expression of a sociologically and economically defined class. Following Ernesto Laclau and Chantal Mouffe (see Chapter 3) as well as Stedman Jones, she saw class consciousness as the creation of a political language founded on hierarchical divisions between groups of people. Women enthusiastically participated in the early Chartist movement, labeling their actions at times as "militant domesticity." Chartist leaders sought to appeal to them by replacing the culture of the pub with tea parties, soirees, and processions aimed at families. There was even the possibility, according to Clark, that the demand for the suffrage would include women as well. In the end, the Chartist leadership adopted the middle-class ideology of separate spheres, demanding a household suffrage founded on the vote for men and untrammeled motherhood for women. The long-term impact of this political discourse, according to Clark, was to restrict discussions of franchise extension to the question of who possessed "respectable manhood," a political setback slowing the drive for universal suffrage.

Rose's book overlapped with, as well as extended, Clark's narrative to the end of the nineteenth century. Her research focused on the northern textile industries – Kidderminster carpet weavers (with longstanding traditions of single-sex working patterns) and Lancashire cotton weavers (where men and women had relatively equal pay). Like Clark, Rose privileged the interconnection between class and gender and the conflicts produced by them. In Rose's words:

> Gender was implicit in the struggle between workers and employers in the nineteenth century, and it was central to some arenas of that struggle. A consequence was that workers' solidarity could easily be diffused by gender politics. In addition, the connection between masculinity and working-class respectability promoted a working class divided along occupational lines (Rose 1992: 153).

Rose treated the second half of the nineteenth century as a transitional phase (Koditschek 1997: 345–46). When it began it still was common for working-class families to depend on the wages of women and children. By the time that it ended, the ideal of men as the sole breadwinner and women presiding over the home had become dominant.

For Rose, an important aspect of this transitional period was parliamentary legislation, notably the Poor Laws and the Factory Acts. The latter were crucial to her argument because they limited and controlled female and child labor in industrial settings. Supported by trade unions that viewed it as a means of limiting competition, state regulation of factory work ultimately restricted women's job opportunities. Protective legislation, Rose argued, made it more difficult for women to compete for better-paid employment, reinforced their status as low-paid workers in the labor market, and contributed to the rise of smaller, unregulated workshops and home manufacturing associated with sweated labor.

Rose likewise charted the process whereby the idea of the family wage and female domesticity infiltrated working-class life, even though during this period the majority of working-class men did not yet earn sufficient wages to adequately support their families. In response to employers' growing reliance on cheap female labor, unions sought to exclude women from employment in their trades. They saw it as an affront to their masculinity and skills. Working-class husbands increasingly equated being the exclusive breadwinner with "respectability." They saw women being wage earners as violating their proper feminine role.

While this representation ultimately became dominant, it also bred conflict. Rose cited instances of men and women's disputes over the desirability of female wages. In letters to the editor of the *Kidderminster Shuttle*, male weavers condemned women who accepted employment that men wanted on the grounds that they were motivated by the desire to purchase frivolities; women responded by accusing them of throwing away their wages on alcohol. As Rose argued, such disputes suggested "the contradictory connections between waged work and womanliness, as much by their silence on the subject as by their proclamations. The waged work a woman did could only detract from her femininity" (ibid.: 136). Ultimately, gender conflicts within the working class made it more difficult for working-class families to stay above water, played into the hands of employers, and served as an obstacle to unified class actions.

Clark and Rose blended the idioms of social and cultural history. They were as interested in the gendered dimension of economic and social conditions as in the way that class experience was shaped by historically constituted understandings of what it meant to be men and women. Carolyn Steedman's work, in many respects, shared these tendencies, but it assumed a less conventional form. Steedman's academic career has itself been highly unconventional. Trained as a social historian, with a Cambridge Ph.D., she only became part of a history department in 1994, when she was given a personal chair at the University of Warwick. Prior to that she was a primary-school teacher; she spent two years working on a research project on bilingualism in early education at the London Institute of Education; and she was a lecturer in arts education at Warwick. In the midst of all of this, she joined the editorial board of *History Workshop Journal* in 1984 (Eley 2005: 172). Although Steedman is clearly a social and cultural historian, her work cuts across several disciplines and engages with multiple audiences. In addition to history it is germane to cultural, women's, and literary studies. It is pertinent to discussions on the structure of narrative, autobiography, the history of class and childhood, psychoanalytic theory, the construction of the self, and postmodernism.

Steedman has addressed issues pertaining to class throughout her career, including a sporadic and oblique engagement with Thompson's work. He seemed to represent for her not just a historian responsible for certain texts: he also personified a historical vision that opened up some avenues and closed down others. In "Culture, Cultural Studies, and the Historians" (Steedman 1992), she spoke of *The Making of the English Working Class* as being in a "transitional stage of life" – about our times rather than those with which it dealt: "Too much has happened for this to operate as a simple historical source; there are too many new items of information – about what women were doing, at that moment, back in Huddersfield, about all the men who were not present at their own class formation, all those who did not 'specially want it to happen' [in W. H. Auden's words]; about recent events in Eastern Europe; about all our lost socialisms" (ibid.: 614). As part of a 1993 seminar honoring Thompson following his death – at the Centre for the Study of Social History at Warwick, a center that he himself founded and directed – Steedman further articulated her thoughts on Thompson's book. She had always resisted Thompson's account of class formation, but only now understood why. It was not because it excluded women: rather it was because it was a "heroic tale" that left out most people (Steedman 1994: 109). In recent work Steedman has acted to redress this hiatus, focusing on domestic servants, one of the largest groups of workers in the eighteenth and nineteenth centuries, yet ignored by Thompson and his followers (Steedman 2002a; 2002b; 2004).

Landscape for a Good Woman: A Story of Two Lives (1986) – arguably Steedman's most important book – was simultaneously autobiography, social history, and cultural studies. Steedman sought to create a narrative for herself as well as for her mother. She reflected on her working-class childhood in south London, which coincided with, and was shaped by, the emerging welfare state of the 1950s. Yet she looked back to the decisive sway of her family background, rooted in Lancashire's crumbling textile industries, where her grandmother had been a weaver and her mother had been a domestic servant. Steedman's own trajectory was unique, but she was one of many who followed the same migratory path from north to south.

Steedman found it difficult to recognize herself in the prevailing modes of understanding available to a feminist on the left. Here, she had in mind psychoanalytic criticism, which exclusively addressed middle-class experience. She also was referring to working-class history and autobiography, which had a narrow and idealistic notion of working people as a collectivity and a male-centered view of the working-class family, with its stereotypical portrait of "our ma'am." Steedman singled out Richard Hoggart and Jeremy Seabrook as being emblematic of this tendency. Growing up in a home with a working mother who was a passionate Tory and a father who had a marginal presence, Steedman's childhood slipped through the cracks of analysis. She sought to discover a narrative that would address it: not in order to produce an alternative grand narrative of working-class history, but to enable others to tell their stories as well – an aspiration that arguably transformed history into fragments of multiple biographies and autobiographies. To achieve this, she used Marxism to interrogate psychoanalysis and vice versa.

Class in this context played a central role, but it had to be rethought in order to embrace subjectivity and individual response, conspicuously absent from people's history and working-class autobiography. Women and children were especially important in this regard for they undermined the conventional narrative. In her words:

> When the mental life of working-class women is entered into the realm of production, and their narrative is allowed to disrupt the monolithic story of wage-labor and capital and when childhood and childhood learning are reckoned with, then what makes the old story unsatisfactory is not so much its granite-like *plot*, built around exploiter and exploited, capital and proletariat, but rather its *timing*: the precise how and why of the development of class consciousness (Steedman 1986: 14).

Steedman advocated focusing on working-class children's unconscious life: "the first loss, the earliest exclusion . . . brought forward later, and articulated through an adult experience of class and class relations" (ibid.: 14).

Steedman's unorthodox, nonlinear, and personal narrative – its blurring of past and present, the subjective and the social, theory and experience, the personal and the political – resonated with the times. In his intellectual autobiography and critical reflections of the trajectory of social and cultural history, *A Crooked Line: From Cultural History to the History of Society* (2005), Geoff Eley saw *Landscape for a Good Woman* as the social- and cultural-history text that best represented the political and intellectual aspirations of the 1980s. In his words: "For those on the left, it struck a particular chord. It authorized reflectiveness at a time when my generation was experiencing a range of uncertainties and disappointments – concerning both the forms of social history we'd expected might explain the world and the types of politics we thought could change it" (Eley 2005: 174). Most important for Eley was Steedman's "original and searching series of arguments about the gendered narratives of class disadvantage and aspiration" (ibid.: 173). *Landscape for a Good Woman* broke with many of social history's protocols, but it echoed the concerns of other British feminist historians discussed in this chapter. Taken together, their work has shed new light on the historical relationship between class and gender.

Conclusion

British feminist historians began in the 1970s by illuminating the lives of women who were hidden from history, extending the class-oriented model of history from below. Subsequently, they came to investigate the process of class formation itself – seeing class and gender as inextricably linked. In this regard, they were participants in a broader movement in the humanities and social sciences that reshaped their fields by integrating the category of gender.

Feminist historians might distance themselves from E. P. Thompson's male-centered account of class formation. However, they followed his efforts to situate the culture, language, and ideologies of historical actors within their material context, without reducing them to representations of objective interests. They were attentive to Joan Scott's discursive understanding of the classed and gendered subject but were reluctant to jettison the category of experience or follow her exclusive focus on discourse. In general, British feminist historians borrowed from social and cultural history approaches without getting involved in the polarizing debates regarding language and class.

If British Marxist social history was susceptible to attacks for its oblivion to gender, British feminist historical practice was vulnerable to critiques that it ignored race. In the United States, where the racial divide was pervasive, divisions between white and black feminists began to appear as early as 1973 (Whelehan 1995: 107). In Britain, where it took longer for racial divisions to be recognized as pivotal, challenges mounted by black feminists surfaced only later. As racial conflicts within the women's movement filtered into scholarly work, they have had a decisive impact on the way that gender was conceived. The implications of race for conceptions of class were no less important – and not only for feminists, as we shall see in the next chapter.

Chapter 7

Foregrounding race

Unlike gender, which only recently became part of the conceptual vocabulary of social sciences and humanities, "race" has a longstanding and complex history. Just as feminists developed the idea of gender to overcome fixed views of innate masculinity and femininity, contemporary theorists of race have combatted culturally ingrained theories that view racial differences as rooted in biology. They have demonstrated that race and racism are founded on culturally and historically based systems of difference, which, of course, does not diminish their impact, consequences, and effects. Some cultural theorists, sociologists, and historians of race have been influenced by poststructuralism's stress on language and discourse; others rely on older intellectual traditions; and still others are indebted to both.

Understanding race and racism is difficult enough. When class is added to the mix, the difficulties are intensified. Much like the feminists discussed in the preceding chapter, scholars analyzing the race/class intersection have confronted the problematic legacy of Marxist theory, which has tended to view race and racism as ultimately being a mere product of economic contradictions. Indeed, the innovation of recent scholars and theorists has been to view race and class as deeply intertwined, resolutely resisting the temptation to give one or the other theoretical priority. In addition, some of these scholars have engaged with feminist thought, which was evolving simultaneously. For these writers, the goal was to investigate the complex intersection of class, race, and gender. This ambition has become a mantra in some quarters of the humanities and the social sciences, but its seemingly ritualistic invocation should not undermine its importance.

In this chapter I examine recent scholarship on the relationship between race and class – and to a lesser extent gender – focusing primarily (but not exclusively) on the black experience in Britain and the United States. Beginning with a discussion of how scholars in cultural studies and sociology have conceived of this relationship, I go on to consider how such ideas have fared in the historical field. I analyze two types of historical work, analytically separable but intertwined in practice. On the one hand, I look at scholarship within and about the black radical tradition by focusing on the African-American historian Robin D. G. Kelley. On the other hand, I consider the rapidly proliferating field of "whiteness" studies, which explore a cultural construction no less important than, and reliant on, its binary opposite – "blackness." My analysis highlights David Roediger's *The Wages of Whiteness* ([1991] 1999) as well as discussions to which the book has given rise.

As I have thought about this chapter, I have been mindful that some of its principal innovators cannot be confined to a single national intellectual tradition, as the black experience itself has been, if anything, transnational. In part, my goal is to provide a glimpse into recent efforts analyzing the relationship between race and class in the context of what Paul Gilroy has described as the "Black Atlantic" (Gilroy 1993).

Theorizing race and class

Let's begin by considering relevant developments in cultural studies and sociology. Here, I consider work that grew out of research and discussions carried out under the auspices of the Centre for Contemporary Cultural Studies (henceforth referred to as the Centre) at the University of Birmingham in the 1970s (see Chapter 3). This work played a powerful role in shaping black British cultural studies. My focus is on Stuart Hall and Paul Gilroy (1956–). I also discuss an influential book by American sociologists Michael Omi and Howard Winant, *Racial Formation in the United States* ([1986] 1994). The British cultural theorists and American sociologists discussed here wrote in different intellectual and political milieus but worked along analogous lines. They both conceived of race as having its own specificity, irreducible to other social, political, and cultural forces – such as class and gender – yet shaped by them as well. And they both reformulated race theory in the context of the ascendancy of new right politics and ideology.

Stuart Hall is among the most influential cultural theorists in the contemporary humanities. He has already been mentioned in this book, for his role in formulating cultural studies and his postmodern-inflected analysis of "new times" and black popular culture (see Chapter 3). His theorization of the race/class relationship is no less important. Born in Jamaica, Hall has lived in Britain since 1951, originally studying literature at Oxford University as a Rhodes scholar. By the time that he became the Centre's director in the 1970s, he had helped establish the British new left in the late 1950s and was the first editor of its journal, *New Left Review* (see Chapter 2). Hall's early intellectual work was influenced by Raymond Williams's cultural theory (see Chapters 2 and 3). Yet Hall was more enthusiastic about mass popular culture than Williams, as evidenced in *The Popular Arts* (Hall and Whannel 1964).

As the Centre's director, Hall played a critical role in articulating the theoretical approaches associated with the "Birmingham school." Roughly speaking, these approaches fused structuralism and humanism, negotiated structure and agency, and drew on semiotics (particularly the version espoused by Roland Barthes), Western Marxist theory (Althusser but especially Gramsci), and British cultural Marxist approaches (Williams and E. P. Thompson). In multi-authored studies – notably *Resistance through Rituals: Youth Subcultures in Post-War Britain* (Hall and Jefferson 1976), *Policing the Crisis: Mugging, the State, and Law and Order* (Hall *et al.* 1978), *Women Take Issue: Aspects of Women's Subordination* (University of Birmingham 1978), and *The Empire Strikes Back: Race and Racism in 70s Britain* (University of Birmingham 1982) – Centre researchers contributed to scholarly discussions on the contemporary media; feminist theory; youth subcultures; working-class life; the modern state; historical theory; ideology; and race, class, and gender.

The first Centre project to systematically explore the connection between race and class in contemporary Britain was *Policing the Crisis*. (Given his importance to articulating its theoretical argument, Hall is henceforth referred to as its author.) The book was produced in a tumultuous climate, conceived in the midst of what seemed like an interminable British crisis. At one level the crisis was economic – a depressed economy accompanied by high unemployment and inflation. At another level it involved multiple challenges to the British state: two miners' strikes, Scottish and Welsh nationalism, the Northern Irish political crisis, and various new social movements. The crisis produced, and was in part produced by, virulent forms of nationalism and racism, spurred on by the emergence of the new right. Racial discord in Britain was by no means new, but its level of intensity and politicization nationally was unprecedented during the 1970s. Postwar immigration – beginning with the *Empire Windrush*'s transport of emigrants from the Caribbean in 1948 – permanently changed Britain.

The impetus for *Policing the Crisis* was a divisive criminal case involving a group of black youths who attacked a white working-class man in Handsworth, a multiracial and working-class neighborhood in Birmingham. The fact that these young men committed the crime was not at issue, but their sentences were excessive, and the case helped precipitate the apparently spontaneous mugging scare that surfaced in the early 1970s. Hall situated the case in a broader ideological context and argued that it was symptomatic of the British crisis. First, he maintained that, far from being spontaneous, the mugging scare resulted from a lengthy and complicated process of ideological preparation, whereby the state and the media exploited fears of race, crime, and youth to create a "moral panic." Second, he regarded this ideological mobilization in relationship to the crumbling of the social-democratic consensus that emerged following World War II. He understood the situation in Gramscian terms, as a crisis in hegemony (see Chapter 2). It was a situation rife for right-wing "authoritarian populism," an emerging hegemonic bloc founded on the ideologies of the free market, nationalism, and the traditional family. Authoritarian populism advanced on the back of orchestrated attacks on socialists, youth, and minorities – the enemy within. The book has been – along with other of Hall's writings at the time (Hall 1988) – rightfully viewed as forecasting the climatic changes that made possible Margaret Thatcher's election as prime minister in 1979, a year after *Policing the Crisis* was published.

Third, Hall maintained that, while blacks in Britain were mostly treated as immigrants, that is, outside of British history and culture, they, in fact, were a diaspora people shaped by the historical experience of the British Empire and global capitalism, thus placing them at the center – rather than the periphery – of British history. They shared with others of the black diaspora a common link to Africa, while being formed by a specifically British context as well. Blacks overwhelmingly belonged to the working class, yet some of their fiercest conflicts were with racist white workers, and they were largely alienated from organized labor. Their class experience was filtered through racial categories.

This last point is given its most cogent expression in "Race, Articulation, and Societies Structured in Dominance" (Hall [1980] 1996). In this essay Hall located himself in relationship to the two prevailing theoretical options: (1) a conventional Marxist perspective viewing ethnic and racial divisions as being rooted in historically grounded economic conditions and (2) a sociological point of view regarding these same divisions as being irreducibly social and cultural. For Hall, racial structures, as Marxists claimed, were historical rather than universal, but they could neither be explained *only* by economic relations nor understood by ignoring them. He sought, in other words, to situate racial dynamics in economically and historically determined conditions, yet insisted on their autonomy and specificity, what he called their "something else."

Hall carved out an intermediate position by rethinking the structural dynamics of the social formation. Borrowing from Althusser, he conceived of society as a "structured totality." Here, various structural levels – the economic, political, cultural, and ideological – were both autonomous and linked by "articulation" – by which Hall meant a loose and contingent connection entailing "no necessary belongingness." Slavery, for example, has historically been "articulated" with racist ideologies, shaping all structural levels, but its articulation with them was purely conditional, as evidenced by slavery in Ancient Greece where race was not a factor. Hall was not suggesting that each level played an equally important role in shaping the final outcome, only that it was not, as envisioned in orthodox Marxism, necessarily the economic one. He conceived of the totality (following Althusser) as a "complex unity structured in dominance."

Hall deployed this model to analyze race and class in contemporary Britain. He argued that race and racism were historically contingent, operated at all levels of the social formation, and involved relationships of domination and subordination. Regarding the black working class, he stated:

> It [race] enters into the way black labor, male and female, is distributed as economic agents at the level of economic practices, and the class struggles which result from it; and into the way the fractions of the black laboring classes are reconstituted, through the means of political representation (parties, organizations, community action centers, publications, and campaigns), as political forces in the "theater of politics" – and the political struggles which result; and the manner in which the class is articulated as the collective and individual "subjects" of emergent ideologies – and the struggles over ideology, culture, and consciousness which result (Hall [1980] 1996: 55).

For Hall, race and racism shaped the whole experience of black workers and, of course, white ones as well. In a memorable formulation he stated that race is "the modality in which class is 'lived,' the medium through which class relations are experienced, the form in which it is appropriated and 'fought through'" (ibid.: 55). Adopting this perspective helped account for the obstacles to class unity, but as this modality was historically contingent, it was not fixed or permanent. It could be transformed through hegemonic struggle. Ultimately, Hall understood race in terms adapted from Gramsci.

Hall's theorization of the race/class nexus helps shed light on what, by any definition, is a complex relationship. Retrospectively, it reads as a last-ditch effort to salvage Marxist categories. In Hall's later theorization of "new times" and black popular culture (see Chapter 3), he continued to insist on historical contingency, hegemonic struggle, and the importance of the economic (although one that had a cultural dimension). He likewise advocated ideas about identity and representation that were more poststructuralist and post-modernist than Marxist. In this later phase Hall was, among other things, helping to define black British cultural studies (Baker *et al.* 1996; Owusu 2000). In this context Paul Gilroy, who received his Ph.D. from the Centre, emerged as a major intellectual figure.

Gilroy was from an English and Guyanese background (his mother being the novelist, children's writer, critic, and teacher Beryl Gilroy), was born in London, and has held academic positions in both Britain and the United States. As a cultural-studies scholar (who is also a musician and has been a DJ), his life, in a sense, has been defined by the "Black Atlantic," a concept that, if he did not actually originate, he nonetheless made part of the common currency of the humanities.

Gilroy's theoretical understanding of race and class is found primarily in earlier work: the multi-authored *The Empire Strikes Back*, published before he received his Ph.D., and, most importantly, "*There Ain't No Black in the Union Jack*" (Gilroy [1987] 1991). Surfing the web, I happened upon a June 2003 BBC news story on Nigel Turner, who launched reFlag (www.reflag.co.uk), a campaign to redesign the British flag – the Union Jack. He advocates adding a touch of black, symbolic of Britain's multicultural and multiracial society. In effect, Turner hopes to achieve what skinheads opposed in their triumphant chant: "There ain't no black in the Union Jack." Turner implicitly or explicitly pays tribute to Gilroy, who nearly twenty years ago helped create a discussion on the connections between class, race, and British national identity.

Gilroy's book is comprised of a series of loosely connected and densely tex-tured essays exploring the dominant cultural constructions connecting race and national belonging in crisis-ridden Britain and the oppositional popular cultures that directly and indirectly contest them. Gilroy began the book by grappling theoretically with the tangled class/race relationship, pursuing a line of argument established by Hall and Centre researchers of which, of course, he was one in the 1970s and early 1980s. Or as he stated it: "'Race' can no longer be reduced to an effect of the economic antagonisms arising from production, and class must be understood in terms qualified by the vitality of the struggles articulated through 'race'" (ibid.: 28). Yet where Hall was critical yet respectful of Marxism, Gilroy seemed to be rapidly running out of patience with it. "One of this book's conclusions," he wrote, "is that if these [new] social struggles (some of which are conducted in and through 'race') are to be called class struggles, then class analysis must itself be thoroughly overhauled. I am not sure whether the labour involved in doing this makes either it a possible or a desirable task" (ibid.: 245). In part, Gilroy's critique was aimed at contemporary Marxist politics, but it also extended to

Marx himself. His Eurocentric vision of capitalist development had relegated many of the peoples of the world, including blacks, to the category of being "historyless."

A central dimension of Gilroy's argument was that the articulation of racial and national discourses had become a central feature of British political culture. In contrast to late nineteenth-century British racism, which was based on biological hierarchy, its late twentieth-century equivalent was founded on cultural differences, which cast blacks as permanent outsiders. In Gilroy's words: "Black settlers and their British born children are denied authentic national membership on the basis of their 'race' and, at the same time, prevented from aligning themselves within the 'British race' on the grounds that their national allegiance inevitably lies elsewhere" (ibid.: 46). For Gilroy, not only had such thinking become a central feature of new-right ideology, but it had also subtly infiltrated left-wing perspectives. When the left sought to reclaim the signifier "Britishness" from their conservative opponents, they left its racial and imperial dimension unexamined:

> Nationhood is not an empty receptacle which can be simply and spontaneously filled with alternative concepts according to the dictates of political pragmatism. The ideological theme of national belonging may be malleable to some extent but its links with the discourses of classes and "races" and the organizational realities of these groups are not arbitrary. They are confined by historical and political factors which limit the extent to which nationalism becomes socialist at the moment that its litany is repeated by socialists (ibid.: 55).

This critique did not apply only to left-wing political efforts to reclaim patriotism in the wake of Thatcherism's colonization of it following the 1982 Falklands War with Argentina. It extended as well to the class analysis of the cultural-studies tradition from which Gilroy's own thinking had emerged. In a later text Gilroy argued that British cultural studies, including the work of Williams and Thompson, was based on ethnocentric assumptions. He sought to move beyond "the limits of the quietly nationalistic vision advanced by British cultural studies' imaginary founding fathers" (Gilroy 1996: 237). He aligned himself with the theoretical path charted by Hall, Gramsci, the postcolonial critic Edward Said (see Chapter 8), and the Trinidadian Marxist C. L. R. James (discussed below) (ibid.: 237). Most importantly, Gilroy explored and, in a sense, helped produce the Black Atlantic intellectual and cultural tradition, "the intercultural flows" linking Africa, the Caribbean, Britain, and America (Puranik 1993).

Like Hall and Gilroy, Omi and Winant wrote *Racial Formation in the United States* in the wake of the ascendancy of the new right, which during the Reagan years, in their words, rewrote "recent history to suggest that discrimination against racial minorities had been drastically curbed and by radically transforming the state institutions which were previously mandated to 'protect' racial minority interests" (Omi and Winant [1986] 1994: 135). Also like their British counterparts, they framed their ideas on race in opposition to views that were (according to them) one dimensional – whether ethnic, economic (some of which were Marxist), or black nationalist. Omi and Winant were like Hall and Gilroy in other ways. They argued that race was an autonomous dimension operating at the micro and macro levels and that racial categories were historically fluid and contested, subject to hegemonic struggle. Omi and Winant described their approach as "racial formation" theory. In their words: it "emphasizes the social nature of race, the absence of any essential racial characteristics, the historical flexibility of racial meanings and categories, the conflictual character of race at both the 'micro-' and the 'macro-social' levels, and the irreducible political aspect of racial dynamics" (ibid.: 4).

Omi and Winant accepted the poststructuralist contention that language and discourse were material forces, while believing that this stress often ignored structural phenomena, for example patterns of racial hierarchies in labor markets or the segregation of neighborhoods. They conceived of race then as simultaneously part of the "social structure" and a form of "cultural representation." "Racial projects," they wrote, "connect what race *means* in a particular discursive practice and the ways in which both social structures and everyday experiences are racially *organized*, based on that meaning" (ibid.: 56). Their view here recalls that of other scholars who, though not writing about race *per se*, sought to bridge the gap between the social and the cultural: Geoff Eley and William Sewell in Chapter 4, James Epstein in Chapter 5, and several of the feminist historians in Chapter 6.

What is the pertinence of racial formation theory for understanding class? In contrast to Hall and Gilroy, Omi and Winant do not systematically address the race/class nexus, partially attributable perhaps to the relative weight of race and class as categories of identification in American and British society. Nonetheless, Omi and Winant's views generally accord with those of their British counterparts. For the two Americans, race, class – and gender – all signify realms of "potential antagonism" and regions of hegemonic struggle, none of which can be accorded theoretical priority. Their view of the interaction of these realms roughly corresponds to Hall's idea of "articulation." Moreover, in language reminiscent of Hall's, Omi and Winant argue that "race is gendered and gender is racialized." Hall and Gilroy would have likely embraced this formulation, while Omi and Winant would likely accept Hall's contention that under contemporary conditions race is the modality in which class is lived. Moreover, Gilroy cites earlier work by Omi and Winant to buttress his own view of race formation (Gilroy [1987] 1991: 42).

Inspired by unique but analogous circumstances, Hall and Gilroy, as well as Omi and Winant, understood the relationship between race and class through a "third way" alternative to the reductionism of existing approaches. For both the British cultural theorists and the American sociologists, the connections between primary forms of social and cultural determinations and identifications – whether race, class, or gender – were entangled yet historically produced, manifested through both micro- and macro-level hegemonic struggles. These men helped produce a theoretical opening that scholars throughout the humanities and the social sciences, including historians, explored.

We are not what we seem

In this section I focus on the African-American historian Robin D. G. Kelley (1962–), who, when only 33, was described by Paul Buhle as "a leading black historian of the age" (Buhle 1996: 41). A social and cultural historian, as well as a political writer and cultural critic, Kelley has grappled with the intersections of race, class, and gender. Kelley sounds very much like the British writers discussed above in his contention "that class is lived through race and gender." He went on to elaborate on this idea:

> There is no universal class identity, just as there is no universal racial or gender or sexual identity. The idea that race, gender, and sexuality are particular whereas class is universal not only presumes that class struggle is some sort of race- and gender-neutral terrain but takes for granted that movements focused on race, gender, or sexuality necessarily undermine class unity and, by definition, cannot be emancipatory for the whole (Kelley 1997: 109).

Kelley's understanding of race, class, and gender in his historical work is found in studies of black working-class history from "way, way below": everyday forms of opposition mounted by ordinary people and the sometimes more articulate expressions of political radicals. Here, I focus primarily on two texts: *Hammer and Hoe: Alabama Communists during the Great Depression* (1990) and *Race Rebels: Culture, Politics, and the Black Working Class* (1994).

I am interested in Kelley's work in its own right. However, since he is in dialogue with numerous intellectual tendencies, his work also lends itself to discussing a wider compass of pertinent scholarship.

Kelley's rapid ascent in the historical profession was far from ordained. From a "low income" Harlem background, he spent his teenage years in southern California, where he attended California State University, Long Beach as a first-generation college student. Graduating in three years, Kelley was accepted into the University of California, Los Angeles Ph.D. program in history, overcoming the handicap of a "third-tier" undergraduate degree. He attributed his acceptance to his "hustling instincts," which perhaps exaggerates what transpired while also having a kernel of truth to it. Kelley pursued a Ph.D. because he believed that it was an indispensable component of political activism: he aspired to be a professional Communist rather than a history professor. Originally an African-history student, Kelley graduated with his Ph.D. in American history, passing his qualifying exams despite having taken only one course on the subject (Winkler 1998; Kelley and Williams 2003).

Kelley's first sustained foray into the world of race and class was his revised dissertation, *Hammer and Hoe*, a book that remains his favorite. The book focused on the small but determined Alabama Communist Party, which in the 1930s and 1940s attracted a constituency overwhelmingly made up of poor, semiliterate, and passionately religious blacks as well as a small group of whites. Drawing on police records, Party newspapers, and interviews, among other things, Kelley sought to recover the Party's history from the "bottom up." He acknowledged that developments in the international and national Communist movement mediated the Alabama Communist Party's strategies, tactics, and agenda, yet he emphasized the shaping influence of local circumstances. "What emerged," in his words, "was a malleable movement rooted in a variety of different pasts, reflecting a variety of different voices, and incorporating countless contradictory tendencies" (Kelley 1990: xii).

In *Hammer and Hoe* Kelley recovered the underground world of Communist militancy. For Kelley, poor blacks regarded the Communist Party as a vehicle for organizing themselves. The Party, despite its emphasis on class-based politics, generated a race organization that represented an alternative to the middle-class-dominated National Association for the Advancement of Colored People (NAACP) and grafted a socialist vision on a tradition of older political struggles of emancipation. Using a formulation reminiscent of Thompson's representation of the English working class as confronting the Industrial Revolution through the oppositional tradition of the freeborn Englishman (see Chapter 2), Kelley suggested that black Communists were not "blank slates" upon their arrival in the movement: "Instead, they were born and reared in communities with a rich culture of opposition – a culture that enveloped and transformed the Party into a movement more reflective of African-American radical traditions than anything else" (ibid.: 99). In the end, the Party was flexible enough to draw from black cultural traditions, while at the same time being unswervingly committed to orthodox Marxism. For rank-and-file black Alabaman Communists, Kelly wrote, "the Bible was as much a guide to class struggle as Marx and Engels's *Communist Manifesto*" (ibid.: 107).

Kelley extended and widened his exploration of the "culture of opposition" in *Race Rebels*, written when he was a faculty member at the University of Michigan in the early 1990s. He has described these years as a "second graduate school experience" in which he engaged with scholars from numerous disciplines – history, anthropology, African-American studies, and American culture (Kelley and Williams 2003). It was the same intellectual environment in which Geoff Eley wrote "Is All the World a Text?" (see Chapter 4).

Race Rebels is a theoretically eclectic and broadly conceived analysis of black working-class resistance. Its first sentence suggests that Kelley has staked out new territory: " 'McDonald's is a Happy Place!' " (Kelley 1994: 1). This ironic comment refers to Kelley's own experience as an employee of the world's largest fast-food chain, in central Pasadena in the late 1970s. The "work was tiring and polyester uniforms unbearable," and employees were underpaid, overworked, and treated as if they were stupid. Yet neither Kelley nor his fellow workers passively capitulated to rules and regulations. They freely "accepted consumption as just compensation": they stole food; they played the "wrong" radio stations; they ignored labor manuals, turning work into performance; and they stretched their breaks. These mostly African-American and Chicano workers, Kelley argued, neither conceived of themselves as belonging to the working class nor "engaged in workplace struggles," but their actions constituted forms of rebellion (ibid.: 1–3).

The point, of course, is that Kelley's fellow workers and others like them had escaped historians' net, even social historians'. The point was underscored by the introduction's subtitle: "Writing Black Working-Class History from Way, Way Below." Kelley, in effect, championed a version of history from below that focused on everyday, frequently cultural forms of political resistance that could be found among black working people. The initiative was not itself new, but it was necessitated by the fact that, according to him, history from below had barely penetrated the writing of African-American history. Kelley recognized that a case existed for considering African-American history as a whole to be quintessentially part of history from below. But he believed that African-American historians had emphasized what Nell Painter called "representative colored men." As a result, historical accounts ignored the lives of countless ordinary people, underplayed class and gender differences, and produced "a very limited and at times monolithic definition of the 'black community'" (ibid.: 6). Kelley strove instead to create a more heterogeneous picture of African-American life: from black workers' subversion of the workplace to their struggle to assert their rights on Birmingham's segregated buses and streetcars, from the interrelationship of Communism and black nationalism to the cultural politics of zoot suits and rap music. Based on original historical research, the creative use of current historiography, and the adaptation of social and cultural theory, the book was at the same time social and cultural history, cultural and political criticism. If it sometimes seemed to romanticize its subjects, the book likewise was a powerful reminder of the power of ordinary people to mount resistance, if only historians dug deep enough.

To create history "from way, way below," Kelley drew from various perspectives: (1) cultural and historical analyses of resistance, (2) African-American and second-wave feminism, and (3) the black radical intellectual tradition. I discuss *Race Rebels* in relationship to these points of view, my goal being to connect Kelley's writing to broader intellectual and political thought.

Kelley's understanding of popular resistance was dependent on multiple sources. He acknowledged the pioneering work of American and British new social and labor history, while noting that its beginnings were very white and very male (ibid.: 6). Given that much of black working-class peoples' resistance was "unorganized, clandestine, and evasive," he was attracted to conceptualizations and analyses of everyday political resistance. He acknowledged the influence of the political anthropologist James Scott, for whom these forms of resistance were "hidden transcripts," expressions of "infrapolitics," which like infrared rays were outside the visible spectrum (ibid.: 8). He was indebted to the ethnographer Lila Abu-Lughod, who believed that everyday forms of resistance were more than instances of integrity and bravery: they provided windows into historically variable power structures (ibid.: 9). And he adapted the French philosopher Michel de Certeau's concept of "wigging," that is, workers' illicit appropriation of slices of their working hours for themselves (ibid.: 20), a conception that could easily have been used to help capture the actions of the McDonald's employees discussed earlier. Kelley deployed it to understand various acts undertaken by southern black workers.

An illustration of Kelley's adaptation of "infrapolitics" was his analysis of black working people's experience on the segregated buses and streetcars of Birmingham, Alabama during World War II. At a time of rising employment, owing to the booming wartime economy, mass transportation used by blacks was on the rise, resulting in increasingly tense interracial relationships between the mostly working-class black and white passengers. Often drivers, conductors, and white passengers maltreated blacks who rode mass transit. Kelley documented cases in which drivers refused to pick up African-Americans; white riders hurled verbal abuse at them; and conductors beat them when they complained that their stop had been passed. But mass transportation was also, according to Kelley, a mobile site of struggle, one in which resistance was spontaneous and fleeting, one in which it was difficult for the police to impose authority. Kelley described black resistance as follows:

> Sitting with whites, for most black riders, was never a critical issue; rather, African Americans wanted more space for themselves, they wanted to receive equitable treatment, they wanted to be personally treated with respect and dignity, they wanted to be heard and possibly understood, they wanted to get to work on time, and above all, they wanted to exercise power over institutions that controlled them or on which they were dependent (ibid.: 75).

Sometimes those asserting these rights were African-American soldiers who equated the segregated South with the fascist regimes that they had fought against in the war. Other times they were demanded by zoot suiters, whose fast-talking hipster style "constructed an identity in which their gendered and racial meanings were inseparable; opposition to racist oppression was mediated through masculinity" (ibid.: 66). Still others involved black women. Indeed, the number of incidents involving women outnumbered those involving men. Black women had a long tradition of opposing the Jim Crow system of public transportation, culminating in Rosa Park's landmark refusal in 1955 to give up her seat to a white passenger, which helped trigger the 1950s and 1960s civil rights movement. All of these protests were embedded in race, class, and gender relationships.

Race Rebels also contributed to recovering the black radical tradition. Here, Kelley extended and broadened what he had begun in *Hammer and Hoe*, delineating a world of African-American Communism, which he described as "a mosaic of racial imagery interpenetrated by class and gender" (ibid.: 120). Kelley acknowledged that black nationalists had a complex and ambivalent association with the Communist movement. However, he argued that black militants, whatever their political roots, believed that revolution was a "man's job" and used "highly masculinist imagery that relied on metaphors from war and emphasized violence as a form of male redemption" (ibid.: 121).

Kelley's sensitivity to the gendered dimension of the black radical tradition was built on a broader understanding of the interweaving of class, race, and gender identities. In this regard his perspective bore the imprint of feminism.

For instance, Kelley's focus on households and families in the making of class consciousness acknowledged Carolyn Steedman, who in *Landscape for a Good Woman* (1986) argued that class formation took place in childhood (see Chapter 6), and Elizabeth Faue, who maintained that class, gender, and race shaped identities long before people entered the work force (Kelley 1994: 37). In addition, Kelley's work drew from the scholarship of African-American feminist historians such as Elsa Barkley Brown and Evelyn Brooks Higginbotham. His historical portrait of the black working-class family relied on Brown's work on the political activism of African-American families during the Reconstruction period. Brown showed that newly liberated African-American families produced an idea of citizenship that conceived of voting as the entire family's property and that men who failed to vote accordingly faced reprimands or ostracism (ibid.: 37–38). Kelley's discussion of southern black working people's "secular forms of congregation" drew from Higginbotham, who analyzed opposing images of church and street in southern black culture, arguing that their meanings were inflected by both class and gender (ibid.: 46).

Brown and Higginbotham are likewise important for this discussion because their understanding of the relationship between class, race, and gender opened up conceptual ground that Kelley was exploring as well. Both Brown and Higginbotham critiqued mainstream white feminism from an African-American feminist perspective. In "Womanist Consciousness: Maggie Lena Walker and the Independent Order of Saint Luke" ([1989] 1996), Brown explored the life of the early twentieth-century activist Maggie Lena Walker (1867–1934), who for 35 years was the Right Worthy Grand Secretary of the Independent Order of Saint Luke, an African-American mutual benefit society, and was best known perhaps as the first female bank president in the United States. For Brown, Walker and the Saint Luke women challenged second-wave feminism's privileging of gender, which misleadingly produced race as a separate and secondary category. Black women such as Walker resisted being categorized exclusively by either their race or their gender. Adopting the multidimensional "womanist" perspective articulated by Alice Walker and Okonjo Ogunyemi, Brown argued: "It is precisely this kind of thinking [white feminism] that makes it difficult to see race, sex, and class as forming one consciousness and the resistance of race, sex, and class oppression as forming one struggle" (Brown [1989] 1996: 468–69).

Like Brown, Higginbotham, in "African-American Women's History and the Metalanguage of Race" ([1992] 1996), attempted to infuse "race" into the theoretical vocabulary of "new wave feminism." White feminists, in her view, still only paid lip service to race, while "continuing to analyze their own experience in ever more sophisticated forms" (Higginbotham [1992] 1996: 184).

Higginbotham sought to bridge the gap between white and black feminist theory, simultaneously drawing on both the African-American intellectual tradition and positions derived from cultural theories of language and discourse. To achieve this, she advocated a three-pronged strategy that, first, involved explicating the "construction" and "technologies" of race, gender, and sexuality. Second, it entailed exploring race as a metalanguage, a language that is prior to and that inflects other languages, by "calling attention to its powerful, all-encompassing effect on the construction and representation of other social and power relations, namely gender, class, and sexuality" (ibid.: 184). Third, it meant viewing race as "providing sites of dialogic exchange and contestation, since race has constituted a discursive tool for both oppression and liberation" (ibid.: 184). Race, in Higginbotham's view, often subsumed gender and class relations, while mystifying the process whereby this had been accomplished: "It precludes unity within the same gender group but often appears to solidify people of opposing economic classes. Whether race is textually omitted or textually privileged, its totalizing effect in obscuring class and gender remains" (ibid.: 186).

Kelley's affinity for feminism thus helps explain one dimension of his take on black radicalism, as well as other aspects of African-American life. We can learn a great deal more both about Kelley's perspective on this tradition and about the tradition itself by looking at a book that Kelley credits with changing his life – Cedric Robinson's *Black Marxism: The Making of the Black Radical Tradition* ([1983] 2000). Kelley first encountered *Black Marxism* as a graduate student, when he was asked to review it. However, he found the book so overwhelming that he was unable to write the review. Instead, he sought out Robinson and prevailed upon him to take him on as a student. Kelley's enthusiasm for *Black Marxism* was not widely shared, or at least so it seems, as the book attracted little attention. Kelley's efforts contributed to the University of North Carolina Press's reprinting of it, with a new preface by Robinson and a foreword by Kelley situating the book in relationship to recent scholarship on African-American history and culture. Kelley's essay has played a critical role in the way I myself regard Robinson's book.

Black Marxism is an interdisciplinary text: it moves back and forth between political theory, historical and cultural analysis, philosophy, and biography. Robinson rethought the relationship between race and class on a global scale as well as elucidating the intellectual and political tradition that inspired such rethinking. First, he critiqued Western Marxist theory, by which he meant Marxism–Leninism. Robinson observed that, as a consequence of its deeply embedded ethnocentrism, Marxism failed to understand the intimate connection between capitalism as it developed in Europe and the global system of slavery and imperialism in other parts of the world. He described this system as "racial capitalism," meaning that racism and capitalism, racial and class formation, were historically inseparable. Racial capitalism resulted from a much older process of European racialization. It was first manifested as intra-European racial hierarchies, but subsequently broadened its scope with European economic and political expansion. Robinson found this mode of racialization not only in the enslavement of African peoples and the extraction of their labor but also, for example, in the English colonization of Ireland, which ultimately made possible the indispensable role of "racially-inferior" Irish workers in early industrialization. As Cornel West has pointed out, Robinson, in effect, criticized E. P. Thompson's oblivion to the connection between Irish anticolonial rebellions, African slaves toiling in the new world, and the ethnocentrism of freeborn English workers in *The Making of the English Working Class* (West 1988: 52–53). For Robinson, the modern class experience always had both a racial and a global dimension.

Second, the obverse side of Robinson's examination of racial capitalism was his analysis of black radicalism. He portrayed it as a black nationalist tradition that created complex, diverse, and potent forms of resistance in response to slavery, colonial violence, and global capitalism, whether in African or new world conditions. It was rooted in shared African cultural experiences that over time evolved in dialectical relationship with the evolving world system, helping produce "not only with a common task but a shared vision" (Robinson [1983] 2000: 166).

On the one hand, the black radical tradition found its embodiment in diverse political movements: from the Haitian slave revolts of the late eighteenth century, which produced the second American republic, to the nineteenth-century armed resistance of the Zulus, who defended their way of life. On the other hand, this tradition was enriched by a varied group of intellectuals, predominantly from the African diaspora, who sought to produce theoretical and political perspectives based on both Marxist and black-radical insights. In the end, they did not succeed in fusing them but left behind a remarkable body of theoretical, historical, and literary work. In *Black Marxism* Robinson investigated the lives and writings of three of these writers – the African-American historian and sociologist W. E. B. Du Bois (1868–1963); the Trinidadian historian, novelist, philosopher, and cultural and literary critic C. L. R. James (1901–1989); and the African-American novelist Richard Wright (1908–1960).

An in-depth discussion of these three writers is beyond this book's scope. However, I want to give some indication of their importance by briefly discussing Du Bois and James, both of whom regarded slavery as a critical component of global capitalism and black resistance as a central element of the modern experience. A founder of the NAACP and one of the most powerful intellectual voices in twentieth-century America, Du Bois is important in this context for his *Black Reconstruction in America, 1860–1880* ([1935] 1998), where he argued that capitalism and slavery, class and race, were structurally related. It was the rebellious slaves, steeped in African traditions, and white agrarian workers who led a frontal assault on capitalism during the Civil War. According to Du Bois, a recalcitrant white working class, infected by racist ideologies and bourgeois promises of social mobility, were obstacles to furthering the class struggle. In effect, their response was shaped as much by their racial as by their class identity. Thus, it was mostly peasants and slaves – not the working class privileged by orthodox Marxism – who were in the forefront of challenging capitalism. Du Bois described what he called the "General Strike" of the Civil War as "the most extraordinary experiments of Marxism that the world, before the Russian Revolution, had seen" (quoted in ibid.: 235).

A leading figure in the development of the Pan-African movement, a renegade Trotskyist, and a leading writer on the game of cricket, C. L. R. James is significant for Robinson's construction of the black radical intellectual tradition, above all, for his historical treatment of the late eighteenth-century Haitian slave revolt in *The Black Jacobins: Toussaint L'Ouverture and the San Domingo Revolution* ([1938] 1963). By situating the slave revolt in the broader context of the French Revolutionary era – in Marxist terms the defining modern political epoch – James linked center and periphery, capitalism and empire, race and class. He portrayed the slaves as producing a revolutionary culture, steeped in African traditions, capable of challenging the existing order, and yet still dependent on the charismatic and authoritarian leadership of Toussaint L'Ouverture, whom James simultaneously respected and criticized. In the course of his life James gradually abandoned his commitment to a Leninist political vanguard in favor of a faith in ordinary people's militancy.

Kelley has pointed out the affinities between Robinson's *Black Marxism* and Gilroy's *The Black Atlantic*, which, though written a decade later, mapped some of the same intellectual and political terrain (Kelley 2000: xviii–xix). Both Gilroy and Robinson viewed Du Bois, James, and Wright as being critical to contemporary political and intellectual discussions. They both stressed the centrality of blacks to the modern experience. And they both viewed this experience as transnational, encompassing Africa, Europe, the Caribbean, and the Americas. Gilroy's notion that the Black Atlantic was a "counterculture of modernity" and that blacks within it experienced a "double consciousness" (an idea adapted from Du Bois) was compatible with Robinson's intellectual vision.

Yet there are differences between Robinson and Gilroy. Robinson flirted with viewing black radicalism as being rooted in an African essence, a criticism first made by West (West 1988: 54). Gilroy regarded it as more fluid, less stable, more fragmented, and characterized by cultural hybridity. Indeed, as Kelley pointed out (Kelley 2000: xix), Gilroy's only acknowledgment of *Black Marxism* was to describe it as both "illuminating and misleading." He critiqued Robinson's notion of the black radical tradition, which "can suggest that it is the radical elements of this tradition which are its dominant characteristics . . . , and because the idea of tradition can sound too closed, too final, and too antithetical to the subaltern experience of modernity which has partially conditioned the development of these cultural forms" (Gilroy 1993: 122). In addition, Gilroy and Robinson had different relationships to Marxism. Robinson was exclusively concerned with combating the reductionism and ethnocentrism of Marxism–Leninism, but he ignored an alternative conception of Western Marxism – which included Gramsci – whose critique of Marxist orthodoxy from within European culture provided a potential basis for a dialogue (see Chapter 2). Gilroy was impatient with Marxism as well, but his thinking developed in conjunction with British cultural Marxism, particularly through his relationship with Hall, who, of course, had been deeply influenced by Gramsci.

Yet all of these men – Gilroy, Kelley, Robinson, and Hall – were part of an intellectual tradition, which they themselves put their stamp on, whose achievements included viewing the race/class nexus in the context of global capitalism and entailed decentering a historical narrative that privileged the position of Europe and the West. For those within this tradition, class, race, and (depending on when, where, and the writer) gender were historically interwoven. These factors were linked together yet retained their specificity; and their relationship was defined through political struggle. This conceptual framework helped explain the potential for unified action between black and white workers, as it did the various forms of resistance engaged in by blacks, so poignantly captured by Kelley. This framework also provided the groundwork for analyzing what kept black and white workers apart. Here, there was no explanation more powerful than Du Bois's: white workers were paid a psychological wage in exchange for choosing race over class solidarity. This half-forgotten idea, articulated during the interwar years, eventually inspired a group of historians exploring the historical resonance of "whiteness."

The point is not to interpret whiteness but to abolish it

This section's title represents a rewriting of Marx's oft-quoted declaration in the "Theses on Feuerbach": "The philosophers have only *interpreted* the world, in various ways; the point, however, is to *change* it" (Tucker 1978: 143). As reworked, it is the name of an essay on the website "Race Traitor: Journal of the New Abolitionism" (Ignatiev 1997). (The website's address is http://racetraitor.org.) Race Traitor is committed, as the essay's title suggests, to ending the white race. This does not, of course, mean exterminating white people; rather, the group takes aim at the culturally constructed systems of meaning that have produced the idea of whiteness and the institutional configurations that those systems underwrite. Race Traitor defines the white race as "a historically constructed social formation" which "consists of all those who partake of the privileges of the white skin in society" (Race Traitor, no date). This view of whiteness shares assumptions about the nature of race found in other writers discussed in this chapter: namely, that race is not a fixed or static category rooted in biological difference but a historically and culturally produced one. As we shall see, "whiteness" is a construction that has been shaped by class as well.

Race Traitor is certainly not a mass party, but it is in the forefront of whiteness studies – an intellectual and political initiative centered in universities, which has garnered a level of public attention not usually given to academic work. This interest is illustrated by Bruce Tinsley's *Mallard Fillmore* cartoon in *The Boston Globe* on 5 October 2002. It pokes fun at Noel Ignatiev – former steel worker, current Harvard professor, editor of Race Traitor, and the author of an influential text in whiteness studies, *How the Irish Became White* (1995). The cartoon questions whether Ignatiev's views are any more enlightened than those of the white racists that he opposes. It lightheartedly suggests that the difference is that he taught at Harvard. That the cartoonist of a major American newspaper thought whiteness studies important enough to make fun of says something about its stature.

The notion that whiteness represents an ideological category bestowing political privileges on the group that it constructs is not new. James Baldwin once wrote: "As long as you think you're white, there's no hope for you" (quoted in Roediger [1991] 1999: 6). More recently, Tony Morrison observed that Americans have a tradition of analyzing the calamitous impact of slavery on blacks, but there has been little "serious intellectual effort to see what racial ideology does to the mind, imagination, and behavior of masters" (quoted in Levine 1994: 11). Whiteness studies have explored the ramifications of such insights, broadening and deepening them along the way. They have, in effect, turned the tables on the study of the "Other." Or as David W. Stowe asks: "What happens to our understanding of race when the dreaded ethnographic gaze is turned back upon itself, away from the (presumably) nonwhite Other to the (presumably) white subject?" (Stowe 1996: 70). In answering this and related questions, whiteness studies have become the academic equivalent of an industry, led by scholars in American, cultural, and ethnic studies; anthropology; education; film studies; geography; history; law; literary criticism; philosophy; and sociology.

Among these fields and disciplines, none has been more influential than history. Much of the work on the subject was produced by activist Marxist historians who located whiteness in the race/class nexus. There was Theodore Allen's monumental two-volume study, *The Invention of the White Race* (1994; 1997). In the first volume he argued that the American system of racial oppression, based on white supremacy, was "Ulster Writ Large," the Protestant system of denomination in Ireland being extended to a different set of economic circumstances. Allen regarded the creation of whiteness as a form of ruling-class social control. European settlers received inducements – the lure of social mobility, citizenship, and property – in exchange for accepting a system of black servitude. Another important study was Alexander Saxton's *The Rise and Fall of the White Republic* (1990), a sweeping historical interpretation of nineteenth-century America, which highlighted the centrality of white supremacy in cementing varying ruling-class partnerships and maintained "that the hard side of racism generally appeared in nineteenth-century America as a corollary to egalitarianism" (Saxton 1990: 186). Deploying an analysis informed by Gramsci's notion of hegemony, Saxton's analysis ranged from American party politics and popular culture (the penny press, theater, blackface minstrelsy, dime novels, folk heroes like Kit Carson) to established literary figures (James Fenimore Cooper, Mark Twain, Harriet Beecher Stowe).

A third book exemplifying historical whiteness studies is Ignatiev's *How the Irish Became White* (briefly alluded to above), which castigated the new labor history for suppressing white-working class racism and advocated viewing the class experience as being racialized. More specifically, it explored how Irish immigrants – starting out in America as an impoverished and oppressed minority and often portrayed by Anglo-Americans as subhuman and "niggers turned inside out" – exchanged "green" identities for "white" status. Rather than reaching out to free blacks and slaves as potential allies in a united class struggle, Irish immigrants insisted on both their whiteness and their racial supremacy. As Ignatiev stated it: "The outcome was not the inevitable consequence of blind historical forces, still less of biology, but the result of choices made, by the Irish and others, from among available alternatives. To enter the white race was a strategy to secure an advantage in a competitive society" (Ignatiev 1995: 2). But the availability of an option to enter the white race was also contingent on the existence of a black one.

Of the historical works on whiteness, arguably the most important has been David Roediger's *The Wages of Whiteness*, an original, sophisticated synthesis that both contributed to whiteness literature as well as drew from it. The book was "written in reaction to the appalling extent to which white male workers voted for Reganism in the 1980s" (Roediger [1991] 1999: 188). But it also had a biographical dimension. Roediger (1952–) was from a German-American working-class and union background. He grew up in Columbia, Illinois, a town outside of St. Louis, Missouri, where racism and white supremacy were taken for granted. Yet his experience of black people contradicted racist stereotypes, and he began to take part in antiracist causes as a high-school student. What Roediger learned from these early experiences, in his words, was "the role of race in defining how white workers look not only at Blacks but at themselves; the pervasiveness of race; the complex mixture of hate, sadness and longing in the racist thought of white workers; the relationship between race and ethnicity" (ibid.: 5).

Roediger explored these themes historically in *The Wages of Whiteness* and related work (Roediger 1994). He adopted a Marxist perspective shorn of its reductive and deterministic tendencies to collapse race and racism into class. Recasting the base–superstructure metaphor, Roediger wrote:

> If, to use tempting older Marxist images, racism is a large, low-hanging branch of a tree that is rooted in class relations, we must constantly remind ourselves that the branch is not the same as the roots, that people may more often bump into the branch than the roots, and that the best way to shake the roots may at times be by grabbing the branch (Roediger [1991] 1999: 8).

In venturing onto this terrain, Roediger found a kindred spirit in the historian Barbara Fields, who argued that race and class were interlocking systems but differently configured (Fields 1982; 1990). Where class systems were founded on objective inequalities, those based on race were wholly ideological, as they were purely rooted in the social imaginary. Roediger embraced Fields' position, while resisting what he saw as her tendency to lapse occasionally into privileging class because it was more "real."

Roediger also drew sustenance from cultural approaches. He conceived of identity as constructed through difference and regarded shifts in signification as important to understanding changes in class and race perception. Indeed, some of the most memorable passages in *The Wages of Whiteness* trace transformations in meaning: the change, for instance, from employer/employee relationships being signified between master and servant to their being represented between hired hand and boss; or how "coon" developed from its early meaning as a white frontiersman to its later one as a racial slur. As an avowed Marxist, Roediger took pains to distance himself from the epistemological radicalism of poststructuralism, while arguing that meaning was always multifaceted and socially contested. His position here recalls Stuart Hall's, which he acknowledged (along with Omi and Winant's) as an important conceptualization of the interpenetration of race and class (Roediger [1991] 1999: 11).

In addition, Roediger situated himself in the Marxist tradition of history from below exemplified by E. P. Thompson and Herbert Gutman (see Chapter 2). Roediger admired the respect that this tradition accorded historical subjects. It portrayed them as agents rather than victims, even in times of iron-clad ruling-class hegemony. This formulation meant that white working-class racism could not be seen simply as being imposed from above. Roediger, like Ignatiev, believed that historians of this stripe often avoided this troubling dimension of working-class life, beginning with Gutman himself, whose "desire to recover antiracist traditions led to a straining of the evidence and an unwillingness to probe the extent of white working-class racism" (Roediger 1994: 41).

Roediger counteracted this tendency by turning to Du Bois, who in *Black Reconstruction* argued that white workers received a "psychological wage" for choosing racial difference over class solidarity. Embracing whiteness conferred upon those in a position to take advantage of it an enhanced standing. In Roediger's words, "status and privileges conferred by race could be used to make up for the alienating and exploitative class relationships, North and South. White workers could, and did, define and accept their class position by fashioning identities as 'not slaves' and as 'not Blacks'" (Roediger [1991] 1999: 13). In this context Roediger owed a debt to psychoanalytic theories of identity, notably as used by George Rawick in the closing chapters of *From Sundown to Sunup: The Making of the Black Community* (1972), an examination of the seventeenth- and eighteenth-century Anglo-European bourgeoisie. Through this work, as well as Frantz Fanon's and Joel Kovel's, Roediger understood whiteness "as the product of specific classes' attempts to come to terms with their class – never simply economic – problems by projecting their longings onto a despised race" (Roediger [1991] 1999: 14).

This understanding of race and class forms the basis of Roediger's historical examination of the 60 years prior to the Civil War. For Roediger, a sense of whiteness and working-class formation proceeded in tandem. He attributed this to the threat that spreading wage labor and capitalist discipline posed for white workers' deeply entrenched commitment to a republican ideology that

stressed individual independence and autonomy and defined itself in relationship to the horrors of slavery (C. Hall 1992b). As "freemen," white workers
resisted "wage slavery," while rejecting the notion that they shared a common
plight with blacks. They might be "hirelings," but they still were free of pater-
nalism and dependence and were socially mobile. To be a freeman involved
the assertion of manly virtues (an important point about gender construction
that is not fleshed out). Most important, it meant not being a slave. To be white
then, as noted above, was the negation of being black; but the implications of
this went beyond mere difference:

> That Blacks were largely noncitizens will surprise few, but it is important to
> emphasize the extent to which they were seen as *anticitizens*, as "enemies
> rather than members of the social compact" . . . The more powerless they
> became, the greater their supposed potential to be used by the rich to make
> freemen unfree. Thus, it was necessary to watch for the smallest signs of
> power among Blacks, and since Blacks were defenseless, it was easy to act
> on perceived threats (Roediger [1991] 1999: 57).

Roediger acknowledged that there were white workers who actively supported the abolitionist cause, but he regarded their efforts as founded on pater-
nalism rather than interracial class solidarity. More typically, working-class
whiteness was embodied in exclusionary, discriminatory, and hostile practices
aimed at free blacks, including racial violence. Only after emancipation could
a forthright assault on "wage slavery" take place. "By that time," Roediger wrote,
"the importance of a sense of whiteness to the white U.S. worker was a long-
established fact, not only politically but culturally as well" (ibid.: 87).

Roediger's argument is achieved primarily through three types of analysis:
examining changes in political language, looking at how the Irish achieved
whiteness through their own agency (a discussion complementing Ignatiev's),
and scrutinizing blackface minstrelsy. The last of these exemplifies the importance that Roediger attributed to popular culture. According to him, the popular blackface performances of the minstrel shows, where white performers
imitated and parodied blacks while never hiding their whiteness, was important for two reasons. First, Roediger regarded it as an important manifestation
of an evolving whiteness, since the performers who assumed black personas
effaced the ethnic differences on which being white depended. Second, he
argued that minstrelsy performances, which represented blacks as preindustrial and in a sense "natural," provided white workers with an outlet for coping
with their own transition to the discipline and repression of becoming a
proletariat. They could take pleasure in the wild sensuality of blackness,

which represented their residual selves, while simultaneously condemning such sensuality as barbaric and uncivilized, thus cementing their newly achieved, and hence fragile, respectability and "superior" white identity.

Writing in 1998, the geographer Peter Jackson observed that "from a position of invisibility only ten years ago, studies in 'whiteness' have now become commonplace" (Jackson 1998: 99). As whiteness studies have proliferated, they have stirred intensive debate – not least in labor history. An inroad into these discussions is a 2001 "scholarly controversy" on "Whiteness and the Historian's Imagination" in *International Labor and Working-Class History*. The "controversy" consisted of Eric Arnesen's thoroughgoing critique, "Whiteness and the Historian's Imagination" (2001a), followed by several responses to Arnesen's essay, and ended with a reply by Arnesen to his respondents (Arnesen 2001b). I explore this multifaceted debate for its implications for understanding the race/class relationship.

Arnesen had both political and intellectual problems with whiteness studies. Politically, he castigated them for their "deep cynicism about the role of white labor." Intellectually, he believed that they either ultimately did not live up to their promise or simply gave a new gloss to old ideas. He criticized whiteness scholars for their sloppy use of evidence, found "whiteness" a vague and ambiguous concept, and ultimately believed that unless the field was recast, it was "time to retire whiteness for more precise historical categories and analytical tools" (Arnesen 2001a: 26).

Pertinent to the present discussion is Arnesen's objection to Roediger's and others' reading and adaptation of Du Bois. For Arnesen, Roediger did not view Du Bois's remarks on the psychological benefits of whiteness in the overall context of his thought; in fact, according to Arnesen, Du Bois saw the benefits of whiteness as material. This assertion led to a more general criticism. In some ways Roediger retained Du Bois's class reductionism (derived from conventional Marxism), seeing white and black workers' failure to unite as a distortion of the historical process. Distancing himself from poststructuralist critiques of social history, though essentially making the same point, Arnesen argued against a formulaic conception of the relationship between class structure and class consciousness that sees the latter as logically flowing from the former. As Arnesen stated it:

> The problem is that at least some of Du Bois's assumptions remain alive and well in the form of a persistent "Marxism lite" – the expectation that common oppression or common enemies should promote unity, that all workers more or less share class interests regardless of race, and that the working class play the role of agent assigned to it by radical theory (ibid.: 12).

Of the historians who responded to Arnesen's essay, only one – James Barrett – had actually used "whiteness" in his/her work. Yet responses ran the full gamut: from enthusiasm for whiteness studies, and misgivings over Arnesen's dismissal of them (Hattam 2001), to ringing endorsements of his critique (Fields 2001; Reed Jr. 2001). There was also a middle ground: scholars who accepted some or many of Arnesen's points, while believing that he underrated whiteness studies' accomplishments and overall potential (Barrett 2001; Brody 2001; Foner 2001). I want to return to what these scholars considered that achievement to be. First, I discuss Victoria Hattam's contribution to the discussion, since she most explicitly addressed Arnesen's contention that Roediger's position was vitiated by its class reductionism.

For Hattam, Arnesen had missed the point. Rather than embracing a form of reductionist Marxism, Roediger had, in fact, viewed class as a form of identification – in her words, "an identity project." Having severed his ties with the classical Marxist notion that class consciousness was shaped by objective class relationships, he explored psychoanalytic theory, since it addressed the complex question of identity formation. Hattam was aware of the problems that arose from using psychoanalytic methods in writing history, yet sympathized with the reason Roediger was interested in them, seeing his position as a trend in whiteness studies as a whole:

> If one breaks with the lingering Marxist materialism, as I believe many whiteness scholars have done, then one needs an account of identification of some kind – an account, it seems to me, that ought not simply to be buried in the empirical details of historical research. Existing research on race, class, and immigration, as I see it, has yet to fully engage this question (Hattam 2001: 62).

By no means sympathetic to whiteness studies, Barbara Fields, in fact, accorded legitimacy to Hattam's interpretation by criticizing the very thing that Hattam enthused over, taking whiteness studies to task for "displacing questions of political, economic and social power" with those of identity and agency (Fields 2001: 54). From this point of view, Roediger and other whiteness scholars might well have (as Arnesen suggested) read Du Bois's observation on the wages of whiteness out of context. If so, perhaps it was strategic, that is, they sought to construct a version of Du Bois that resonated with our very different times.

I mentioned previously that there were scholars participating in the discussion, Hattam among them, who believed that historical whiteness studies were responsible for opening up important intellectual avenues. According to these scholars, two accomplishments stand out. First, whatever specific problems the concept of whiteness studies might have, whiteness scholars spoke to the political crisis of the contemporary left, which could not rejuvenate itself without addressing racial divisions among working-class people (Foner 2001: 59). Second, whiteness studies "denaturalized" race, viewing it as culturally and historically constructed yet having very real consequences (Barrett 2001: 40; Hattam 2001: 63). Among some whiteness scholars this concept held for class as well. Roediger was, above all, concerned with how class was produced through a racially inflected experience. Such thinking provided the groundwork for conceiving of race and class – and gender – as being deeply intertwined, with none of the three being accorded a theoretically privileged position. There is no doubt that historical work on whiteness has a disheartening quality to it. Racism is not a pleasant subject. However, when it is seen as being founded on a culturally and historically constituted construction, however deeply engrained, there is always the potential for a reshaping of consciousness.

Conclusion

In this chapter I have examined attempts by cultural theorists, sociologists, and historians to come to terms with the interpenetration of race and class. Several conclusions can be drawn from this discussion. First, despite the differences in perspective and orientation of the various writers examined, many share a view of class and race and (depending on the circumstances and writer) gender as being historically intertwined, culturally constructed, linked together yet retaining their specificity, and defined through political struggle. Second, several of the writers discussed deployed poststructuralist notions of language and discourse to understand shifts in cultural and political meaning and to free themselves from the pitfalls of the binary model of social being and social consciousness. Yet, as several writers have taken pains to make clear, by no means has this fact led them to embrace the more radical epistemological implications of poststructuralism. Third, some of the work discussed here has a transnational dimension, both insofar as it has been produced through an intellectual and cultural network that does not always fit easily into neat national parcels and because the experience of blacks and/or whites has been conceptualized in the context of a global capitalist system. This is certainly true of Cedric Robinson's understanding of the black radical tradition and Paul Gilroy's concept of the Black Atlantic, but it is not limited to these.

In the end, the work discussed here has enriched our understanding of the complexity of class, particularly how it has been understood in connection to other determinations and identities. Yet it is conceivable that this very achievement threatens to obliterate the distinctiveness of class analysis. Class retains an importance among the writers discussed to varying degrees, but its weight is attenuated when compared with the Marxist accounts of the new social history (see Chapter 2). Thinking about class in relationship to race and gender poses formidable challenges. If other dimensions of experience are added to the equation – region, religion, nationality, ethnicity, space, age, and so forth – there is the potential for class to be dwarfed by the sheer weight of social, cultural, political, and historical complexity. Moreover, as several writers in this chapter have made clear, despite its universal aspirations, the class narrative was produced within a Eurocentric understanding of history, which marginalized the historical role of peoples outside of the West.

The Eurocentric nature of the class narrative has been a central concern for the South Asian historians of the Subaltern Studies group. Conceiving inequality in the colonial and postcolonial world of India, a very different context than either Western Europe or the United States, they drew from the rich theoretical language of class struggle in a situation where class consciousness was rarely visible. To understand oppression and resistance, these South Asian historians turned to Gramsci's notion of "the subaltern," a reworking of the idea of the oppressed classes. Their interpretation not only challenged the foundations of class theory and analysis but also ultimately called into question the premises of existing historical practices. Their scholarship had ripple effects among scholars worldwide.

Chapter 8

Class and beyond

The Subaltern Studies group is comprised of South Asian historians, who in books, monographs, and an essay series, *Subaltern Studies*, have explored oppression and resistance within the colonial and postcolonial setting of South Asia. In the process they have challenged class theory's foundations. They have also questioned whether mainstream historical practices – steeped in colonialist and Eurocentric modes of thought – can do justice to the specificity of South Asian history and, by implication, the non-Western world more generally. Founders of Subaltern Studies – notably Dipesh Chakrabarty, Partha Chatterjee, and Ranajit Guha – have achieved international reputations in their own right. But Subaltern Studies also came to symbolize something wider than any individual scholar who was part of it. Its wider project had ripple effects worldwide.

Subaltern historians in some ways replicated the movement from social to cultural history described in earlier chapters. They took their original cue from the British Marxist tradition of history from below. By "subaltern," they meant "subservient classes." They adapted the term from Gramsci, who used it to signify the oppressed classes of early twentieth-century Italy. These South Asian historians defined subalterns as those who were not part of the elite classes. Subalterns inhabited an autonomous realm that stood aloof from dominant historical narratives – colonialist and nationalist alike. They stood outside of the realm of representation.

Linguistic and cultural approaches challenged Subaltern Studies' original social-history perspective, although the former were present from an early point. The focus on recovering subaltern groups was challenged by the argument that – rather than constituting the history of actual groups of people with attendant forms of consciousness – the subaltern was a category owing its existence, in fact, to language and discourse. This argument drew support from the fact that few historical documents were produced from a subaltern perspective. Critics of social-history approaches argued that subalternity was gleaned from the silences, gaps, and contradictions of the dominant discourses.

This remapping of subalternity produced fractures among the original group of Subaltern historians and drew additional scholars into its orbit. The shift from social to cultural history was accompanied by a dialog with post-colonial criticism, whose deconstruction of the universal claims of Western understanding proved indispensable for interrogating the historical models used to analyze colonial and postcolonial conditions. In this later phase Subaltern Studies was influenced by two influential postcolonial literary scholars based in the United States – Edward Said (1935–2005) and Gayatri Chakravorty Spivak (1942–) – both of whom inspired, as well as lent support to, this new direction.

Subaltern Studies scholarship, at its best, manifested a tension between recovering oppressed and silenced groups and developing sophisticated reading strategies for finding alternative and critical spaces within disciplinary conventions and discourses. These often-contradictory aspirations challenged the border between social and cultural history and converged with developments in literary and cultural studies. Rooted in Marxist class theory, Subaltern Studies stretched it to its limits, arguably beyond all recognition. To show what these limits are, we shall on occasion have to look at what lies beyond them.

Origins and background

The Subaltern Studies group was comprised of historians based in India, Australia, Britain, and North America. It was spearheaded by Ranajit Guha (1922–) and consisted of a fluctuating group of participants from multiple generations. In addition to Guha, the original cluster consisted of Shahid Amin, David Arnold, Gautam Bhadra, Dipesh Chakrabarty, Partha Chatterjee, David Hardiman, and Gyanendra Pandey. Guha has memorably described the collective as "an assortment of marginalized academics – graduate students yet to complete their dissertations, two or three very young scholars only recently admitted to the teaching profession, and an older man stuck at its lowest rung apparently for good – it had the advantage of owing no loyalty to any department, faculty, school or party" (Guha 1997a: xiv).

The group is best known for *Subaltern Studies*, first published in 1982. There are now eleven volumes in the series (the most recent being published in 2002). Forty-four authors have written essays, many being translated from their original language of English (Ludden 2002a: 1). In addition, there are now four book-length collections, which either reproduce articles from *Subaltern Studies* or reprint critical essays from the mushrooming literature that has developed in wake of the group's work (Guha and Spivak 1988; Guha 1997b; Chaturvedi 2000a; Ludden 2002b).

The immediate context for Subaltern Studies was the 1970s crisis in Indian democracy and the resulting political disappointments. On the one hand, the group's historians were dismayed by the suppression of democratic institutions under the state of emergency (1975–1977) declared by Prime Minister Indira Gandhi, which, according to Chatterjee "was in effect seen as a symptom of a virtually terminal illness afflicting the Indian state" (Shaikh 2003). On the other hand, they were disappointed over the defeat of the Naxalite political movement. A late 1960s and early 1970s armed peasant struggle, led by militants inspired by Maoist thought, the Naxalite movement took its name from a small village in the state of West Bengal in eastern India. Chakrabarty recalled that the 1962 war between India and China demonstrated the hollowness of official nationalism and "eventually gave rise to a fascination with Maoism among urban, educated young people in India." The Naxolite movement accordingly "drew many urban youths into the countryside in the late 1960s and early 1970s" (Chakrabarty 2002: 6–7). According to Shahid Amin and Gautam Bhadra, as a result of engagement with Maoist students, Guha deserted his planned study of Gandhi to pursue the investigation of peasant insurgencies (Amin and Bhadra 1994: 224). The decision proved momentous.

The historian arguably most responsible for putting his stamp on the group's direction was Guha, who David Arnold and David Hardiman described as being "more than just the founder of the series: he has been the intellectual driving force behind it" (Arnold and Hardiman 1994). Guha was born in Siddhakati village in eastern Bengal and was from a family of medium-sized landed proprietors. He attended the prestigious Presidency College in Calcutta and later Calcutta University, where he received an M.A. in History. He never submitted a thesis to complete his Ph.D., the reason quite possibly being his activism in the Communist Party, a major part of his life between 1942 and 1956. He left the Party as a result of his opposition to the Soviet Union's invasion of Hungary. Guha has taught in universities in India, Britain, and Australia. In 1980 an appointment as a senior research fellow to the Research School of Pacific Studies in the Australian National University, Canberra allowed more time for his own research as well as for editing the first six volumes of *Subaltern Studies* between 1982 and 1989 (Amin and Bhadra 1994: 222–25).

As with many intellectual and political initiatives, Subaltern historians were unified by what they opposed, in this case elitist views of modern Indian history. In what can be construed as the *Subaltern Studies* manifesto, "On Some Aspects of the Historiography of Colonial India" ([1982] 1988a), Guha articulated the principal targets in the first volume of the series:

> The historiography of Indian nationalism has for a long time been dominated by elitism – colonialist elitism and bourgeois-nationalist elitism. Both originated as the ideological product of British rule in India, but have survived the transfer of power and been assimilated to neo-colonialist and neo-nationalist forms of discourse in Britain and India respectively (Guha [1982] 1988a: 37).

Subaltern historians combatted three forms of elitist historiography. First, they opposed the views of historians who portrayed the recent Indian past as a heroic contest waged by the nationalists against the British, one in which the independence movement had created a unified Indian people. Subaltern historians regarded this historiography as reproducing the nationalist movement's self-image at the cost of downplaying class and other conflicts. Second, the group's historians distinguished their own vantage point from what is known as the Cambridge school, which adopted a materialist understanding of history emphasizing group self-interest rather than rhetoric. For historians of this persuasion, the key to understanding the Indian nationalist movement was not its stated ideals: they emphasized the material benefits that an independent state brought to India's native elite. Subaltern historians commended the Cambridge school for highlighting the gap between Indian nationalists' actions and creed. But they rejected its dismissal of ideals altogether, its privileging of elite classes, and its narrow view of politics and interests. Third, the group contrasted its own Marxist-inspired views with those of orthodox Marxists. While the latter had an interest in popular social movements, they were confined, according to Subaltern historians, by a narrow and mechanistic understanding of the base–superstructure relationship, had a reductive concept of class dynamics, and were as enamored with state power and elite politics as nationalist historians. Indeed, for Subaltern historians, the nationalist and Marxist perspectives converged at times.

Subaltern historians undoubtedly overstated their differences with their intellectual adversaries. They, in fact, represented their opponents as the "other," which in turn provided the binary opposition for articulating their own vantage point. In the group's manifesto Guha clearly articulated what that was:

For parallel to the domain of elite politics there existed throughout the colonial period another domain of Indian politics in which the principal actors were not the dominant groups of the indigenous society or the colonial authorities but the subaltern classes and groups constituting the mass of the labouring population and the intermediate strata in town and country – that is, the people. This was an *autonomous* domain, for it neither originated from elite politics nor did its existence depend on the latter (ibid.: 40).

Here we see the principal chord struck by Subaltern Studies, especially as developed in its early social-history phase. These historians argued that neocolonialist, nationalist, and orthodox Marxist versions of Indian history were elitist; and they insisted on the autonomy, modernity, and centrality of the subalterns or "the people," defined as the laboring classes. Subalterns expressed their grievances and aspirations politically but were "hidden from history," a phrase used to portray the plight of women but one that was just as applicable here (see Chapter 6). Subalterns were autonomous not because they were separate, since they were, in fact, structurally linked to elite classes; but rather because they could not be appropriated to dominant narratives. Let's examine this general orientation more concretely, remembering – but not being detoured by – Rajnarayan Chandavarkar's apt observation: "Any attempt to treat the corpus [of Subaltern Studies] as a whole must leave a trail of exceptions in its wake" (Chandavarkar [1997] 2000: 54).

Subaltern Studies in context

Subaltern Studies' early volumes mostly consisted of scholarship conceived in the vein of the new social history. The essays encompassed a wide chronological range: from the seventeenth century to the edge of the contemporary world, with most focusing on the nineteenth and twentieth centuries. Contributors explored the practices of various overlapping categories of subalterns: smallholding peasants, agricultural laborers, workers, sharecroppers, and so forth. Their essays ranged from theoretical reflection and argument to detailed empirical studies, often deploying highly original research strategies. Many of the essays focused on riots, rebellions, and protests. These flash points served as windows through which to examine multifaceted social and political conflicts. Subalterns usually entered the historical record at what Sumit Sarkar called "moments of explosion," but he added: "What one needs to keep in mind is a vast and complex continuum of intermediate attitudes

of which total subordination and open revolt are only the extreme poles"
(Sarkar 1984: 274).

We can learn a great deal about the group's early scholarship by surveying
Selected Subaltern Studies, which consisted of essays from the first five volumes
of the *Subaltern Studies* series, from 1982 to 1987. The anthology included
Guha's articulation of the group's principles – its manifesto discussed above –
and a second essay, "The Prose of Counter-Insurgency" ([1983] 1988),
discussed below. Chosen also was Shahid Amin's essay on the relationship
between the Awadh peasants' revolt and Indian nationalism in the 1920s
(Amin [1984] 1988) and Gyanendra Pandey's on subaltern groups' construction of Mahatma Gandhi in the midst of their protests against their landlords
(Pandey [1982] 1988). The anthology also included Gautam Bhadra's account
of four subaltern leaders of the 1857 Indian Mutiny against British authority
(Bhadra [1985] 1988) and Pandey's recovery of peasant consciousness through
a reading of a nineteenth-century chronicle written by a member of a Muslim
landowning family and a diary kept by a weaver (Pandey [1984] 1988).

The anthology was rounded out by three instances of rethinking South
Asian history via a critical engagement with Marx and Marxism and Foucault.
As Chakrabarty commented about his attitude towards Marx: "we are arguing
with Marx and not against him" (Chakrabarty [1983] 1988: 179). Here,
Chakrabarty explored the differences between governmental production of
knowledge of factory conditions in Britain and India (discussed below)
(Chakrabarty [1983] 1988). Chatterjee adapted a Marxist mode-of-production
analysis to specify the structural transformation of a society (like India) whose
transition from feudalism to capitalism was mediated by colonialism (Chatterjee
[1983] 1988). David Arnold examined governmental actions and indigenous
response during the early twentieth-century phase of the Indian plague.
Conflicts over the treatment of the body "provide an important illustration
of the complex interplay of coercion and co-operation, resistance and hegemony, class and race in the colonial situation" (Arnold [1987] 1988: 426).

To better appreciate the achievements of Subaltern historians in relationship
to class theory and analysis, I analyze their understanding and deployment of
"subaltern" in their scholarship. As part of this discussion, I examine the group's
understanding of the term in relationship to Gramsci's original usage. I also
compare Subaltern historians' project – primarily focusing on Guha's historical work – with British Marxist historians' (see Chapter 2). Although British
Marxists did not explicitly use the term "subaltern," they were motivated
by the same aspiration to uncover the history of marginalized peoples prior
to industrialization and were an initial inspiration for Subaltern historians.
Situating the Subaltern Studies group in relationship to the British historians
helps sheds light on the distinctiveness of the group's project.

There was an unresolved tension in the group's definition of "subaltern." By and large, Subaltern historians stayed within the confines of a conventional Marxist understanding of class, equating subalterns with the exploited laboring classes, who rarely expressed themselves in the class-conscious political forms found in industrial societies. Chakrabarty argued that this class milieu did not only exist in the past: it existed in the present as well. He described it as "the composite culture of resistance to and acceptance of domination and hierarchy," arguing that it "is a characteristic of class relations in our society, where the veneer of bourgeois equality barely masks the violent, feudal nature of much of our systems of power and authority" (Chakrabarty 1985: 376).

But this conventional Marxist usage is not the only one. In his preface to the first volume of *Subaltern Studies* (henceforth referred to as the Preface), Guha initially defined "subaltern" as "of inferior rank," his source being the *Concise Oxford English Dictionary*. Significantly, Guha's definition was not specifically Marxist: its frame of reference was wider than the relations of production (see Chapter 1). Guha described subalterns as those whose subordination was "expressed in terms of class, caste, age, gender and office or in any other way" (Guha [1982] 1988b: 35). More generally, he simply described them as "the people," defined as those not of the elite. Guha was aware that diverse groups inhabited this category and that there were difficulties in establishing its boundaries at the margins, but he argued that the category was coherent. A critical reading might hold that what was true at the margins was true at the supposed center as well: subalternity was irreducibly heterogeneous, unstable, plural, contradictory, and fluid. However rooted his position may have been in the Marxist paradigm, Guha's analysis of subaltern looked beyond the confines of class, suggesting a broader, more flexible framework for analyzing dominance, subordination, and resistance. It was by no means the definition uppermost in Subaltern historians' early work, but, as historians in the group gravitated from social to cultural history, and new scholars were drawn into the group's orbit, the tendency became more prominent.

In the Preface, Guha referred to Gramsci, whose analysis of the subaltern classes in *The Prison Notebooks* (Hoare and Smith 1971), written while he was imprisoned by Mussolini's fascist regime, was groundbreaking. Guha expressed the hope that the essays in *Subaltern Studies* "may even remotely match the six-point project" imagined by the Italian Marxist in "Notes on Italian History," a major text for understanding Gramsci's analysis of subalterns. It is widely acknowledged that the Subaltern Studies group adapted their idea of the subaltern from Gramsci, but what precisely does this mean? My analysis of Gramsci draws on David Arnold's "Gramsci and Peasant Subalternity in India" (Arnold [1984] 2000), the only sustained analysis of Gramsci's theoretical relevance for studying South Asian history by a group member. It is simultaneously a perceptive analysis of Gramsci and an important text for understanding Subaltern Studies.

As Arnold observed, Gramsci was mostly read in the 1980s for his acute political analysis of industrial capitalist societies and the modern state, adopting a Marxist analysis that gave full weight to ideological conflicts (ibid.: 24). But since he was centrally concerned with early twentieth-century Italy in historical context – where peasants and small producers constituted major social groups – he grappled with a social and political world beyond that of the industrial proletariat. Writing for, above all, a political purpose, Gramsci embraced a wider notion of struggle than the opposition between capitalists and proletarians. He described the oppressed classes as subalterns: a blanket category comprising workers, peasants, artisans, agricultural laborers, and other such groups.

When thinking of the subalterns, however, Gramsci undoubtedly was thinking, first and foremost, about the peasantry. Where Marx conceived of peasants as an obsolete class, likened them to a sack of potatoes, and talked of the "idiocy of rural life," Gramsci took their aspirations and culture seriously, knowing full well that working-class hegemony could not be achieved without a genuine alliance. Peasants engaged in "passive" and "turbulent" behavior and were often ideologically subservient to hegemonic ruling-class groups, who mobilized them for conservative and reactionary political causes. But the peasantry's slowness to change also provided an obstacle to embracing new ruling-class ideas. Moreover, if they received cultural forms from the ruling class, peasants gave it their own meanings. For example, they placed their own stamp on the Roman Catholicism that they received from above. This example is indicative of the importance that Gramsci attributed to religious practices: he conceived of them as neither self-deception nor false consciousness, but as a specific way of apprehending the world and daily life. In sum, subalternity, for Gramsci, was riddled with contradictions. It was, as Arnold wrote, "engaged in a continuing dialectical tussle within itself, between its active and its passive voice, between acceptance and resistance, between isolation and collectivity, between disunity and cohesion" (ibid.: 30).

There is a clear affinity, allowing for the writers' different situations, between Gramsci's and Subaltern Studies' intellectual endeavor. Like Gramsci, Subaltern historians conceived of society and politics as characterized by a power struggle between the people and the ruling class. Both had an inclusive view of subalternity, while grounding their conception of it in their analysis of peasants. Obviously both were also preoccupied with the working class as well, but both India and Italy had small industrial sectors and hence little in the way of the working-class consciousness found in Britain. Moreover,

Gramsci and the Subaltern Studies group were both sensitive to the contradictory nature of the subaltern realm. Both also viewed religious perspectives from the subaltern's point of view. The historians most clearly differed from Gramsci insofar as they envisioned the subaltern classes as constituting an autonomous realm, although one that was structurally dependent on elite groups. This view is certainly at odds with Gramsci's contention that subalterns seldom developed a political initiative of their own.

The perspective of Subaltern historians likewise shared common ground with British Marxist historians, who, of course, likewise were influenced by Gramsci's ideas (see Chapter 2). I am not thinking here of E. P. Thompson's *The Making of the English Working Class* ([1963] 1968), which rescued English workers from the condescension of history, although Thompson's book and Subaltern Studies scholarship certainly shared intellectual and political aspirations. More relevant in the present context, I believe, are historical writings on preindustrial revolts: Rodney Hilton's on peasant resistance in medieval England, Christopher Hill's on radicals in the seventeenth-century English Revolution, Eric Hobsbawm's on bandits and "primitive rebels," and Thompson's on eighteenth-century popular resistance (see Chapter 2). Indeed, Thompson's conception of preindustrial English society as a class struggle without class or as a conflict between patricians and plebeians resonated with Subaltern Studies' own binary conception of Indian society as a conflict between subalterns and elites. Both groups of historians reworked Marxist class theory in order to consider conditions other than those of workers in a fully developed world of industrial capitalism. In both cases a more inclusive and fluid way of thinking about oppression and resistance resulted.

Given the affinity between these two intellectual formations, Arif Dirlik has suggested that Subaltern Studies represented a transplanted version of British history from below to an Indian context (Dirlik [1994] 1996: 302). But, as Chakrabarty persuasively argued, from the onset there were fundamental differences, which helped account for the "postcolonial" path that Subaltern Studies would take. For one, the Subaltern Studies project critiqued British Marxists' – or at least Hobsbawm's – implicit assumption that there was a universal model of capitalist development. This perspective – derived from Marx and Marxism but more generally indebted to the Enlightenment tradition's penchant for constructing universal models or metanarratives – implicitly denied that its frame of reference was European conditions.

Following Chakrabarty, we can see this critique of Hobsbawm's Eurocentric views in Guha's influential historical study of the structure of peasant resistance, *Elementary Aspects of Peasant Insurgency in Colonial India* (1983), and related writings. The book was clearly indebted to British Marxist historians

– as references to Hill, Hilton, Hobsbawm, and Thompson make clear – but in its introduction Guha set forth an important distinction between his and Hobsbawm's analysis of peasant resistance. He took issue with Hobsbawm's contention that peasant insurgencies were prepolitical – that is, that they constituted acts of people "who have not yet found, or only begun to find, a specific language in which to express their aspirations about the world" (Hobsbawm [1959] 1965: 2). Guha did not overtly challenge the validity of Hobsbawm's assertion for European history, from which the latter's evidence was mostly derived. But he certainly believed that it did not capture the sub-continent's historical experience; or in his words: "Whatever its validity for other countries the notion of prepolitical peasant insurgency helps little in understanding the experience of colonial India. For there was nothing in the militant movements of its rural masses that was not political" (Guha 1983: 6). In the group's manifesto Guha was even more adamant that peasant or subaltern movements in India were modern and political. He wrote that the subaltern domain "was traditional only in so far as its roots could be traced to pre-colonial times, but it was by no means archaic in the sense of being outmoded ... As modern as indigenous elite politics, it was distinguished by its rela-tively greater depth in time as well as in structure" (Guha [1982] 1988a: 40).

Guha implicitly questioned Hobsbawm's unstated faith in the validity of a universal Marxist model. In Guha's view, there were multiples forms of – and paths to – modernity. India's transition to capitalism was shaped by the British colonial presence. It consisted of two systems of oppression and exploitation; and it was comprised of two layers of elites, one British and one native. This same dualism was inscribed in Indian political institutions, which relied "on the colonial adaptations of British parliamentary institutions and the residua of semi-feudal political institutions of the pre-colonial period" (ibid.: 40). Thus, in contrast to the West, where capitalism gave rise to the modern state and the bourgeoisie's political hegemony, the Indian context produced a different relationship between civil society and state. In Guha's words: "the originality of the South Asian colonial state lay precisely in this difference: a historical paradox, it was an autocracy set up and sustained in the East by the foremost democracy of the Western world. And since it was nonhegemonic, it was not possible for that state to assimilate the civil society of the colonized to itself" (Guha 1997c: xii). Ingeniously adapting Gramsci's terminology to analyze an imperial setting, Guha described political power in British India as "dominance without hegemony."

Guha's analysis of the colonial state had implications for Indian nationalism as well. While Indian nationalists spoke in the name of the people, their strug-gle against British rule was frequently a conflict between two elite formations.

In the end, they founded a state based on democratic institutions but one that ultimately reproduced the elite and subaltern relationship, thus continuing nonhegemonic power. As Chakrabarty wrote: "For the greater part of our daily experience, class relations express themselves in that other language of politics, which is the politics of nation without 'citizens'" (Chakrabarty 1985: 376).

Gyanendra Pandey's "Peasant Revolt and Indian Nationalism: The Peasant Movement in Awadh, 1919–1922" ([1982] 1988) was one among many essays by Subaltern historians that demonstrated the elite nature of the Indian nationalist movement and its struggle to contain subaltern aspirations. According to Pandey, in its attempts to organize a movement, the Awadh peasantry had "overcome many, though, by no means all, of its own traditionalist limitations," but to be successful it needed an alliance with a more powerful, better organized anti-imperial force (Pandey [1982] 1988: 281). While the nationalist Congress movement was initially drawn into the conflict, it eventually came to see the peasants' movement as a threat to its own aspirations. As Pandey argued, Congress leaders appealed to national unity, which meant a united front of landlords and peasants. In other words, it "was a statement in favour of the *status quo* and against any radical change in the social set-up when the British finally handed over the reins of power" (ibid.: 277).

Another way in which Subaltern and British Marxist historians differed was in their attitude towards the linguistic turn. Both faced difficult challenges in gleaning evidence of ordinary peoples' experience from existing sources. Because almost all the traces of plebian life came from documents produced by and for the powers that be, both were compelled to read the documents as much for what they did not say as for what they did. British Marxist and Subaltern historians – and other social historians as well – tended to read primary sources by filtering the content for bias and prejudice. But some in the Subaltern Studies group developed an alternative strategy. The colonial regime created archival sources and a historiography founded on them, resulting in ideologically inflected representations of the laboring classes and the poor. Yet, given the dearth of alternative texts, these archives provided the only ground on which any alternative history could be written. Some in the group accordingly grappled with the discursive underpinnings of archival sources and became interested in theories of textual production and narrative construction. In short, they were not only interested in what texts meant: they also sought to understand how they produced meaning. They were, accordingly, drawn first to structuralism and later to poststructuralism. To borrow the terminology of Alun Munslow, Subaltern historians were "deconstructionists." They believed that history was derived as much by *how* it was represented as by *what* sources it deployed. This position was far removed from the "constructionist"

mindset of British Marxist history from below, which held that it was possible to generate concepts that produced "meaningful patterns" from existing
evidence, the assumption being that the form and the content were separable
(Munslow 2003: 5–6).

"The Prose of Counter-Insurgency" (Guha [1983] 1988) exemplified
Subaltern historians' early interest in the discursive dimension of archival
sources. In this essay Guha argued that contemporary elite historiography
unconsciously reproduced the colonial powers' perspective of peasant revolts
by never questioning the discursive structure of "counterinsurgency" that
pervaded the archival sources. His goal was to show the historical process
whereby these discursive structures were reproduced. Or as he expressed it:
"For an answer one could start by having a close look at its constituting
elements and examine those cuts, seams and stitches – those cobbling marks –
which tell us about the material it is made of and the manner of its absorption
into the fabric of writing" (ibid.: 47). Using a structuralist method of reading
derived from Roland Barthes (see Chapter 3), Guha examined the creation
of historical meaning, tracing it through a three-stage process of primary,
secondary, and tertiary texts, each "differentiated from the other two by the
degree of its formal and/or acknowledged (as opposed to real and/or tacit)
identification with an official point of view, by the measure of its distance from
the event to which it refers, and by the ratio of the distributive and integrative
components in its narrative" (ibid.: 47). As a result, he was able to pinpoint
the way in which assumptions, inscribed in colonial officials' letters written in
immediate response to peasant rebellions, carried over into later officials' more
reflective histories of peasant movements, and consequently underpinned
nationalist historians' rewriting of those histories from their own perspective.
Despite pronounced differences between these various texts, none granted
peasants their own autonomous sphere of action or took their political aspirations, often framed in religious terms, seriously.

The attraction of the linguistic turn is also apparent in Chakrabarty's
"Conditions for Knowledge of Working-Class Conditions: Employers,
Government and the Jute Workers of Calcutta, 1890–1940" ([1983] 1988),
which explored the colonial regime's efforts at producing knowledge about
Calcutta jute mill workers' labor conditions between 1890 and 1940. In this
essay Chakrabarty probed Foucault's contention that surveillance, crucial to
the functioning of modern institutions, "insidiously objectified those on whom
it applied." As Chakrabarty stated it: "It was thus in the nature of capitalist
authority that it [surveillance] operated by forming 'a body of knowledge'
about its subjects. In this it was different from, say, pre-capitalist domination
which worked more by deploying 'the ostentatious signs of sovereignty' and
could do without a knowledge of the dominated" (Chakrabarty [1983] 1988:

182). According to Chakrabarty, such aspirations were present in Indian industrial development. But despite governmental initiative and varying degrees of capitalist compliance, the documents produced about workers' conditions were filled with gaps, distortions, and outright falsification. Chakrabarty suggested that the narrow range of data collected resulted from the jute mill owners' indifference to the project. In Britain factory owners frequently required a relatively healthy and well-trained workforce and thus benefited from reliable knowledge about working-class life. However, the capitalists in Chakrabarty's study were primarily interested in a continual flow of laborers and were indifferent to data regarding their state of being.

Most important, Chakrabarty stressed that workplace organization was responsible for systematic distortions. Here, he focused on the *sardar* – a supplier and supervisor of labor and the immediate employer of ordinary workers. The *sardar* thrived on money lending and bribery, often helping workers acquire housing. He served the interests of capital, as he performed tasks that in the West were often performed by owners. But his authority stemmed from precolonial and precapitalist institutions adapted to industrial circumstances. The *sardar*'s role in falsifying data signified his power and influence over other workers:

> When the Government of India grafted a disciplinary apparatus of documentation on the culture that supported (and sometimes resisted) the *sardar*'s domination, these documents found their own place and meaning within that culture: as additional vehicles of the *sardar*'s power and authority. The *sardar* now proved his power by bending rules and falsifying documents. Hence the phenomenon of "false fines," "cooked up charges," "wrongful dismissals," etc. (ibid.: 229–30).

In short, capitalism might dictate producing knowledge regarding its subjects, but the case of Calcutta jute workers proved that this endeavor was mediated by cultural relationships. These relationships were revealed through the gaps, distortions, and silences in knowledge production.

Thus, the Subaltern Studies project, despite clear affinities with British Marxist history, marked out a distinct path of its own. Insofar as it aimed at recovering marginalized historical subjects, it clearly shared common ground with British history from below and hence the new social history. *Subaltern Studies* originally conceived of the subaltern within the parameters of Marxist class theory, while its conception of this domain pointed beyond these original confines. But historians in the group were also interested in theoretical developments associated with the linguistic turn, ideas that were producing the new cultural history. As the group developed, it did not reject social approaches wholesale, yet cultural perspectives came to play a more dominant role in its scholarship. As some of the group's participants moved in a post-structuralist and postmodern direction, they were drawn into the orbit of an emergent postcolonial scholarship on which they put an indelible stamp. Their conception of subalternity was transformed in the process.

The postcolonial turn

Subaltern Studies' original goal had been to rescue the oppressed from history's indifference, to peel away the layers of colonial and nationalist prejudice and at last allow the people to speak. But as the project developed, some in the group questioned whether this goal was attainable. By the time of its second conference in Calcutta in 1986, the group was torn in two directions. David Hardiman suggested that the Subaltern Studies project stood "at something of a crossroads": "One road leads towards greater concentration on textual analysis and a stress on the relativity of all knowledge; another towards the study of subaltern consciousness and action so as to forward the struggle for a socialist society" (Hardiman 1986: 290). In retrospect Hardiman's description appears oversimplified, but it dramatically captures the idea, so prevalent in historiographical debates, that such approaches are polar opposites (see Chapter 5). Following the Latin American historian Florencia Mallon, I see the conceptual space carved out by Subaltern Studies scholarship as negotiating between these two directions rather than adopting one or the other, which, of course, meant that both would be transformed in the process As Mallon perceptively observes regarding this possibility: "Herein lies the deepest, most irresolvable, and also the most fertile tension in the Subaltern Studies project" (Mallon 1994: 1497).

Partha Chatterjee has described the group in the late 1980s as going through a "poststructuralist moment" (Chatterjee 1999: 416). It was in this phase that the notion of the subaltern developed beyond the class-based perspective of the group's original vision. It came to stand for a wider, more decentered, more fluid, and less stable understanding of oppression and resistance, revealed through the silences, gaps, fissures, and contradictions produced by elite sources and historiography. Gyan Prakash, a more recent group participant, gave a good description of what this development entailed:

> Subalternity thus emerges in the paradoxes of power, in the functioning of the dominant discourse as it represents and domesticates peasant agency as

a spontaneous and "pre-political" response to colonial violence. No longer does it appear outside the elite discourse as a separate domain, embodied in a figure endowed with a will that the dominant suppress and overpower but do not constitute. Instead, it refers to that impossible thought, figure, or action without which dominant discourse cannot exist and which is acknowledged in its subterfuges and stereotypes (Prakash 1994: 1483).

Discussing this later phase of the group's scholarship, Chatterjee recalled: "we began looking for much more relational or textual, more fragmentary kinds of evidence and the assumption, well, even the certitude, that these fragments would not necessarily add up to a structure" (Chatterjee 1999: 416). He perhaps had in mind Gyanendra Pandey's remarkable "In Defense of the Fragment: Writing about Hindu–Muslim Riots in India Today" ([1992] 1997). Like other subalternists, Pandey investigated the means by which dominant nationalist discourses foreclosed recovering the actions of ordinary people. Here, he focused on the Bhagalpur "riots" of 1989. Part of a ten-member team sent by the People's Union for Democratic Rights, Delhi, to investigate the causes of the sectarian strife, Pandey charted the obstacles to producing an account that did not trivialize or sanitize the violence that took place, portray it as an aberration, or view it strictly as a consequence of economic determinations.

"Fragments" in Pandey's title had multiple meanings. First, it referred to the subalterns of Indian society: "the smaller religious and caste communities, tribal sections, industrial workers, and activist women's groups" that failed to become part of India's "'mainstream' (Brahmanical Hindu, consumerist) national culture" (Pandey [1992] 1997: 3). Second, it described the one-sided accounts and explanations produced by official sources, which, in fact, comprised "fragments" of history. Third, the term referred to the shreds of evidence that provided the basis for producing alternative narratives. It was through the third meaning of "fragment" – rather than the second totalizing and dominant one – that dissident subaltern voices, the first meaning, could have their agency restored. By implication Pandey rejected the possibility that a totalizing discourse such as Marxism could find a place for subalterns.

An important influence in facilitating Subaltern Studies' move in a post-structuralist and postcolonial direction was the deconstructionist and feminist literary critic Gayatri Spivak. She was originally known for her translation of Derrida's *Of Grammatology* (1976), but by the 1980s she was helping shape the contours of postcolonial criticism. Like "postmodernism" and "post-structuralism," and other important terms defined throughout this book, the "postcolonial" is intensely contested. Before discussing Spivak's connection to Subaltern Studies, I offer a definition aimed at grounding the discussion that follows.

"Postcolonial" initially signified the newly formed states that won their independence from colonial regimes in the aftermath of World War II. It was subsequently used to describe the new literatures that grew up within those states. As a term referring to practices in literary criticism, cultural studies, and history, postcolonial did not become common currency until the 1980s and 1990s, although the impulses it represented surfaced much earlier, a pivotal moment being the publication of Edward Said's *Orientalism* ([1978] 1995) (discussed below). Roughly speaking, postcolonial thought constitutes a body of scholarly and critical practices, undertaken following the demise of European colonial rule, which wrestled with colonialism's legacy in both the formerly colonized regions and the metropolis. Scholars, in broad sympathy with peoples subject to various forms of the colonial experience, were its producers. Postcolonial criticism has focused on, among other things, the general discursive structures underpinning the imperial endeavor, while offering in-depth analyses of the material impact of those discursive formations in historically specific localities and contexts. An important dimension of this intellectual endeavor has been to challenge the cultural assumptions underpinning the universal claims of Western or European modes of thought.

Spivak's initial contribution to *Subaltern Studies* was "Subaltern Studies: Deconstructing Historiography" ([1985] 1988), subsequently reprinted in *Selected Subaltern Studies* (Guha and Spivak 1988), which she coedited with Guha. Here, she memorably caught the tension between the group's aspiration to recover subaltern consciousness and its realization that this endeavor was "subject to the cathexis of the elite, that it is never fully recoverable, that it is always askew from its received signifiers, indeed, that it is effaced even as it is disclosed, that it is irreducibly discursive" (Spivak [1985] 1988: 11). Spivak described this unresolved duality "as a *strategic* use of positivist essentialism in a scrupulously visible political interest"; that is, Subaltern historians were aware of the problems that postulating subaltern consciousness entailed, yet believed it was politically justified (ibid.: 13).

Spivak extended her critique of Subaltern Studies' essentialism in her essay "Can the Subaltern Speak?" (1988), a text critical not only to debates pertaining to subaltern histories but also to defining the contours of postcolonial criticism and influencing debates in feminist theory. Spivak criticized Subaltern historians' oblivion to the category of gender. She attributed this to the discursive apparatuses of colonial rule, but she contended that Subaltern historians reproduced its silencing of women. In an important passage for both postcolonial and feminist criticism, she wrote:

Within the effaced itinerary of the subaltern subject, the track of sexual difference is doubly effaced. The question is not of female participation in insurgency, or the ground rules of the sexual division of labor, for both of which there is "evidence." It is, rather, that, both as object of colonialist historiography and as subject of insurgency, the ideological construction of gender keeps the male dominant. If, in the context of colonial production, the subaltern has no history and cannot speak, the subaltern as female is even more deeply in shadow (Spivak 1988: 287).

To explore the discursive silencing of "the subaltern as female" in historical terms, Spivak analyzed nineteenth-century debates over *sati* or Hindu widow sacrifice. The silencing of women, she argued, had taken place, not because there was not enough evidence of their experience, but because the controversy's unfolding precluded them from having a speaking position. This silencing had long-term political ramifications. "Between patriarchy and imperialism, subject-constitution and object-formation, the figure of the woman disappears, not into a pristine nothingness, but into a violent shuttling which is the displaced figuration of the 'third-world woman' caught between tradition and modernization" (ibid.: 306). Ultimately for Spivak, the subaltern could not speak, but this did not mean that the oppressed were doomed to silence. "Her point is that no act of dissent or resistance occurs on behalf of an essential subaltern subject entirely separate from the dominant discourse that provides the language and the conceptual categories with which the subaltern voice speaks" (Ashcroft *et al.* 1998: 219).

Deconstructing elite sources and historiography had been part of the Subaltern Studies project from the beginning, but in later work the group's historians probed more deeply into the epistemological underpinnings of their discipline, extending the earlier critique to encompass the Eurocentrism of historical production more broadly. According to Prakash: "The Subaltern Studies' relocation of subalternity in the operation of dominant discourses leads it necessarily to the critique of the modern West. For if the marginalization of 'other' sources of knowledge and agency occurred in the functioning of colonialism and its derivative, nationalism, then the weapon of critique must turn against Europe and the modes of knowledge it instituted" (Prakash 1994: 1483).

Edward Said, who wrote an appreciative introduction to *Selected Subaltern Studies*, provided a major impetus for this direction in the group's work. In *Orientalism* ([1978] 1995) he scrutinized Western scholars' ideological construction of the "Orient," showing that it revealed more about the Western imagination than the people that it objectified. Said drew on both Foucault and Gramsci. Following Foucault, he analyzed the "networks of interests" and discursive frameworks that produced the Orient as "other": a fixed, static, and a historical image transforming diverse peoples into a homogeneous object. He saw this scholarly apparatus in Gramscian terms, as an act of Western dominance or hegemony. "My contention," wrote Said, "is that Orientalism is fundamentally a political doctrine willed over the Orient because the Orient was weaker than the West, which elided the Orient's difference with its weakness" (Said [1978] 1995: 204).

The spirit of Said's critique among Subaltern historians was found in essays, written in the 1990s, comprising Chakrabarty's influential book, *Provincializing Europe: Postcolonial Thought and Historical Difference* (2000). Chakrabarty, in effect, extended Said's critique of Orientalist scholarship to encompass the historical enterprise itself. Historical practice, though claiming universal applicability, was shackled with assumptions reflecting European experience. "'Europe,'" in his words, "remains the sovereign, theoretical subject of all histories, including the ones we call 'Indian,' 'Chinese,' 'Kenyan,' and so on. There is a peculiar way in which all these other histories tend to become variations on a master narrative that could be called 'the history of Europe'" (Chakrabarty 2000: 27). Chakrabarty was not advocating the rejection of European modes of thought: in fact, no historical practice was possible without them. But in deconstructing or "provincializing" Europe, it became possible to understand India in other terms than as having achieved an incomplete form of modernity, with Europe tacitly being the fully realized model of modernization.

What is the implication of Chakrabarty's thinking for conceptualizing the subaltern? On the one hand, it seemed that, for Chakrabarty, the subaltern realm no longer signified just the popular classes: it encompassed all that went against the grain of European metanarratives. But he also continued to understand the subaltern in terms closer to the spirit of the original project, although mediated by his critique of European universality. Here, Chakrabarty sought to align himself with (1) the critical spirit of Marxism and (2) postmodern theories of difference undermining Marxism's totalizing and universal claims. He defined the subaltern as "that which constantly, from within the narrative of capital, reminds us of other ways of being human than as bearers of the capacity to labor" (ibid.: 94). And he argued that subaltern history existed within a Marxist understanding of global capitalism without being grounded in it. Chakrabarty's aspiration to provincialize Europe was an impossible task, for its vision of radical heterogeneity was only conceivable through intellectual protocols that undermined that vision in the first place. The same may be said of his attempt to fuse Marxist theory and postmodern notions of difference;

but this did not mean that – as in the case of the aspiration to provincialize Europe – the tension between the two modes of thought did not generate a creative intellectual space.

As in British social history (see Chapter 5), debates surrounding these newer directions in Subaltern Studies pitted social and cultural approaches, Marxism and postmodernism, against each other. One notable example was an exchange between Prakash, on the one hand, and Rosalind O'Hanlon and David Washbrook, on the other (Prakash [1990] 2000; [1992] 2000; O'Hanlon and Washbrook [1992] 2000). Prakash rejected totalizing systems; advocated a post-Saidian, postfoundational history that represented India "in relationships and processes that have constructed contingent and unstable identities"; aligned himself with a postmodern "politics of difference"; championed the Subaltern Studies project; and enthused over a historiography "located at the point where post-structuralist, Marxist and feminist theories converge and intersect" (Prakash [1990] 2000: 178, 180). He drew the fire of O'Hanlon and Washbrook, who questioned whether it was, in fact, possible to ride the horse of both critical Marxism and postmodernism at the same time (O'Hanlon and Washbrook [1992] 2000: 216).

In addition, Sumit Sarkar, an original contributor to Subaltern Studies, wrote a critical essay on the group's later work, "The Decline of the Subaltern in *Subaltern Studies*" ([1996] 2000), in which he argued that the project had lamentably shifted ground. According to Sarkar, Subaltern Studies "has encouraged a virtual folding back of all history into the single problematic of Western colonial cultural domination" and had consequently imposed "a series of closures and silences" and threatened "simultaneously to feed into shallow forms of retrogressive indigenism," by which he meant a resurgent Hindu nationalism (Sarkar [1996] 2000: 316). Important for both critiques were Subaltern Studies' retreat from Marxism and its abandonment of class theory. As it turned out, these critiques were part of a much broader discussion on Subaltern Studies: the subaltern was going global.

The subalternity effect

By the 1990s the Subaltern Studies collective had achieved worldwide influence. Vinayak Chaturvedi has described it as attaining "the status of a global academic institution" (Chaturvedi 2000b: vii). David Ludden has concurred: he called the collective "a weapon, magnet, target, lightening rod, hitching post, icon, gold mine, and fortress for scholars ranging across disciplines from history to political science, anthropology, sociology, literary criticism, and cultural studies" (Ludden 2002a: 2). Subalternity had penetrated fields as varied as African, Irish, Latin American, and Palestinian studies.

Ranajit Guha observed that when *Subaltern Studies* was launched he never imagined that it would appeal to readers outside of India, as the British colonial regime and academic establishment had always represented the subcontinent abroad (Guha 2001: 35). He was speaking to a group of scholars of Latin America. They were mostly in literary and cultural studies and predominantly based in North America. They were founders of the Latin American Subaltern Studies group, which aspired to loosely emulate the South Asian historians' blend of informal democratic organization and politically engaged scholarship. Coming together in the wake of the Sandinistas' defeat in the 1990 Nicaraguan elections, and having lost faith in Marxist revolutionary theory, the Latin American Subaltern Studies group regarded itself as confronting political and intellectual challenges analogous to those faced by their South Asian colleagues. In the words of Ileana Rodríguez: "While the South Asian Subaltern Collective was criticizing the postcolonial liberal state and the nationalist independence and anticolonialist movements from the Left, we were criticizing leftist states and party organizations for their liberalism. It was the same question attacked from the pre- and postrevolutionary fronts" (Rodríguez 2001: 3–4). The Latin American scholars felt an affinity with their South Asian counterparts, for both had experienced nationalist politics and had ties with the Western academic world. Their convergence was "a case of South–South dialogue, but paradoxically it passes through the North" (ibid.: 5).

Latin American Subaltern Studies rethought the connection between the nation, state, and "people" at a time when rampant globalization was rewriting that relationship. Participants viewed the subaltern within a framework that drew from Subaltern Studies' blend of history from below and deconstruction of dominant discourses. On the one hand, Latin American Subaltern Studies scholars' commitment to subaltern histories was manifested in their privileging of the political practices of the poor and their vow to produce scholarship that showed that in "the failure to recognize the poor as active social, political, and heuristic agents reside the limits and thresholds of our present hermeneutical and political condition" (ibid.: 3). Moreover, the group sought to go beyond class theory, viewing the nation, as their founding statement stated, as "multiple fractures of language, race, ethnicity, gender, class, and the resulting tensions between assimilation (ethnic dilution and homogenization) and confrontation (passive resistance, insurgency, strikes, terrorism)" (Latin American Subaltern Studies Group 1993: 118).

On the other hand, Latin American Subaltern Studies also embraced post-modern, poststructuralist, and deconstructionist perspectives, as evidenced in their aspiration to capture "the blank space where it [the subaltern] speaks as a sociopolitical subject" (ibid.: 119). As its founding statement stated: "We can find the subaltern only in the seams of the previously articulated sociocultural and administrative practices and epistemologies, in the cloning of cultural mentalities, and in the contingent social pacts that occur at every transitional juncture" (ibid.: 119). Like Prakash and Chakrabarty, and other South Asian historians, the Latin American collective sought to ride Marxist and postmodern horses simultaneously. On balance it was the latter of these two approaches that was most conspicuous in its scholarship.

Among the most intriguing migrations of Subaltern Studies beyond its original geographical confines in South Asian studies was its appearance in an Irish context, primarily because of the literary scholar and cultural theorist David Lloyd. Lloyd was the first writer to publish in *Subaltern Studies* about a non-Indian topic (Lloyd 1996). Ireland was Britain's oldest colony and con-stituted the British Empire's first postcolonial state (aside from a settler colony like the United States). Yet, as Lloyd acknowledged, analyzing Ireland via a postcolonial framework, as he proposed to do, immediately brought forth objections. First, the very idea of a "postcolonial" Ireland presupposed that the six northern counties under British sovereignty, in fact, remained "colo-nial," a proposition bound to be contentious. Second, no less contentious was the notion that Ireland's historical trajectory had more in common with India's than with comparatively recent independent European states produced by nationalist movements, whether Italy, Hungary, or Poland. Could Ireland be conceived of as a third-world country, given its recent economic growth, which took place within the framework of the European Union?

For Lloyd, both these reservations presupposed a constricted understand-ing of what the idea of a postcolonial Ireland signified: they either assumed a narrow political focus or held to a constricting modernization metanarrative. Like the South Asian historians, Lloyd saw both arguments as enmeshed in elitist discourses. Ireland was, in fact, "anomalous," "both a small European country and a decolonized nation," both of the First and Third World. Lloyd found Subaltern Studies stimulating precisely because it allowed for such formulations. "Both the terms 'post-colonial' and 'subaltern,'" he wrote, "designate in different but related ways the desire to elaborate social spaces that are recalcitrant to any straightforward absorption – ever more inevitable though this often seems – of Ireland into European modernity" (ibid.: 263).

For Lloyd, subalternity in Ireland was bound up with elitist historiography. In critical respects the Irish historiographical context was different than the

Indian. "Revisionist" historians were in the forefront of critiquing Irish nationalist historiography – Roy Foster (1949–) being the best known. They deconstructed the nationalist "story of Ireland," recapturing historical uncertainties and contingencies and recovering the voices of historical actors on their own terms. Yet for Lloyd, nationalists and revisionists shared a common focus on the state's political formation and its institutions that ignored subaltern groups, much as historians of India had. Lloyd championed recent work in Irish history, which, though not produced by an organized effort, had recovered subaltern voices across a wide front, most importantly in feminist accounts of women's and gender history. In his words: "The insistence of the new histories on the *contemporaneity* of marginal and dominant social forms, and on their differential construction, is in this respect a profoundly instructive corrective to the self-evidences of developmental historiographies which over and again relegate differences to anteriority" (ibid.: 277).

Lloyd's thought here echoed Raymond Williams's understanding of hegemony as the complex relationship between dominant, residual, and emergent cultures (see Chapter 2). Accordingly, Lloyd regarded these new histories as potentially providing the basis for emergent "radical imaginaries." Like the Subaltern Studies group, Lloyd conceived of the "subalternity effect" as present in the gaps, contradictions, and fissures of elite historiography and retrievable through non-elite histories. "That is, the social space of the 'subaltern' designates not some sociological datum of an objective and generalizable kind, but is an effect emerging in and between historiographical discourses" (ibid.: 263). Lloyd advocated bringing together a postmodern emphasis on heterogeneity and irreducible difference with cultural Marxism's emphasis on recovering the lives of marginalized peoples. His position, like Chakrabarty and others discussed in this section, moved beyond the confines of Marxist class theory, but it nonetheless bore its imprint.

Conclusion

The Subaltern Studies group originally developed and expanded class theory by producing histories of subaltern groups, its project being inspired by Gramsci and British Marxist historians. Its historical practice was also shaped by the linguistic turn. Confronted with archives and historical writing formed by colonial discourses, these South Asian historians honed deconstructive reading strategies, discovering the subaltern in the gaps, recesses, and silences of the historical archives and elitist historiography – colonial and nationalist.

The group's development in some ways mirrored the movement from social to cultural history described in earlier chapters. However, Subaltern historians increasingly became drawn to an emerging postcolonial criticism, to which they also contributed. A principal feature of this development was their deconstruction of the universal claims of Enlightenment reasoning, especially as pertaining to history – embodied by Chakrabarty's provocative aspiration to provincialize Europe. As a result of this focus, the subaltern became identified with virtually the third world itself, by any definition beyond the limits of class theory.

More overtly germane to exploring the concept of class was the ramification of this postcolonial critique for Marxism, conceived as a Eurocentric narrative that distorted the historical development of non-Western societies. Some of the group's historians resisted Marxism's totalizing ambitions, while continuing to insist on its critical force. They attempted to fuse Marxist critique with a postmodern acceptance of irreducible social and cultural differences. Here, the historians regarded subalternity as irreducibly plural: various forms of dissidence and antagonisms to the totalizing ambitions of metanarratives. Thus, though rooted in Marxist class theory, Subaltern Studies stretched this tradition beyond its previous limits. Their aspiration to recover the "small voice of history" (Guha 1996) in colonial and postcolonial settings inspired scholars worldwide.

Conclusion

In this book I have traced contemporary conceptions and usages of social class among sociologists, cultural studies scholars, and, most importantly, historians, based on the premise that class explanations and narratives have been in the throes of a crisis. My goal has been to produce an intellectual history of the present, situating contemporary discussions on class in their historical context. I have viewed class theory's assumptions, its objects of analysis, the changes it has undergone, and its political aspirations as deeply intermingled. I have sought to explain why a crisis has arisen, analyzed the critiques and debates comprising it, and discussed scholarly work steeped in these discussions.

Pronouncements of class's demise are exaggerated, but its status as an explanatory concept has been significantly and perhaps irrevocably diminished. I have also suggested that the intellectual turmoil has led to fresh and original ways of thinking, imaginative revisions of established positions, and vital discussions and debates. Where once class narratives provided unity to diverse intellectual endeavors, fragmentation now reigns. This provides an intellectual opening for a more complex and sophisticated understanding of society, culture, politics, identity, and history, in which "class" potentially plays a still vital, if muted, role.

Many scholars discussed in this book avidly believed in class and the social as central organizing features of society and history, but they subsequently developed reservations regarding their explanatory power. One form that these reservations took was postmodern and poststructuralist critique, which frequently involved according to culture, language, and discourse a privileged status. Another reservation concerned the privileged position of class. This skepticism led to the development of the class concept in complex and imaginative ways, frequently viewing class as interwoven with other determinations and identities. These directions in class analysis often – but not necessarily – led to abandonment of the concept altogether, although often individuals who trod such a path never entirely freed themselves of the binary assumptions from which they began. Just as Marx turned Hegel on his head, but his ideas were marked by the encounter, so critics of the primacy of "class" and the "social" put forward alternatives that often bore traces of what it was that they sought to overthrow. Those who privileged language, discourse, culture, and politics at the expense of the social and the economic often seemed to be marked by the same theoretical forms as what they were rejecting; only they were inverting them. Class, in other words, remains vital, even in its absence. In this final chapter, I revisit the scholarship pertaining to class and the social and the principal debates regarding them. Having reexamined where we have been, I then conclude the book by discussing where we are now, speculating on what future directions class theory and analysis might take.

Recapitulation

While it was not Marxists alone who developed class theory and analysis – followers of Max Weber's ideas being the most formidable competitors – the Marxist tradition powerfully influenced the contours of scholarly work on class. Whether derived directly or indirectly from Marx's writings, class theory was dualistic. It was founded on the distinction between an objective socio-economic structure, or "social being," and forms of understanding and awareness or "social consciousness." "Experience" provided the link between them. Just as being shaped consciousness, people's experience of an inequitable class structure, rooted in the relations of production, led to class consciousness and collective action. When expected forms of consciousness – notably working-class political action – did not surface, the challenge was to explain why. Such assumptions lent themselves to reductionist interpretations, but the model was more complex that this. Engels observed that the superstructure – politics, ideology, religion, and philosophy – shaped the contours of the base as well as being shaped by it. When Marx analyzed the class dynamic in concrete situations, he represented human agency as being fundamental to historical outcomes. In short, Marxist class theory had a built-in tension between structure and action, free will and determinism. Its "orthodox" defenders did not always appreciate this fact.

By any definition the sociological and historical scholarship of the 1960s and 1970s – founded on a critique of orthodox Marxism's reductionism and an unprecedented attention to culture and ideology – comprised an intellectual renaissance. This renaissance was informed by a confrontation with social, political, and cultural transformations in the two decades following World War II, and, most importantly, changes in working-class experience, manifested in debates about affluence and classlessness. The rebirth was also part of a flowering of cultural, political, and intellectual initiatives symbolized by "1968," but whose roots were traceable to the previous decade. The new thinking was deeply interfused with the rise of the new left, and an important direction of the scholarship associated with it was a vastly enlarged notion of the political.

Despite pronounced differences in orientation, the historians and sociologists who enriched class theory and interpretation in the 1960s and 1970s shared the assumptions of the Marxist dualistic model. They also adhered to (using Alun Munslow's terminology) "constructionist" ideas regarding the relationship between theory and evidence; that is, they believed that theories and concepts gave coherence to the vast array of evidence and made it possible for the historical and social process to be objectively knowable. Sociologists – notably John Goldthorpe, David Lockwood, and Erik Olin Wright – produced refined mappings of objective class relationships in order to make connections between structural location, life opportunities, forms of consciousness, and collective action. Historians elaborated on the process of class formation and class experience. They helped produce the new social and labor history, which was rooted in the primacy of the "social," based on the aspiration to write "total history," and founded on a "bottom-up" perspective. Central here was E. P. Thompson's inspirational book, *The Making of the English Working Class*. Thompson aspired to recover working-class formation within a materialist framework, but he insisted that it was a cultural and political process that disclosed human agents making their own history.

By the 1980s and 1990s, class theory and analysis – and social approaches more generally – were subject to serious attack, most importantly by left-wing scholars. The latter were rethinking their commitment to Marxism or had abandoned it altogether, yet were still committed to a radical democratic vision. There was always something slightly nostalgic about scholars' privileging of class in the 1960s and 1970s, since it coincided with the beginning of the break up of the very working-class culture that was often being privileged. By the time of the Reagan and Thatcher eras, it was undeniable that a fundamental shift had taken place, as observers began to flesh out an emerging postmodern society. These "new times" were not as "new" as often portrayed, but they undeniably posed challenges to the traditional left and socialism, which only intensified following the demise of Communism. A crucial element in this context was the emergence of identity politics and new social movements – traceable to movements such as the Campaign for Nuclear Disarmament of the 1950s and the civil rights movement – which were transforming the political terrain. There was a contrast between the labor movement's class-based notion of identity – centered on white male skilled workers – and the more fluid and open-ended notion of identity that was emerging in the new social movements such as feminism.

These identity shifts resonated with postmodernism's opposition to universal narratives and essentialist thought; its insistence on pluralism in the social, political, and cultural fields; and its tendency to think in terms of fragmented subjects – all of which challenged the totalizing aspirations of class narratives. Many of these ideas were explored in the burgeoning field of cultural studies. They were intertwined with an emerging post-Marxism, as evidenced in Ernesto Laclau and Chantal Mouffe's *Hegemony and Socialist Strategy* and *Marxism Today*'s *New Times* project. Despite pronounced differences, both advocated a "politics of difference," emphasizing the contingency, heterogeneity, and autonomy of social movements and human subjects. Such views represented inversions of the Marxist belief in the triumph of the proletariat – the universal human subject – and socialism, based on appeals to the laws of history.

Along analogous lines, Jan Pakulski and Malcolm Waters in *The Death of Class* advocated abandoning the class concept entirely in favor of multiple forms of status. In addition, Zygmunt Bauman in *Intimations of Postmodernity* and other writings advocated "sociality" – rather than "society." He stressed contingency, fluidity, under-determination, randomness, and local and autonomous practices. Bauman soundly rejected the binary model of structure and action, class structure and class consciousness on which classical social theory had been founded. Even stalwart advocates, such as John Goldthorpe, defended a version of class theory that left little of its original scope or aspiration intact (Goldthorpe and Marshall [1992] 1996).

A major challenge to the social basis of the class model was the linguistic or cultural turn associated with poststructuralism. Here, language was viewed as playing a constitutive role in constructing the reality that it described. Given that experience and consciousness were linguistically ordered, individual and group interests were not seen as being rooted in an objective structure: they were, in fact, produced through language and culture. The thrust of the linguistic turn was to reclaim the social and cultural representations of historical actors. This included, following Foucault, the historicizing of the categories in which actors thought and took action. In short, in the poststructuralist view, it was not structure that produced consciousness. Instead it was the other way around: consciousness produced structure. The effect of such developments was to give new life to the political realm, which was freed from its dependence on socio-economic determinants; but it was not by any means exclusively the world of high politics – diplomacy and government – that social historians had treated as being secondary. Politics was seen as having added depth and breadth, in accordance with the feminist contention that the personal was political and Foucault's belief that political power was diffuse rather than being centralized.

The ramifications of the linguistic turn for the new social history were profound, for the very foundation of social history and history in general was potentially undermined. Poststructuralist approaches challenged the idea of a materialist "total history." They disputed the notion that "the social" could provide the ground for historical explanations, arguing that this very term, the social, needed to be historicized. Rather than conceiving of class consciousness as developing in the context of an objectively analyzable class structure, cultural historians regarded such forms of awareness as part of the "social imaginary." Where social historians tended to view political and ideological conflicts as being rooted in the class structure, cultural historians inverted this formulation. They were prone to viewing the political and ideological sphere as producing our sense of class and the social. They subscribed to, again in Munslow's terminology, a deconstructionist view of historical knowledge, meaning that the act of representation played an active role in shaping the object of knowledge.

In the course of this book, I have analyzed various instances where cultural and linguistic perspectives have reshaped history's priorities and challenged class narratives. In French revolutionary historiography the dominant Marxist model was first dethroned by a group of revisionist historians who disputed the empirical foundation of the Marxist interpretation. But critical of the socio-economic assumptions of both was François Furet's *Rethinking the French Revolution*, which emphasized the role of political culture – "centres of democratic sensibility" – in the making of the French Revolution. Similarly, Lynn Hunt in *Politics, Culture, and Class in the French Revolution* stressed the autonomy of political culture and the cultural and symbolic dimension of politics, while arguing that analyzing the French class structure failed to shed light on the course of revolutionary politics. Labor historians of France reconfigured their subject as well. William Sewell advocated a post-materialist labor history, which problematized the idea that economic explanations were any more "real" than cultural ones. He acknowledged that class cultures had to be viewed in their historical context, but he also conceived of them as having their own discursive logic and in turn an impact on historical outcomes.

As discussed in Chapter 5, the most wide-ranging debates regarding social history and class interpretations took place among social historians of Britain. Here, Gareth Stedman Jones turned the field on its head in "Rethinking Chartism" – one of the essays in *Languages of Class*. He rejected the dominant Marxist-inflected social interpretation of the Chartist movement in favor of a discursive and political one. For Stedman Jones, the Chartist movement was best understood as an outgrowth of an older tradition of political radicalism, whose discursive structure set limits to and pressures on working-class political action. Thompson's "class struggle" model was put on trial in seemingly endless debates that followed in the wake of Stedman Jones's book. As the debate entered the 1990s, Patrick Joyce widened the attack on social history, advocating a postmodern history of the social, which, following the spirit of Foucault, historicized the categories – class among them – that social historians took for granted. In other words, class itself was seen to be a discursive category and not a fundamental social fact. While Joyce's polemic was divisive, by the beginning of the new millennium the historiographical ground undeniably had shifted, producing a greater focus on political discourse. An intermediate ground was also becoming more visible, as evidenced by James Epstein's advocacy of drawing on both cultural and social approaches in his essays comprising *In Practice*.

Epstein was not alone. Despite polarizing debates between social and cultural historians in British history, there was also a group of historians – in Britain and elsewhere – who sought in practice to combine cultural and social approaches, viewing class as being intertwined with multiple identities and determinations. I have fleshed out this outlook in the book's final three chapters on British feminist historians (Chapter 6), British and American theorists and historians of race (Chapter 7), and the South Asian Subaltern Studies group (Chapter 8).

In the 1970s British feminist historians followed a "bottom-up" approach, extending the class-oriented model of history from below to include women. By the 1980s they had begun to analyze the process of class formation from a feminist and gendered perspective. Here, *Family Fortunes* was the pivotal text. Beginning from the premise that class was gendered, Davidoff and Hall focused on the importance of separate-spheres ideology to the process of Victorian middle-class formation. They critiqued Thompson's account of the working class, for its oblivion to gender. But they followed him in situating culture, language, and ideologies within a materialist framework. Along similar lines, Anna Clark in *The Struggle for the Breeches* and Sonya Rose in *Limited Livelihoods* rewrote the narrative of nineteenth-century working-class formation by interweaving class and gender conflicts. The accomplishments of many of the historians in this chapter were not incompatible with the discursive analysis of gender and class advocated by Joan Scott, but their work continued to give credence to material factors.

Although they have distinctive styles of thought and politics, the scholars who studied black culture, whiteness, and racial dynamics in Chapter 7 all helped produce a theoretical opening in which class and race and (in many cases) gender were conceptualized as being historically intertwined, culturally constructed, and defined in the course of political struggle. Cultural theorists Stuart Hall and Paul Gilroy – as well as sociologists Michael Omi and Howard Winant – held these views. So did Robin Kelley in his retrieval of the lives of black working-class people in *Race Rebels*. David Roediger espoused a similar perspective in his sober reflections on the formation of the nineteenth-century American white working class in *The Wages of Whiteness*. The theoretical effort to analyze race and class simultaneously, while holding on to the specificity of both, was unforgettably captured in Hall's influential formulation: race is "the modality in which class is 'lived,' the medium through which class relations are experienced, the form in which it is appropriated and 'fought through'" (Hall [1980] 1996: 55).

Some of the writers discussed in this chapter combined materialist and discursive analyses. Omi and Winant sought to bring together poststructuralist notions of cultural representation with the analysis of socio-economic structures. David Roediger focused on transformations in racially charged language, seeing the cultural representation of whiteness and blackness as defining each other. As a committed Marxist, Roediger was careful to distinguish his own position from what he considered to be the more radical versions of poststructuralism. In his view, the close scrutiny of texts found in poststructuralism led to skepticism about knowledge of the past altogether. Yet, like other historians discussed in these final chapters, he drew from both social and cultural perspectives.

One of the most potent criticisms of the class model made by African-American and black British scholars was that it was Eurocentric. Gilroy, Hall, Kelley, and Cedric Robinson all made this critique. Their appraisal was built on the labors of earlier black intellectuals, notably W. E. B. Du Bois and C. L. R. James. Robinson, responsible for the most developed version of this position, attempted to decenter a narrative of capitalist development and modernity, which portrayed the European working class as the universal agent of history and which failed to register the intimate connections between European capitalism and the global system of slavery and imperialism. He described this evolving global system as "racial capitalism." He argued that racism and capitalism, racial and class formation, were historically inseparable.

Historians of South Asia, who comprised the Subaltern Studies group, developed a critique of the universal pretensions of the class model along analogous lines. They originally enriched class theory and interpretation by retrieving the lives of subaltern groups, whose political acts had been appropriated to neocolonial and nationalist historical narratives. Their understanding of the subaltern came from Gramsci, and they modeled their project after that of the British Marxist historians. But they also were drawn to the linguistic turn. They discovered traces of the subaltern in the gaps, recesses, and silences of the historical archives and elitist historiography.

As Subaltern Studies evolved, its work developed in a more cultural than social direction, although it drew from both, and it was informed by postcolonial theory. Subaltern scholars argued that the Marxist historical analysis of modernity – as well as Enlightenment universalism more generally – was Eurocentric. At points their understanding of the subaltern seemed to encompass the third world itself, an indication of the distance they had traveled from the initial project of recovering the lives of the laboring classes. Yet Subaltern historians still retained a commitment to recover what Ranajit Guha described as the "small voice in history" – a reiteration of Subaltern Studies' original aspiration (Guha 1996). Subaltern historians had moved well beyond the confines of Marxist class theory, but their work continued to bear its imprint. Their trajectory was by no means unique.

Class matters

Scholars who have viewed class as either one determination or one identity among many have produced an important intellectual space, drawing on social and cultural approaches. While this scholarship reaffirms that class perspectives retain their potential to illuminate the historical process, it is clearly not the conquering version of class that once dominated discussions in history and sociology 30 years ago. In addition, as I have previously suggested, such work, while producing more complex and sophisticated understanding of class dynamics, threatens to eradicate what was distinctive about class analysis in the first place. Analyzing the intertwined relationship of class, race, and gender poses difficult challenges. When other factors are considered – region, religion, nationality, ethnicity, space, age, and so forth – class may disappear under a mountain of social, cultural, political, and historical specialty. The idea of the subaltern, for instance, which (as pointed out previously) began as a concept signifying the laboring classes, evolved into something more indistinct and amorphous. This shift captures what can happen to class interpretations when scholars seek to understand multidimensional forms of power and resistance.

Despite the potential to lose its distinctiveness, I do not believe that "class" is at the end of its rope. I began this book by citing statistics about the widening income gap within the United States and between different parts of the world. It is difficult to imagine analyzing inequalities in today's world without mapping global capitalism and its regional and local variations. Some version of class is necessary here, which does not mean, of course, that it is the only concept that is to be deployed. "Class," from this point of view, is an important dimension of the signification of our contemporary situation, one that is inseparable from the political commitments that we bring to the analysis. Potentially there are other ways of expressing what "class" does, yet does it make sense to abandon a concept that still has purchase in public political discourse? We need fresh ways to analyze structured forms of inequality and political resistance, but it seems preferable to retain the language of class – part of peoples' everyday toolkit for negotiating the social, cultural, and political world – rather than inventing a new, purely "academic" discourse.

In addition, although the old working-class cultures of the industrial world will certainly not reemerge, it is conceivable that political movements and cultures may yet surface that coalesce at least partially around fighting economic inequalities and producing an egalitarian economic and political order. Where such social imaginaries might surface or how they might combine with other discourses cannot be known in advance. Whether they originate in politics, culture, or society – or a combination of the three – is less important than that they might serve as the basis to unite people in specific contexts. Certainly social imaginaries involving class will inevitably be mediated by race and gender (and potentially a host of other factors); they will be shaped by existing cultural and political discourses; and they will be steeped in the langue of popular culture. They are likely to be in response to the uneven and unequal process of globalization. Even if such aspirations do not materialize in formal political movements, they might still be detectable "way, way below," in Robin Kelley's phrase. This phrase bears the imprint of multiple sources – anthropologists, historians, and cultural theorists. But certainly one is the British cultural Marxism associated with E. P. Thompson. There are limits to Thompson's thinking, as several critics in this book have made clear. But it is difficult not to appreciate his achievement and just how widespread his influence has been. The multiple engagements with his work described in the preceding chapters suggest the powerful hold he has had on historians. He remains a figure with which to be reckoned.

In sum, it is still important, resorting to Marx's terminology, to analyze "class in itself," seen as those relationships that people enter into independent of their will, although such an idea must include the discursive as well as the material groundings of those relationships. It is likewise possible that "class for itself" – conceived as a social and cultural imaginary – might yet emerge as a way of bridging differences between diverse groups of people, although it might – as it has in the past – be exclusionary as well. But if "class in itself" and "class for itself" might still be conceived as relevant ideas, that does not mean that the former lends itself, via experience, to producing the latter. The linkage between structure, interest, experience, consciousness, and action, so critical to the classical model of class, cannot be assumed, even in the abstract. Discontinuities between links in the chain are as likely as continuities. All of these terms involve the others simultaneously. Their relationship(s) can only be understood in specific historical contexts.

Finally, we still can benefit from the kind of materialist analysis characteristic of the best social history, but we also can profit from the historical scholarship produced through the linguistic and cultural turn. Bringing together the insights of both ways of conceiving of historical practice could be a boon to scholarship. I am not advocating a new synthesis that would replace the existing fragmentation of the field. I see little chance for that. But I believe that the scholarship discussed in this book might provide the ground on which this conceptual space could be more fruitfully explored. William Sewell has recently advocated bringing together social and cultural approaches. He argued for

> a conception of the social in which every sphere of life – from production, to art, to family life, to the state – is constituted by both discursive and extradiscursive logics that are always tightly intertwined in social practice. Although one of the tasks of sociocultural historians is to disentangle these logics, to assess their autonomous presences and dynamics, it is also important to remember that they are always merged in practice, that, for example, questions of meaning, spatiality, relative scarcity, and coercion are conjoined in the world in a dance of mutual and simultaneous determination. According to this social ontology, the economic, the political, the cultural and the geographic are not distinct institutional spheres of social existence; they are distinguishable but mutually constituting dimensions of social life, dimensions that are present in all institutional spheres (Sewell 2001: 222–23).

Along similar lines, Geoff Ely and Keith Nield have advocated a rapprochement between social and cultural history, one that marries Gramsci's notion of

hegemony and Foucault's emphasis on the microphysics of power and resistance. Eley and Nield believed that adopting a discursive approach did
not negate the project of social history, and they defended social history's
"carefully and archivally grounded studies" and its potential to inspire future
forms of political agency. However, when it came to class, they favored a view
whose point of departure was a poststructuralist conception of subjectivity:

> Class *discursively* understood, we would argue, is a better starting point for
> the study of class formation than the classical approaches of economics and
> social structure, because it was at this discursive level that a new operational
> collectivity (class in its actually existing forms) was defined – who got to be
> included, who formed the boundaries, who set the tone, and who won the
> recognized voice (Eley and Nield 2000: 18).

Eley and Nield were not arguing that economics and social considerations were
unimportant. Yet they insisted that "class emerged historically as a set of discursive claims about the social world seeking to reorder the latter in terms of
itself" (ibid.: 19).

Ely and Nield's attempt to bridge the gap between social and cultural
approaches is timely, but it is an open question whether it will produce the
dialogue that they have in mind. Responses to their argument in the spring
2000 issue of *International Labor and Working-Class History* often tended to
reinforce – rather than mend – existing divisions among historians. Yet, as I
have argued, there have been historians who, whether they would accept the
particular emphasis of Eley and Nield's argument, would likely approve of the
spirit underpinning it. From Catherine Hall, Sonya Rose, and Anna Clark to
David Roediger, James Epstein, Robin Kelley, and Ranajit Guha, their work
shows the ways the fusing of the social and the cultural can take place.

The same may be said for the class concept. I remember hearing an old
Jewish story involving a rabbi and a skeptical young man. When the young
man tells the rabbi he has doubts about God's existence, the rabbi replies
that it is less important to believe in God than to act as if God exists. However
problematic "class" may be as a concept, however contested it has become,
however elusive it sometimes seems, and however limited its reach sometimes
may appear, "class" allows for mapping economic forms of inequality that
invade peoples' lives in a way that no other concept makes possible. Class provides a means of discussing manifestations of politics, culture, and language
that neither status nor gender nor race allows. It is perhaps less important that
we come to a consensus regarding what class means: more crucial that we act
as if it exists.

Guide to key reading

By any measure "class" is a daunting subject. This guide to key reading highlights texts that I have found important in writing this book. It is organized by chapter, which in some cases necessitates mentioning readings in multiples places. These I have indicated in parentheses: (cited under Introduction), for example.

Introduction

As is fitting for a subject as important and large as "class," a hefty general and introductory literature has surfaced. When I was formulating this project, I benefited enormously from Paul Fussell's witty and entertaining *Class* (New York: Ballantine Books, 1983), which convincingly dispels the myth of an American classless society. I also have relied on more academic studies: Rosemary Crompton, *Class and Stratification: An Introduction to Current Debates* (Cambridge: Polity Press, 2nd Edn 1998), Gary Day, *Class* (London: Routledge, 2001), Anthony Giddens, *The Class Structure of the Advanced Societies* (New York: Harper & Row, 1975), Andrew Milner, *Class* (London: Sage, 1999), and Jeremy Seabrook, *The No-Nonsense Guide to Class, Caste and Hierarchies* (London: New Internationalist Publications in association with Verso, 2002). In a category by itself is Patrick Joyce (Ed.), *Class* (Oxford: Oxford University Press, 1995): it consists of extracts from important texts on class in the humanities and social sciences (especially history); it includes relevant excerpts from classical social theory; and it is conceived from a post-modern perspective.

Chapter 1

The history of the idea of "class" has been treated by a small group of scholars. Readers should consult Asa Briggs's classic 1960 essay, "The Language of 'Class' in Early Nineteenth-Century England," *The Collected Essays of Asa Briggs* (Urbana, IL: University of Illinois Press, 1985, Vol. 1, pp. 3–33), followed by the entry for "class" in Raymond Williams's indispensable *Keywords: A Vocabulary of Culture and Society* (London: Fontana Paperbacks, 1983, pp. 60–69). For the development of "class" in the working-class movement see Iorwerth Prothero, "William Renbow and the Concept of the 'The General Strike,'" *Past and Present*, 1974, 63: 132–71. Peter Calvert, *The Concept of Class: An Historical Introduction* (London: Hutchinson, 1982) is the most sustained historical treatment, although it stresses political theory. Pertinent here also is Penelope J. Corfield (Ed.), *Language, History and Class* (Oxford: Basil Blackwell, 1991), a collection of essays in the aftermath of the linguistic turn. The classical theorists of "class" and the "social" – Karl Marx and Max Weber – are discussed in Calvert, Crompton, and Milner, and selections from Marx's and Weber's writings pertaining specifically to class are found in Joyce (all cited under Introduction). An excellent introduction to the foundational ideas of modern social theory is found in Anthony Giddens, *Capitalism and Modern Social Theory: An Analysis of the Writings of Marx, Durkheim and Max Weber* (Cambridge: Cambridge University Press, 1971). Also worthwhile is Norman Birnbaum, "Conflicting Interpretations of the Rise of Capitalism," *The British Journal of Sociology*, 1953, 4: 125–41.

Chapter 2

Crompton and Milner, as well as Giddens, *The Class Structure of the Advanced Societies* (all cited under Introduction), are good places to begin investigating post-World War II class theory. For David Lockwood see *The Blackcoated Worker: A Study in Class Consciousness* (London: Allen & Unwin, 1958) and "Sources of Variation in Working-Class Images of Society," *Sociological Review*, 1966, 14: 249–67. For John Goldthorpe see Goldthorpe *et al.*, *The Affluent Worker in The Class Structure*, *The Affluent Worker: Industrial Attitudes and Behaviour*, and *The Affluent Worker: Political Attitudes and Behaviour*, published in 1968 by Cambridge University Press.

The Marxist intellectual renaissance – including the recovery of an older Western Marxist tradition – which forms the background to Erik Olin Wright's work and much else in this book, are traced in Perry Anderson, *Considerations on Western Marxism* (London: NLB, 1976) and Martin Jay, *Marxism and Totality: The Adventures of a Concept from Lukács to Habermas* (Berkeley, CA: University of California Press, 1984). Louis Althusser's most important writings are found in *For Marx* (London, Verso, 1996), *Lenin and Philosophy and Other Essays* (New York: Monthly Review Press, 2001), and with Etienne Balibar, *Reading Capital* (London: Verso, 1998). For Nicos Poulantzas, the two most important works in relationship to class are *Political Power and Social Classes* (London: NLB, 1973) and *Classes in Contemporary Capitalism* (London: NLB, 1975). Antonio Gramsci's most important writings are found in two collections: Quintin Hoare and Geoffrey Nowell-Smith (Eds), *Selections from the Prison Notebooks of Antonio Gramsci* (New York: International Publishers, 1971) and David Forgacs (Ed.), *The Gramsci Reader: Selected Writings, 1916–1935* (New York: New York University Press, 2000). An important essay on Gramsci is Perry Anderson, "The Antinomies of Antonio Gramsci," *New Left Review*, 1976, 100: 5–78. Erik Olin Wright's development can be traced by reading *Class, Crisis, and the State* (London: NLB, 1978), *Classes* (London: Verso, 1985), and *Class Counts: Comparative Studies in Class Analysis* (Cambridge: Cambridge University Press, 1997). Critical evaluations of Wright's thought comprise Erik Olin Wright et al., *The Debate on Classes* (London: Verso, 1998).

Currently, the best guide to the new social history is Geoff Eley, *A Crooked Line: From Cultural History to the History of Society* (Ann Arbor, MI: University of Michigan Press, 2005). The book is an intellectual memoir that traces the shift from "social" to "cultural" history. See also Georg G. Iggers, *New Directions in European Historiography* (Middletown, CT: Wesleyan University Press, 1975). For the *Annales* School, readers should consult Peter Burke, *The French Historical Revolution: The Annales School, 1929–89* (Stanford, CA: Stanford University Press, 1990) and Traian Stoianovich, *French Historical Method: The Annales Paradigm* (Ithaca, NY: Cornell University Press, 1976). For the British Marxist historians, especially E. P. Thompson, readers should begin with Harvey J. Kaye's highly sympathetic treatment, *The British Marxist Historians: An Introductory Analysis* (New York: Polity Press, 1984), followed by Dennis Dworkin's more critical one: *Cultural Marxism in Postwar Britain: History, the New Left and the Origins of Cultural Studies* (Durham, NC: Duke University Press, 1997).

E. P. Thompson's two masterpieces of social history are *The Making of the English Working Class* (Harmondsworth: Penguin, 1968) and *Whigs and*

Hunters: The Origin of the Black Act (New York: Pantheon Books, 1975). Also see Dorothy Thompson (Ed.), *The Essential E. P. Thompson* (New York: New Press, 2001). In addition to the discussion of Thompson's work in Kaye and Dworkin cited above, the reader should look at Bryan D. Palmer's *The Making of E. P. Thompson: Marxism, Humanism, and History* (Toronto: New Hogtown Press, 1981) and *E. P. Thompson: Objections and Oppositions* (London: Verso, 1994). Also important is Harvey J. Kaye and Keith McClelland (Eds), *E. P. Thompson: Critical Perspectives* (Philadelphia, PA: Temple University Press, 1990).

Chapter 3

In this chapter I analyzed shifts in the social sciences and the humanities that comprise the "cultural" or "linguistic" turn and that converge with post-modernist thought and the idea of postmodernity. These changes have some-times directly, sometimes indirectly, affected class theory and analysis. There are endless books describing the nature of the linguistic turn. In my own reading, three stand out: Terry Eagleton, *Literary Theory: An Introduction* (Minneapolis, MN: University of Minnesota Press, 1983), Richard Harland, *Superstructuralism: The Philosophy of Structuralism and Poststructuralism* (London: Methuen, 1987), and Terence Hawkes, *Structuralism and Semiotics* (Berkeley, CA: University of California Press, 1977). For an overview of cul-tural theory and cultural studies, no text is better than Chris Barker, *Cultural Studies: Theory and Practice* (London: Sage, 2000). In addition, readers should consult Francis Mulhern, *Culture/Metaculture* (London: Routledge, 2000). Also important here are the essays that constitute Lawrence Grossberg *et al.* (Eds), *Cultural Studies* (New York: Routledge, 1992). For British cultural studies, an excellent survey is Graeme Turner, *British Cultural Studies: An Introduction* (New York: Routledge, 3rd Edn 2003). A historical treatment of early British cultural studies is found in Dworkin (cited under Chapter 2). The best introduction to Stuart Hall's writings is the essays, interviews, and critical responses that constitute David Morley and Kuan-Hsing Chen (Eds), *Stuart Hall: Critical Dialogues in Cultural Studies* (London: Routledge, 1996). Valuable essays on Hall are found in Paul Gilroy *et al.* (Eds), *Without Guarantees: In Honour of Stuart Hall* (London: Verso, 2000).

The literature on postmodernism and postmodernity, like that on the lin-guistic turn, is seemingly infinite. For the historically minded, there is no bet-ter introduction to the subject than Hans Bertens, *The Idea of the Postmodern:*

A History (London: Routledge, 1995). In addition, see the following: David Harvey, *The Condition of Postmodernity: An Enquiry into the Origins of Cultural Change* (Oxford: Blackwell, 1989), Fredric Jameson, *Postmodernism, or, The Cultural Logic of Late Capitalism* (Durham, NC: Duke University Press, 1991), and Charles Jencks, *What is Post-Modernism?* (London: Academy Editions, 3rd Rev. and Enlarged Edn 1989). The attempt to couple Gramsci and postmodernism is found in Stuart Hall and Martin Jacques (Eds), *New Times: The Changing Face of Politics in the 1990s* (London: Verso, 1990). The "classic" text of post-Marxist political theory is Ernesto Laclau and Chantal Mouffe, *Hegemony and Socialist Strategy: Towards a Radical Democratic Politics* (London: Verso, 1985). An important refutation of post-Marxism is found in Ellen Meiksins Wood, *The Retreat from Class: A New "True" Socialism* (London: Verso, Rev. Edn 1998).

The crisis of class theory in sociology is the subject of David J. Lee and Bryan S. Turner (Eds), *Conflicts About Class: Debating Inequality in Late Industrialism: A Selection of Readings* (London: Longman, 1996). Readers should also look at Crompton (cited under Introduction), Rosemary Crompton *et al.* (Eds), *Renewing Class Analysis* (Oxford: Blackwell/The Sociological Review, 2000), John R. Hall (Ed.), *Reworking Class* (Ithaca, NY: Cornell University Press, 1997), and Scott G. McNall *et al.* (Eds), *Bringing Class Back in: Contemporary and Historical Perspectives* (Boulder, CO: Westview Press, 1991).

To discover more about radical critiques of the tenets of sociology, social theory, and the structure–action model – all of which implicitly and explicitly involve attacks on class theory – a good place to begin is with Joyce (cited under Introduction). See also Peter Beilharz *et al.* (Eds), *Between Totalitarianism and Postmodernity: A Thesis Eleven Reader* (Cambridge, MA: MIT Press, 1992). Zygmunt Bauman's important books in this context are *Intimations of Postmodernity* (London: Routledge, 1992), *Postmodern Ethics* (Oxford: Blackwell, 1993) and *Postmodernity and its Discontents* (New York: New York University Press, 1997). The most influential works of Jean Baudrillard are found in Mark Poster (Eds), *Selected Writings: Jean Baudrillard* (Stanford, CA: Stanford University Press, 2nd Edn 2001).

Chapter 4

A groundbreaking text on cultural history is Lynn Hunt (Ed.), *The New Cultural History* (Berkeley, CA: University of California Press, 1989). Geoff

Eley's reflections on the historical profession give great insights into the rise of cultural history. See "Is All the World a Text? From Social History to the History of Society Two Decades Later," in *The Historic Turn in the Human Sciences*, Ed. by Terrence J. McDonald (Ann Arbor, MI: University of Michigan Press, 1996, pp. 93–243) and *A Crooked Line* (cited under Chapter 2).

No thinker has been more influential on the new cultural history than Michel Foucault. Two collections of Foucault's writings are good introductions to the range of his thought: Paul Rabinow (Ed.), *The Foucault Reader* (New York: Pantheon Books, 1984) and Paul Rabinow and Nikolas Rose (Eds), *The Essential Foucault: Selections from the Essential Works of Foucault, 1954–1984* (New York: New Press, 2003). An accessible overview to Foucault's thought is Sara Mills, *Michel Foucault* (London: Routledge, 2003). Foucault's relevance for historians is analyzed in Patrick H. Hutton, "The Foucault Phenomenon and Contemporary French Historiography," *Historical Reflections/Réflexions Historiques*, 1991, 17: 77–102. Critical to shifts in French historiography are debates on the French Revolution. Anthologies that capture trends in recent scholarship on the revolutionary decades are Gary Kates (Ed.), *The French Revolution: Recent Debates and New Controversies* (London: Routledge, 1998) and Ronald Schechter (Ed.), *The French Revolution: The Essential Readings* (Malden, MA: Blackwell, 2001). A revisionist Marxist perspective is found in George C. Comninel, *Rethinking the French Revolution: Marxism and the Revisionist Challenge* (London: Verso, 1987).

The impact of the cultural and linguistic turn on French social and labor history is the subject of Lenard R. Berlanstein (Ed.), *Rethinking Labor History: Essays on Discourse and Class Analysis* (Urbana, IL: University of Illinois Press, 1993). For William Reddy, see "The Concept of Class," in *Social Orders and Social Classes in Europe since 1500: Studies in Social Stratification*, Ed. by M. L. Bush (London: Longman, 1992, pp. 13–25). William Sewell's attempt to grapple with the linguistic turn is found in "Toward a Post-Materialist Rhetoric for Labor History," in *Rethinking Labor History*, pp. 15–38 (cited above). Sewell's recent theoretical reflections have been published as *Logics of History: Social Theory and Social Transformation* (Chicago, IL: University of Chicago Press, 2005). Jacques Rancière's major work in the field of labor history is *The Nights of Labor: The Workers' Dream in Nineteenth-Century France* (Philadelphia, PA: Temple University Press, 1989). Not to be missed is Donald Reid's introduction (pp. xv–xxxvii).

Chapter 5

Readers can learn about recent trends in British social history by consulting David Cannadine, *Class in Britain* (London: Penguin, 2000) and James Thompson, "After the Fall: Class and Political Language in Britain, 1780–1900," *The Historical Journal*, 1996, 39: 785–806. The historical development of Chartist historiography is sketched out by two of its leading contemporary interpreters – Gareth Stedman Jones and Dorothy Thompson. See the former's "Rethinking Chartism," in *Languages of Class: Studies in English Working Class History, 1832–1983* (Cambridge: Cambridge University Press, 1983, pp. 90–178) and the latter's "Chartism and the Historians," in *Outsiders: Class, Gender and Nation* (London: Verso, 1993, pp. 19–44). Also important is Miles Taylor, "Rethinking the Chartists: Searching for Synthesis in the Historiography of Chartism," *The Historical Journal*, 1996, 39: 479–95. Thompson's key works are *The Early Chartists* (Columbia, SC: University of South Carolina Press, 1971) and *The Chartists: Popular Politics and the Industrial Revolution* (London: Temple Smith, 1984). For Stedman Jones, the pivotal text is, of course, *The Languages of Class* (cited above). Stedman Jones's later views are found in "The Determinist Fix: Some Obstacles to the Further Development of the Linguistic Approach to History in the 1990s," *History Workshop Journal*, 1996, 42: 19–35.

To better appreciate debates surrounding Stedman Jones's – and subsequently Patrick Joyce's – work, it is important to view them in the context of earlier controversies within British Marxism and later ones regarding postmodernism. The Marxist intellectual milieu is discussed in Dworkin (cited under Chapter 2). For the impact of postmodernism on historiography, a good starting point is Keith Jenkins (Ed.), *The Postmodern History Reader* (London: Routledge, 1997). Two books by Alun Munslow are also important: *Deconstructing History* (London: Routledge, 1997) and *The New History* (Harlow, England: Pearson Longman, 2003).

For Patrick Joyce – the most articulate advocate of postmodernism among British social/cultural historians – the following are important: the edited collection *The Historical Meanings of Work* (Cambridge: Cambridge University Press, 1987), *Visions of the People: Industrial England and the Question of Class, 1848–1914* (Cambridge: Cambridge University Press, 1991), and *Democratic Subjects: The Self and the Social in Nineteenth-Century England* (Cambridge: Cambridge University Press, 1994). For James Vernon, see *Politics and the People: A Study in English Political Culture, c.1815–1867* (Cambridge: Cambridge University Press, 1993). Thompsonian social history and the tradition of Chartist historiography as developed by Dorothy Thompson is defended in Neville Kirk (Ed.), *Social Class and Marxism: Defences and Challenges* (Aldershot, England: Scolar Press, 1996). James Epstein has sought to create a dialog between the cultural Marxist tradition and the linguistic turn. See *In Practice: Studies in the Language and Culture of Popular Politics in Modern Britain* (Stanford, CA: Stanford University Press, 2003).

Chapter 6

Good introductions to the variety of feminisms are two highly readable surveys: Imelda Whelehan, *Modern Feminist Thought: From the Second Wave to "Post-Feminism"* (New York: New York University Press, 1995) and Rosemarie Putnam Tong, *Feminist Thought: A More Comprehensive Introduction* (Boulder, CO: Westview Press, 2nd Edn 1998). A reader that includes excerpts from many of the most influential feminist texts is Maggie Humm (Ed.), *Modern Feminisms: Political, Literary, Cultural* (New York: Columbia University Press, 1992). Black feminism is explored in Patricia Hill Collins, *Black Feminist Thought: Knowledge, Consciousness, and the Politics of Empowerment* (New York: Routledge, 2nd Edn 2000). A good introduction to British feminism is Terry Lovell (Ed.), *British Feminist Thought: A Reader* (Oxford: Blackwell, 1990). Sheila Rowbotham is undoubtedly the most influential British feminist historian associated with 1970s women's history and remains the best known to this day. Her prodigious output includes *Hidden from History: 300 Years of Women's Oppression and the Fight Against It* (London: Pluto Press, 1973) and *A Century of Women: The History of Women in Britain and the United States in the Twentieth Century* (New York: Penguin, 1999).

For the relationship between gender and history, readers should begin with Laura Lee Downs, *Writing Gender History* (London: Hodder Arnold, 2004). From there, they should move on to Laura L. Frader and Sonya O. Rose (Eds), *Gender and Class in Modern Europe* (Ithaca, NY: Cornell University Press, 1996) and Robert Shoemaker and Mary Vincent (Eds), *Gender and History in Western Europe* (London: Arnold, 1998). Joan Scott's pathbreaking essays of the 1980s are found in *Gender and the Politics of History* (New York: Columbia University Press, 1988). Responses to Scott's 1980s essays are voluminous. A good indication of what is stake is found in the exchange between Laura Lee Downs and Scott in *Comparative Studies in Society and*

History, 1993, 35: Downs, "If 'Woman' is Just an Empty Category, Then Why Am I Afraid to Walk Alone at Night? Identity Politics Meets the Postmodern Subject," pp. 414–37, Scott, "The Tip of the Volcano," pp. 438–43, and Downs, "Reply to Joan Scott," pp. 444–51.

The pathbreaking British-history text that explores the relationship between gender and class is Leonore Davidoff and Catherine Hall, *Family Fortunes: Men and Women of the English Middle Class, 1780–1850* (London: Routledge, Rev. Edn 2002). Noteworthy is the new introduction, which reflects on the book in light of subsequent research and debates. For Hall's development see *White, Male and Middle-Class: Explorations in Feminism and History* (New York: Routledge, 1992); for Davidoff's see *Worlds Between: Historical Perspectives on Gender and Class* (New York: Routledge, 1995).

For the gendering of the working class, the best starting point is Theodore Koditschek, "The Gendering of the British Working Class," *Gender and History*, 1997, 9: 333–363. In addition to Anna Clark, *The Struggle for the Breeches: Gender and the Making of the British Working Class* (Berkeley: University of California Press, 1995) and Sonya O. Rose, *Limited Livelihoods: Gender and Class in Nineteenth-Century England* (Berkeley, CA: University of California Press, 1992), two important books are Deborah Valenze, *The First Industrial Woman* (New York: Oxford University Press, 1995) and Ellen Ross, *Love and Toil: Motherhood in Outcast London, 1870–1918* (New York: Oxford University Press, 1993). Besides *Landscape for a Good Woman: A Story of Two Lives* (London: Virago, 1986), Carolyn Steedman's work pertaining to class and gender includes "Culture, Cultural Studies, and the Historians," in *Cultural Studies*, pp. 613–22 (cited under Chapter 3) and "The Price of Experience: Women and the Making of the English Working Class," *Radical History Review*, 1994, 59: 109–119.

Chapter 7

Stuart Hall's and Paul Gilroy's ideas about race and class developed in the context of the now defunct Centre for Contemporary Cultural Studies at the University of Birmingham. For an introduction to the Centre's work in the 1960s and 1970s see Dworkin (cited under Chapter 2) and Turner (cited under Chapter 3). For black British cultural studies, see Houston A. Baker Jr. *et al.* (Eds), *Black British Cultural Studies: A Reader* (Chicago, IL: University of Chicago Press, 1996) and Kwesi Owusu (Ed.), *Black British*

Culture and Society: A Text Reader (London: Routledge, 2000). Citations for Hall's work can be found under chapter three above. Gilroy's trajectory can be traced via *"There Ain't No Black in the Union Jack": The Cultural Politics of Race and Nation* (Chicago: University of Chicago Press 1991), *The Black Atlantic: Modernity and Double Consciousness* (London: Verso, 1993), and *Against Race: Imagining Political Culture Beyond the Color Line* (Cambridge, MA: Harvard University Press, 2000).

Robin Kelley's principal works are *Hammer and Hoe: Alabama Communists during the Great Depression* (Chapel Hill, NC: University of North Carolina Press, 1990), *Race Rebels: Culture, Politics, and the Black Working Class* (New York: Free Press, 1994), *Yo' Mama's Disfunktional!: Fighting the Culture Wars in Urban America* (Boston, MA: Beacon Press, 1997), and *Freedom Dreams: The Black Radical Imagination* (Boston, MA: Beacon Press, 2002). The black radical tradition is magnificently captured by Cedric Robinson in *Black Marxism: The Making of the Black Radical Tradition* (Chapel Hill, NC: University of North Carolina Press, 2000), with a superb foreword by Kelley, who situates Robinson's work in its broader intellectual and political context and teases out its importance.

"Whiteness" scholarship is a small industry. An indication of its range is found in Mike Hill (Ed.), *Whiteness: A Critical Reader* (New York: New York University Press, 1997), and a useful introduction is found in David W. Stowe, "Uncolored People: The Rise of Whiteness Studies," *Lingua Franca*, 1996, September–October: 68–77. Among historical studies of whiteness, there is Theodore Allen's two-volume *The Invention of the White Race* (London: Verso) [*Radical Oppression and Social Control* (Vol. 1, 1994) and *The Origin of Radical Oppression in Anglo-America* (Vol. 2, 1997)], Noel Ignatiev, *How the Irish Became White* (New York: Routledge, 1995), George Lipsitz, *The Possessive Investment in Whiteness: How White People Profit from Identity Politics* (Philadelphia, PA: Temple University Press, 1998), Eric Lott, *Love and Theft: Blackface Minstrelsy and the American Working Class* (New York: Oxford University Press, 1993), Michael Paul Rogin, *Blackface, White Noise: Jewish Immigrants in the Hollywood Melting Pot* (Berkeley, CA: University of California Press, 1996), and Alexander Saxton, *The Rise and Fall of the White Republic: Class Politics and Mass Culture in Nineteenth-Century America* (London: Verso, 1990). David Roediger's major works are *The Wages of Whiteness: Race and the Making of the American Working Class* (London: Verso, Rev. Edn 1999), *Towards the Abolition of Whiteness: Essays on Race, Politics, and Working Class History* (London: Verso, 1994), and *Colored White: Transcending the Racial Past* (Berkeley, CA: University of California Press, 2002).

Chapter 8

A starting point for exploring Subaltern Studies is the two collections of the group's work edited by Ranajit Guha: the earlier phase (edited with Gayatri Chakravorty Spivak), *Selected Subaltern Studies* (New York: Oxford University Press, 1988) and the later phase, *A Subaltern Studies Reader, 1986–1995* (Minneapolis, MN: University of Minnesota Press, 1997). In writing this chapter I drew heavily on the writings of Dipesh Chakrabarty and Guha. For the former, see *Rethinking Working-Class History: Bengal, 1890–1940* (Princeton, NJ: Princeton University Press, 1989), *Provincializing Europe: Postcolonial Thought and Historical Difference* (Princeton, NJ: Princeton University Press, 2000), and *Habitations of Modernity: Essays in the Wake of Subaltern Studies* (Chicago: University of Chicago Press, 2002). For the latter, see *Elementary Aspects of Peasant Insurgency in Colonial India* (New Delhi: Oxford University Press, 1983) and *Dominance without Hegemony: History and Power in Colonial India* (Cambridge, MA: Harvard University Press, 1997). Selections of critical essays and debates on Subaltern Studies comprise Vinayak Chaturvedi (Ed.), *Mapping Subaltern Studies and the Postcolonial* (London: Verso, 2000) and David Ludden (Ed.), *Reading Subaltern Studies: Critical History, Contested Meaning and the Globalization of South Asia* (London: Anthem, 2002). A selection of essays by the Latin American Subaltern Studies collective is found in Ileana Rodríguez (Ed.), *The Latin American Subaltern Studies Reader* (Durham, NC: Duke University Press, 2001). David Lloyd's reflections on subaltern studies and postcolonial theory in relationship to Ireland are the subject of *Ireland After History* (Notre Dame, IN: University of Notre Dame Press in association with Field Day, 1999).

Like other important modes of thought, postcolonialism has a huge literature. Three anthologies that serve as introductions are Bill Ashcroft *et al.* (Eds), *The Post-Colonial Studies Reader* (London: Routledge, 1996), Padmini Mongia (Ed.), *Contemporary Postcolonial Theory: A Reader* (London: Arnold, 1995), and Patrick Williams and Laura Chrisman (Eds), *Colonial Discourse and Post-Colonial Theory* (New York, Columbia University Press, 1994). Good introductions to postcolonial theory are Bill Ashcroft *et al.*, *Key Concepts in Post-Colonial Studies* (London: Routledge, 1998) and Leela Gandhi, *Postcolonial Theory: A Critical Introduction* (Edinburgh: Edinburgh University Press, 1998). In my view Robert J. C. Young is unparalleled among commentators and critics of postcolonial theory. His *Postcolonialism: A Very Short Introduction* (Oxford: Oxford University Press, 2003) provides a point of entry to his work. His *Postcolonialism: An Historical Introduction* (Malden, MA: Blackwell, 2001) is unsurpassed.

References

Alexander, Sally (1984) "Women, Class and Sexual Differences in the 1830s and 1840s: Some Reflections on the Writing of Feminist History," *History Workshop Journal*, 17: 125–49.

Alexander, Sally and Davin, Anna (1976) "Feminist History," *History Workshop Journal*, 1: 4–6.

Allen, Theodore (1994) *The Invention of the White Race: Racial Oppression and Social Control*, Vol. 1, London: Verso.

Allen, Theodore (1997) *The Invention of the White Race: The Origin of Racial Oppression in Anglo-America*, Vol. 2, London: Verso.

Amin, Shahid ([1984] 1988) "Gandhi as Mahatma: Gorakhpur District, Eastern UP, 1921-2," in Ranajit Guha and Gayatri Chakravorty Spivak (Eds), *Selected Subaltern Studies*, New York: Oxford University Press, pp. 288–348.

Amin, Shahid and Bhadra, Gautam (1994) "Ranajit Guha: A Biographical Sketch," in David Arnold and David Hardiman (Eds), *Subaltern Studies VIII: Essays in Honour of Ranajit Guha*, New Delhi: Oxford University Press, pp. 222–25.

Aminzade, Ronald (1993) "Class Analysis, Politics, and French Labor History," in Lenard R. Berlanstein (Ed.), *Rethinking Labor History*, Urbana, IL: University of Illinois Press, pp. 90–113.

Anderson, Perry (1992) *English Questions*, London: Verso.

Arnesen, Eric (2001a) "Whiteness and the Historians' Imagination," *International Labor and Working-Class History*, 60: 3–32.

Arnesen, Eric (2001b) "Assessing Whiteness Scholarship: A Response to James Barrett, David Brody, Barbara Fields, Eric Foner, Victoria Hattam, and Adolph Reed," *International Labor and Working-Class History*, 60: 81–92.

Arnold, David ([1987] 1988) "Touching the Body: Perspectives on the Indian Plague: 1896-1900," in Ranajit Guha and Gayatri Chakravorty Spivak (Eds), *Selected Subaltern Studies*, New York: Oxford University Press, pp. 391–426.

Arnold, David ([1984] 2000) "Gramsci and Peasant Subalternity in India," in Vinayak Chaturvedi (Ed.), *Mapping Subaltern Studies and the Postcolonial*, London: Verso, pp. 24–49.

Arnold, David and Hardiman, David (1994) "Preface," in David Arnold and David Hardiman (Eds), *Subaltern Studies VIII: Essays in Honour of Ranajit Guha*, New Delhi: Oxford University Press.

Ashcroft, Bill, Griffiths, Gareth and Tiffin, Helen (1998) *Key Concepts in Post-Colonial Studies*, London: Routledge.

Auslander, Leora (1993) "Perceptions of Beauty and the Problem of Consciousness: Parisian Furniture Makers," in Lenard R. Berlanstein (Ed.), *Rethinking Labor History: Essays on Discourse and Class Analysis*, Urbana, IL: University of Illinois Press, pp. 149–81.

Baker, Houston A., Jr, Diawara, Manthia and Lindeborg, Ruth H. (Eds) (1996) *Black British Cultural Studies: A Reader*, Chicago, IL: University of Chicago Press.

Barker, Chris (2000) *Cultural Studies: Theory and Practice*, London: Sage.

Barrett, James R. (2001) "Whiteness Studies: Anything Here for Historians of the Working Class?," *International Labor and Working-Class History*, 60: 33–42.

Barrett, Michèle ([1980] 1988) *Women's Oppression Today: The Marxist/Feminist Encounter*, Rev. Edn, London: Verso.

Bauman, Zygmunt (1992) *Intimations of Postmodernity*, London: Routledge.

Belchem, John and Kirk, Neville (Eds) (1997) *Languages of Labour*, Aldershot, England: Ashgate.

Bell, Daniel (1973) *The Coming of Post-Industrial Society: A Venture in Social Forecasting*, New York: Basic Books.

Benenson, Harold (1983) "Victorian Sexual Ideology and Marx's Theory of the Working Class," *International Labor and Working-Class History*, 25: 1–23.

Berlanstein, Lenard R. (1993a) "Introduction," in Lenard R. Berlanstein (Ed.), *Rethinking Labor History: Essays on Discourse and Class Analysis*, Urbana, IL: University of Illinois Press, pp. 1–14.

Berlanstein, Lenard R. (Ed.) (1993b) *Rethinking Labor History: Essays on Discourse and Class Analysis*, Urbana, IL: University of Illinois Press.

Bertens, Hans (1995) *The Idea of the Postmodern: A History*, London: Routledge.

Bhadra, Gautam ([1985] 1988) "Four Rebels of Eighteen-Fifty-Seven," in Ranajit Guha and Gayatri Chakravorty Spivak (Eds), *Selected Subaltern Studies*, New York: Oxford University Press, pp. 129–75.

Bourdieu, Pierre (1987) "What Makes a Social Class? On the Theoretical and Practical Existence of Groups," *Berkeley Journal of Sociology*, 32: 1–17.

Braudel, Fernand ([1949] 1972) *The Mediterranean and the Mediterranean World in the Age of Philip II*, New York: Harper & Row.

Braudel, Fernand (1981) *Civilization and Capitalism, 15th–18th Century*, New York: Harper & Row.

Briggs, Asa (Ed.) (1959) *Chartist Studies*, London: Macmillan.

Briggs, Asa ([1960] 1985) "The Language of 'Class' in Early Nineteenth-Century England," *The Collected Essays of Asa Briggs*, Vol. 1, Urbana, IL: University of Illinois Press, pp. 3–33.

Brody, David (2001) "Charismatic History: Pros and Cons," *International Labor and Working-Class History*, 60: 43–47.

Brown, Elsa Barkley ([1989] 1996) "Womanist Consciousness: Maggie Lena Walker and the Independent Order of Saint Luke," in Joan Wallach Scott (Ed.), *Feminism and History*, Oxford: Oxford University Press, pp. 453–76.

Buhle, Paul (1996) "Race Rebels, Class Rebels," *Monthly Review: An Independent Socialist Magazine*, 47: 41–48.

Burke, Peter (1980) *Sociology and History*, London: George Allen & Unwin.

Calvert, Peter (1982) *The Concept of Class: An Historical Introduction*, London: Hutchinson.

Cannadine, David (2000) *Class in Britain*, London: Penguin.

Canning, Kathleen (1992) "Gender and the Politics of Class Formation: Rethinking German Labor History," *The American Historical Review*, 97: 736–68.

Canning, Kathleen (1994) "Feminist History after the Linguistic Turn: Historicizing Discourse and Experience," *Signs: Journal of Women in Culture and Society*, 19: 368–404.

Chakrabarty, Dipesh (1985) "Invitation to a Dialogue," in Ranajit Guha (Ed.), *Subaltern Studies IV*, New Delhi: Oxford University Press, pp. 364–76.

Chakrabarty, Dipesh ([1983] 1988) "Conditions for Knowledge of Working-Class Conditions: Employers, Government and the Jute Workers of Calcutta, 1890–1940," in Ranajit Guha and Gayatri Chakravorty Spivak (Eds), *Selected Subaltern Studies*, New York: Oxford University Press, pp. 179–230.

Chakrabarty, Dipesh (2000) *Provincializing Europe: Postcolonial Thought and Historical Difference*, Princeton, NJ: Princeton University Press.

Chakrabarty, Dipesh (2002) *Habitations of Modernity: Essays in the Wake of Subaltern Studies*, Chicago, IL: University of Chicago Press.

Chandavarkar, Rajnarayan ([1997] 2000) "'The Making of the Working Class': E. P. Thompson and Indian History," in Vinayak Chaturvedi (Ed.), *Mapping Subaltern Studies and the Postcolonial*, London: Verso, pp. 50–71.

Chartier, Roger (1988) *Cultural History: Between Practices and Representations*, Ithaca, NY: Cornell University Press.

Chatterjee, Partha ([1983] 1988) "More on Modes of Power and the Peasantry," in Ranajit Guha and Gayatri Chakravorty Spivak (Eds), *Selected Subaltern Studies*, New York: Oxford University Press, pp. 351–90.

Chatterjee, Partha (1999) "Partha Chatterjee: In Conversation with Anuradha Dingwaney Needham, Oberlin College," *Interventions: International Journal of Postcolonial Studies*, 1: 413–25.

Chaturvedi, Vinayak (Ed.) (2000a) *Mapping Subaltern Studies and the Postcolonial*, London: Verso.

Chaturvedi, Vinayak (2000b) "Introduction," in Vinayak Chaturvedi (Ed.), *Mapping Subaltern Studies and the Postcolonial*, London: Verso, pp. vii–xix.

Childs, Michael (1998) "Labor History," in D. R. Woolf (Ed.), *A Global Encyclopedia of Historical Writing*, Vol. 2, New York: Garland Publishing, pp. 525–28.

Clark, Alice ([1919] 1982) *Working Life of Women in the Seventeenth Century*, London: Routledge & Kegan Paul.

Clark, Anna (1995) *The Struggle for the Breeches: Gender and the Making of the British Working Class*, Berkeley, CA: University of California Press.

Cohen, Patricia (2004) "Forget Lonely. Life is Healthy at the Top," *New York Times*, 15 May.

Contemporary Authors Online (2001) "Leonore Davidoff". The Gale Group, available online from The Literature Resource Center: www.gale.com/LitRC.

Corfield, Penelope J. (1991) "Class by Name and Number in Eighteenth-Century Britain," in Penelope J. Corfield (Ed.), *Language, History and Class*, Oxford: Basil Blackwell, pp. 101–30.

Cott, Nancy F. ([1977] 1997) *The Bonds of Womanhood: "Woman's Sphere" in New England, 1780–1835*, 2nd Edn, New Haven, CT: Yale University Press.

Crompton, Rosemary (1996) "Gender and Class Analysis," in David J. Lee and Bryan S. Turner (Eds), *Conflicts About Class: Debating Inequality in Late Industrialism: A Selection of Readings*, London: Longman, pp. 115–26.

Crompton, Rosemary (1998) *Class and Stratification: An Introduction to Current Debates*, 2nd Edn, Cambridge: Polity Press.

Cronin, James E. (1986) "Language, Politics and the Critique of Social History," *Journal of Social History*, 20: 177–84.

Davidoff, Leonore (1995) *Worlds Between: Historical Perspectives on Gender and Class*, New York: Routledge.

Davidoff, Leonore ([1974] 1995) "Mastered for Life: Servant and Wife in Victorian and Edwardian England," *Worlds Between: Historical Perspectives on Gender and Class*, New York: Routledge, pp. 18–40.

Davidoff, Leonore ([1979] 1995) "Class and Gender in Victorian England: The Case of Hannah Cullwick and A. J. Munby," *Worlds Between: Historical Perspectives on Gender and Class*, New York: Routledge, pp. 103–50.

Davidoff, Leonore and Hall, Catherine ([1987] 2002) *Family Fortunes: Men and Women of the English Middle Class, 1780–1850*, Rev. Edn, London: Routledge.

Dawley, Alan (1978–1979) "E. P. Thompson and the Peculiarities of the Americans," *Radical History Review*, 19: 33–60.

Derrida, Jacques (1976) *Of Grammatology*, Baltimore, MD: Johns Hopkins University Press.

Dickens, Charles ([1854] 2001) *Hard Times*, Norton Critical Edn, New York: W.W. Norton.

Dirlik, Arif ([1994] 1996) "The Aura of Postcolonialism: Third World Criticism in the Age of Global Capitalism," in Padmini Mongia (Ed.), *Contemporary Postcolonial Theory: A Reader*, London: Arnold, pp. 294–320.

Downs, Laura Lee (1993a) "If 'Woman' is Just an Empty Category, Then Why Am I Afraid to Walk Alone at Night? Identity Politics Meets the Postmodern Subject," *Comparative Studies in Society and History*, 35: 414–37.

Downs, Laura Lee (1993b) "Reply to Joan Scott," *Comparative Studies in Society and History*, 35: 444–51.

Downs, Laura Lee (2004) *Writing Gender History*, London: Hodder Arnold.

Doyle, William (1988) *Origins of the French Revolution*, 2nd Edn, Oxford: Oxford University Press.

Doyle, William (1990) "Reflections on the Classic Interpretation of the French Revolution," *French Historical Studies*, 61: 744–48.

Du Bois, W. E. B. ([1935] 1998) *Black Reconstruction in America, 1860–1880*, New York: Free Press.

Dworkin, Dennis (1997) *Cultural Marxism in Postwar Britain: History, the New Left and the Origins of Cultural Studies*, Durham, NC: Duke University Press.

Economist (2002) Editorial: "Marx after Communism," *Economist*, 21 December.

Eley, Geoff (1979) "Some Recent Tendencies in Social History," in Georg G. Iggers and Harold T. Parker (Eds), *International Handbook of Historical Studies: Contemporary Research and Theory*, Westport, CT: Greenwood Press, pp. 55–70.

Eley, Geoff (1996) "Is All the World a Text? From Social History to the History of Society Two Decades Later," in Terrence J. McDonald (Ed.), *The Historic Turn in the Human Sciences*, Ann Arbor, MI: University of Michigan Press, pp. 193–243.

Eley, Geoff (2005) *A Crooked Line: From Cultural History to the History of Society*, Ann Arbor, MI: University of Michigan Press.

Eley, Geoff and Nield, Keith (1980) "Why Does Social History Ignore Politics?," *Social History*, 5: 249–71.

Eley, Geoff and Nield, Keith (1995) "Starting Over: The Present, the Post-Modern and the Moment of Social History," *Social History*, 20: 355–64.

Eley, Geoff and Nield, Keith (2000) "Farewell to the Working Class?," *International Labor and Working-Class History*, 57: 1–30.

Eley, Geoff and Nield, Keith (2007) *The Future of Class in History: What's Left of the Social?* Ann Arbor, MI: University of Michigan Press.

Epstein, James (1986) "Rethinking the Categories of Working-Class History," *Labour/Le Travail*, 18: 195–208.

Epstein, James (1989) "Understanding the Cap of Liberty: Symbolic Practice and Social Conflict in Early Nineteenth-Century England," *Past and Present*, 122: 75–118.

Epstein, James (2003) *In Practice: Studies in the Language and Culture of Popular Politics in Modern Britain*, Stanford, CA: Stanford University Press.

Epstein, James and Thompson, Dorothy (Eds) (1982) *The Chartist Experience: Studies in Working-Class Radicalism and Culture, 1830–60*, London: Macmillan.

Fields, Barbara J. (1982) "Ideology and Race in American History," in J. Morgan Kousser and James M. McPherson (Eds), *Region, Race and Reconstruction: Essays in Honor of C. Vann Woodward*, New York, pp. 143–77.

Fields, Barbara J. (1990) "Slavery, Race and Ideology in the United States of America," *New Left Review*, 181: 95–118.

Fields, Barbara J. (2001) "Whiteness, Racism, and Identity," *International Labor and Working-Class History*, 60: 48–56.

Foner, Eric (2001) "Response to Eric Arnesen," *International Labor and Working-Class History*, 60: 57–60.

Forgacs, David (Ed.) (1988) *An Antonio Gramsci Reader: Selected Writings, 1916–1935*, New York: Schocken Books.

Foster, John (1974) *Class Struggle and the Industrial Revolution: Early Industrial Capitalism in Three English Towns*, New York: St. Martin's Press.

Foster, John (1985) "The Declassing of Language," *New Left Review*, 150: 29–45.

Foucault, Michel (1980) *Power/Knowledge: Selected Interviews and Other Writings, 1972–1977*, New York: Pantheon Books.

Genovese, Eugene D. (1974) *Roll, Jordan, Roll: The World the Slaves Made*, New York: Pantheon Books.

Gerth, H. H. and Mills, C. Wright (Eds) ([1946] 1958) *From Max Weber: Essays in Sociology*, New York: Oxford University Press.

Giddens, Anthony (1975) *The Class Structure of the Advanced Societies*, New York: Harper & Row.

Giddens, Anthony (1982) "Hermeneutics and Social Theory," *Profiles and Critiques in Social Theory*, Berkeley, CA: University of California Press, pp. 1–17.

Gilroy, Paul ([1987] 1991) *"There Ain't No Black in the Union Jack": The Cultural Politics of Race and Nation*, Chicago, CA: University of Chicago Press.

Gilroy, Paul (1993) *The Black Atlantic: Modernity and Double Consciousness*, London: Verso.

Gilroy, Paul (1996) "British Cultural Studies and the Pitfalls of Identity," in Houston A. Baker, Jr., Manthia Diawara and Ruth H. Lindeborg (Eds), *Black British Cultural Studies: A Reader*, Chicago, IL: University of Chicago Press, pp. 223–39.

Goldthorpe, John H. (1984) "The End of Convergence: Corporatist and Dualist Tendencies in Modern Western Societies," in John H. Goldthorpe (Ed.), *Order and Conflict in Contemporary Capitalism*, Oxford: Oxford University Press, pp. 315–43.

Goldthorpe, John H. and Lockwood, David (1963) "Affluence and the British Class Structure," *Sociological Review*, 11: 133–63.

Goldthorpe, John H. and Marshall, Gordon ([1992] 1996) "The Promising Future of Class Analysis," in David J. Lee and Bryan S. Turner (Eds), *Conflicts About Class: Debating Inequality in Late Industrialism: A Selection of Readings*, London: Longman, pp. 98–109.

Goldthorpe, John H., Lockwood, David, Bechhofer, Frank and Platt, Jennifer (1969) *The Affluent Worker in the Class Structure*, London: Cambridge University Press.

Gorz, André (1982) *Farewell to the Working Class: An Essay on Post-Industrial Socialism*, Boston, MA: South End Press.

Gray, Robert (1986) "The Deconstructing of the English Working Class," *Social History*, 11: 363–73.

Guha, Ranajit (1983) *Elementary Aspects of Peasant Insurgency in Colonial India*, Delhi: Oxford.

Guha, Ranajit ([1982] 1988a) "On Some Aspects of the Historiography of Colonial India," in Ranajit Guha and Gayatri Chakravorty Spivak (Eds), *Selected Subaltern Studies*, New York: Oxford University Press, pp. 37–44.

Guha, Ranajit ([1982] 1988b) "Preface," in Ranajit Guha and Gayatri Chakravorty Spivak (Eds), *Selected Subaltern Studies*, New York: Oxford University Press, pp. 35–36.

Guha, Ranajit ([1983] 1988) "The Prose of Counter-Insurgency," in Ranajit Guha and Gayatri Chakravorty Spivak (Eds), *Selected Subaltern Studies*, New York: Oxford University Press, pp. 45–86.

Guha, Ranajit (1996) "The Small Voice of History," in Shahid Amin and Dipesh Chakrabarty (Eds), *Subaltern Studies IX*, New Delhi: Oxford University Press, pp. 1–12.

Guha, Ranajit (1997a) "Introduction," in Ranajit Guha (Ed.), *A Subaltern Studies Reader, 1986–1995*, Minneapolis, MN: University of Minnesota Press, pp. ix–xxii.

Guha, Ranajit (Ed.) (1997b) *A Subaltern Studies Reader, 1986–1995*, Minneapolis, MN: University of Minnesota Press.

Guha, Ranajit (1997c) *Dominance without Hegemony: History and Power in Colonial India*, Cambridge, MA: Harvard University Press.

Guha, Ranajit (2001) "Subaltern Studies: Projects for Our Time and Their Convergence," in Ileana Rodríguez (Ed.), *The Latin American Subaltern Studies Reader*, Durham, NC: Duke University Press, pp. 35–46.

Guha, Ranajit and Spivak, Gayatri Chakravorty (Eds) (1988) *Selected Subaltern Studies*, New York: Oxford University Press.

Gullickson, Gay L. (1993) "Commentary: New Labor History from the Perspective of a Women's Historian," in Lenard R. Berlanstein (Ed.), *Rethinking Labor History: Essays on Discourse and Class Analysis*, Urbana, IL: University of Illinois Press, pp. 200–13.

Gutman, Herbert George (1976) *Work, Culture, and Society in Industrializing America: Essays in American Working-Class and Social History*, New York: Knopf.

Hall, Catherine (1991) "Politics, Post-Structuralism and Feminist History," *Gender and History*, 3: 204–10.

Hall, Catherine (1992a) *White, Male and Middle-Class: Explorations in Feminism and History*, New York: Routledge.

Hall, Catherine (1992b) "White Identities," *New Left Review*, 193: 114–19.

Hall, Catherine (2002) *Civilising Subjects: Colony and Metropole in the English Imagination, 1830–1867*, Chicago, IL: University of Chicago Press.

Hall, John R. (1997) "The Reworking of Class Analysis," in John R. Hall (Ed.), *Reworking Class*, Ithaca, NY: Cornell University Press, pp. 1–37.

Hall, Stuart (1988) *The Hard Road to Renewal: Thatcherism and the Crisis of the Left*, London: Verso.

Hall, Stuart (1992) "Cultural Studies and its Theoretical Legacies," in Lawrence Grossberg, Cary Nelson and Paula A. Treichler (Eds), *Cultural Studies*, New York: Routledge, pp. 277–94.

Hall, Stuart ([1980] 1996) "Race, Articulation, and Societies Structured in Dominance," in Houston A. Baker Jr., Manthia Diawara, and Ruth H. Lindeborg (Eds), *Black British Cultural Studies: A Reader*, Chicago, IL: University of Chicago Press, pp. 16–60.

Hall, Stuart ([1986] 1996) "On Postmodernism and Articulation: An Interview with Stuart Hall," in David Morley and Kuan-Hsing Chen (Eds), *Stuart Hall: Critical Dialogues in Cultural Studies*, London: Routledge, pp. 131–50.

Hall, Stuart ([1989] 1996) "New Ethnicities," in David Morley and Kuan-Hsing Chen (Eds), *Stuart Hall: Critical Dialogues in Cultural Studies*, London: Routledge, pp. 441–49.

Hall, Stuart ([1992] 1996) "What Is This 'Black' in Black Popular Culture?," in David Morley and Kuan-Hsing Chen (Eds), *Stuart Hall: Critical Dialogues in Cultural Studies*, London: Routledge, pp. 465–75.

Hall, Stuart and Jacques, Martin (Eds) (1990) *New Times: The Changing Face of Politics in the 1990s*, London: Verso.

Hall, Stuart and Jefferson, Tony (Eds) (1976) *Resistance through Rituals: Youth Subcultures in Post-War Britain*, London: Hutchinson.

Hall, Stuart and Whannel, Paddy (1964) *The Popular Arts*, London: Hutchinson Educational.

Hall, Stuart, Critcher, Chas, Jefferson, Tony, Clarke, John and Roberts, Brian (1978) *Policing the Crisis: Mugging, the State, and Law and Order*, London: Macmillan.

Hardiman, David (1986) "'Subaltern Studies' at Crossroads," *Economic and Political Weekly*, 21: 288–90.

Hartmann, Heidi ([1979] 1981) "The Unhappy Marriage of Marxism and Feminism: Towards a More Progressive Union," in Lydia Sargent (Ed.), *Women and Revolution: A Discussion of the Unhappy Marriage of Marxism and Feminism*, Boston, MA: South End Press, pp. 1–41.

Hattam, Victoria C. (2001) "Whiteness: Theorizing Race, Eliding Ethnicity," *International Labor and Working-Class History*, 60: 61–68.

Hawkes, Terence (1977) *Structuralism and Semiotics*, London: Methuen.

Hewitt, Nancy (1985) "Beyond the Search for Sisterhood: American Women's History in the 1980s," *Social History*, 10: 299–321.

Higginbotham, Evelyn Brooks ([1992] 1996) "African-American Women's History and the Metalanguage of Race," in Joan Wallach Scott (Ed.), *Feminism and History*, Oxford: Oxford University Press, pp. 183–208.

Higgins, Charlotte (2005) "Marx Voted Top Thinker," *Guardian*, 14 July.

Hill, Christopher (1972) *The World Turned Upside Down: Radical Ideas during the English Revolution*, New York: Viking Press.

Hilton, R. H. (1973) *Bond Men Made Free: Medieval Peasant Movements and the English Rising of 1381*, London: Temple Smith.

History Workshop Journal (1985) Editorial: "Women's History and Men's History," *History Workshop Journal*, 19: 1–2.

Hoare, Quintin and Smith, Geoffrey Nowell (Eds) (1971) *Selections from the Prison Notebooks of Antonio Gramsci*, New York: International Publishers.

Hobsbawm, Eric (1962) *The Age of Revolution, 1789–1848*, New York: New American Library.

Hobsbawm, Eric (1964) *Labouring Men: Studies in the History of Labour*, London: Weidenfeld & Nicolson.

Hobsbawm, Eric ([1959] 1965) *Primitive Rebels: Studies in Archaic Forms of Social Movement in the 19th and 20th Centuries*, New York: W. W. Norton.

Hobsbawm, Eric (1975) *The Age of Capital, 1848–1875*, New York: Scribner.

Hobsbawm, Eric (1984) *Workers: Worlds of Labor*, New York: Pantheon Books.

Hobsbawm, Eric ([1971] 1984) "Notes on Class Consciousness," *Workers: Worlds of Labor*, New York: Pantheon Books, pp. 15–32.

Hobsbawm, Eric (1987) *The Age of Empire, 1875–1914*, New York: Pantheon Books.

Hobsbawm, Eric (1994) *The Age of Extremes: A History of the World, 1914–1991*, New York: Pantheon Books.

Hobsbawm, Eric ([1972] 1997) "From Social History to the History of Society," *On History*, New York: New Press, pp. 71–93.

Hobsbawm, Eric ([1969] 2000) *Bandits*, 4th Rev. Edn, New York: New Press.

Hobsbawm, Eric, Jacques, Martin and Mulhern, Francis (Eds) (1981) *The Forward March of Labour Halted?*, London: NLB in association with *Marxism Today*.

Holton, Robert ([1989] 1996) "Has Class Analysis a Future? Max Weber and the Challenge of Liberalism to Gemeinschaftlich Accounts of Class," in David J. Lee and Bryan S. Turner (Eds), *Conflicts About Class: Debating Inequality in Late Industrialism: A Selection of Readings*, London: Longman, pp. 26–41.

Hunt, Lynn (1984) *Politics, Culture, and Class in the French Revolution*, Berkeley, CA: University of California Press.

Hunt, Lynn (1986) "French History in the Last Twenty Years: The Rise and Fall of the *Annales* Paradigm," *Journal of Contemporary History*, 21: 209–24.

Hunt, Lynn (Ed.) (1989a) *The New Cultural History*, Berkeley, CA: University of California Press.

Hunt, Lynn (1989b) "Introduction: History, Culture, and Text," in Lynn Hunt (Ed.), *The New Cultural History*, Berkeley, CA: University of California Press, pp. 1–22.

Hutton, Patrick H. (1991) "The Foucault Phenomenon and Contemporary French Historiography," *Historical Reflections/Réflexions Historiques*, 17: 77–102.

Iggers, Georg, G. (1975) *New Directions in European Historiography*, Middletown, CT: Wesleyan University Press.

Ignatiev, Noel (1995) *How the Irish Became White*, New York: Routledge.

Ignatiev, Noel (1997) "The Point Is Not to Interpret Whiteness but to Abolish it," *Race Traitor*, available online at: http://racetraitor.org/.

Jackson, Peter (1998) "Constructions of 'Whiteness' in the Geographical Imagination," *Area*, 30: 99–106.

James, C. L. R. ([1938] 1963) *The Black Jacobins: Toussaint L'Ouverture and the San Domingo Revolution*, 2nd Edn, New York: Vintage Books.

Jameson, Fredric (1984) "Postmodernism, or the Cultural Logic of Late Capitalism," *New Left Review*, 146: 53–92.

Jencks, Charles (1987) *What is Post-Modernism?*, 2nd Rev. Edn, London: Academy Editions.

Jenkins, Keith (Ed.) (1997) *The Postmodern History Reader*, London: Routledge.

Johnson, Christopher (1983) "Response to J. Rancière 'Le Mythe de L'Artisan,'" *International Labor and Working-Class History*, 24: 21–25.

Johnson, Christopher (1993) "Lifeworld, System, and Communicative Action: The Habermasian Alternative in Social History," in Lenard R. Berlanstein (Ed.), *Rethinking Labor History: Essays on Discourse and Class Analysis*, Urbana, IL: University of Illinois Press, pp. 55–89.

Joyce, Patrick (1991) *Visions of the People: Industrial England and the Question of Class, 1848–1914*, Cambridge: Cambridge University Press.

Joyce, Patrick (1993) "The Imaginary Discontents of Social History: A Note of Response to Mayfield and Thorne, and Lawrence and Taylor," *Social History*, 18: 81–85.

Joyce, Patrick (1994) *Democratic Subjects: The Self and the Social in Nineteenth-Century England*, Cambridge: Cambridge University Press.

Joyce, Patrick (Ed.) (1995a) *Class*, Oxford: Oxford University Press.

Joyce, Patrick (1995b) "The End of Social History?," *Social History*, 20: 73–91.

Joyce, Patrick (1996) "The End of Social History? A Brief Reply to Eley and Nield," *Social History*, 21: 96–98.

Joyce, Patrick (1998) "The Return of History: Postmodernism and the Politics of Academic History in Britain," *Past and Present*, 158: 207–35.

Joyce, Patrick (2001) "More Secondary Modern Than Postmodern," *Rethinking History*, 5: 367–82.

Kates, Gary (Ed.) (1998) *The French Revolution: Recent Debates and New Controversies*, London: Routledge.

Katznelson, Ira (1986) "Working-Class Formation: Constructing Cases and Comparisons," in Ira Katznelson and Aristide R. Zolberg (Eds), *Working-Class Formation: Nineteenth-Century Patterns in Western Europe and the United States*, Princeton, NJ: Princeton University Press, pp. 3–41.

Kelley, Robin D. G. (1990) *Hammer and Hoe: Alabama Communists during the Great Depression*, Chapel Hill, NC: University of North Carolina Press.

Kelley, Robin D. G. (1994) *Race Rebels: Culture, Politics, and the Black Working Class*, New York: The Free Press.

Kelley, Robin D. G. (1997) *Yo' Mama's Disfunktional!: Fighting the Culture Wars in Urban America*, Boston, MA: Beacon Press.

Kelley, Robin D. G. (2000) "Foreword," in Cedric J. Robinson, *Black Marxism*, Chapel Hill, NC: University of North Carolina Press, pp. xi–xxiii.

Kelley, Robin D. G. and Williams, Jeffrey (2003) "History and Hope: An Interview with Robin D. G. Kelley," *The Minnesota Review*, 58–60: 93–109.

Kelly, Joan (1983) "The Doubled Vision of Feminist Theory," in Judith L. Newton, Mary P. Ryan and Judith R. Walkowitz (Eds), *Sex and Class in Women's History*, London: Routledge & Kegan Paul, pp. 259–70.

Kirk, Neville (1987) "In Defence of Class: A Critique of Recent Revisionist Writing upon the Nineteenth-Century English Working Class," *International Review of Social History*, 32: 2–47.

Kirk, Neville (1994) "History, Language, Ideas, and Post-Modernism: A Materialist View," *Social History*, 19: 221–40.

Kirk, Neville (1995) "Conference Report," *Labour History Review*, 60: 2–15.

Kirk, Neville (Ed.) (1996) *Social Class and Marxism: Defences and Challenges*, Aldershot, England: Scolar Press.

Kirk, Neville (1998) *Change, Continuity and Class: Labour in British Society, 1850–1920*, Manchester: Manchester University Press.

Koditschek, Theodore (1997) "The Gendering of the British Working Class," *Gender and History*, 9: 333–63.

Krugman, Paul (2002) "For Richer," *New York Times*, 20 October.

Laclau, Ernesto and Mouffe, Chantal (1985) *Hegemony and Socialist Strategy: Towards a Radical Democratic Politics*, London: Verso.

Latin American Subaltern Studies Group (1993) "Founding Statement," *Boundary 2*, 20: 110–21.

Lawrence, Jon and Taylor, Miles (1993) "The Poverty of Protest: Gareth Stedman Jones and the Politics of Language – A Reply," *Social History*, 18: 1–15.

Lee, David J. and Turner, Bryan S. (1996) "Editorial Introduction: Myths of Classlessness and the 'Death' of Class Analysis," in David J. Lee and Bryan S. Turner (Eds), *Conflicts About Class: Debating Inequality in Late Industrialism: A Selection of Readings*, London: Longman, pp. 1–20.

Lefebvre, Georges (1924) *Les Paysans du Nord pendant la Révolution française*, Paris: Lile.

Lefebvre, Georges ([1932] 1973) *The Great Fear of 1789: Rural Panic in Revolutionary France*, New York: Pantheon Books.

Levine, Judith (1994) "The Heart of Whiteness: Dismantling the Master's House," *Voice Literary Supplement*, September: 11–16.

Liddington, Jill and Norris, Jill (1978) *One Hand Tied Behind Us: The Rise of the Women's Suffrage Movement*, London: Virago.

Lloyd, David (1996) "Outside History: Irish New Histories and the 'Subalternity Effect,'" in Shahid Amin and Dipesh Chakrabarty (Eds), *Subaltern Studies IX*, New Delhi: Oxford University Press, pp. 261–77.

Lockwood, David (1956) "Some Remarks on 'The Social System,'" *British Journal of Sociology*, 7: 134–46.

Lockwood, David (1958) *The Blackcoated Worker: A Study in Class Consciousness*, London: Allen & Unwin.

Lockwood, David (1966) "Sources of Variation in Working Class Images of Society," *Sociological Review*, 14: 249-67.

Lucas, Colin, Hunt, Lynn and Sutherland, Donald (1990) "Commentaries on the Papers of William Doyle and Michel Vovelle," *French Historical Studies*, 61: 756-65.

Ludden, David (2002a) "Introduction: A Brief History of Subalternity," in David E. Ludden (Ed.), *Reading Subaltern Studies: Critical History, Contested Meaning and the Globalization of South Asia*, London: Anthem Press, pp. 1-39.

Ludden, David (Ed.) (2002b) *Reading Subaltern Studies: Critical History, Contested Meaning and the Globalization of South Asia*, London: Anthem Press.

Lyotard, Jean François (1984) *The Postmodern Condition: A Report on Knowledge*, Minneapolis, MN: University of Minnesota Press.

Mallon, Florencia E. (1994) "The Promise and Dilemma of Subaltern Studies: Perspectives from Latin American History," *American Historical Review*, 99: 1491-1515.

Manza, Jeff and Brooks, Clem (1996) "Does Class Analysis Still Have Anything to Contribute to the Study of Politics?," *Theory and Society*, 25: 717-24.

Marx, Karl and Engels, Frederick (1969) *Selected Works*, Vol. 1, Moscow: Progress Publishers.

Mayfield, David and Thorne, Susan (1992) "Social History and its Discontents: Gareth Stedman Jones and the Politics of Language," *Social History*, 17: 165-188.

Mayfield, David and Thorne, Susan (1993) "Reply to 'The Poverty of Protest' and 'The Imaginary Discontents,'" *Social History*, 18: 219-33.

McCord, Norman (1985) "Adding a Touch of Class," *History*, 70: 410-19.

McNall, Scott G., Levine, Rhonda F. and Fantasia, Rick (Eds) (1991) *Bringing Class Back in: Contemporary and Historical Perspectives*, Boulder, CO: Westview Press.

Meacham, Standish (1985) "Languages of Class," *Victorian Studies*, 29: 162-64.

Milner, Andrew (1999) *Class*, London: Sage.

Mitchell, Juliet ([1966] 1984) *Women, The Longest Revolution: Essays on Feminism, Literature, and Psychoanalysis*, London: Virago.

Mulhern, Francis (2000) *Culture/Metaculture*, London: Routledge.

Munslow, Alun (2003) *The New History*, Harlow, England: Pearson Longman.

Newman, Louise M. (1991) "Critical Theory and the History of Women: What's at Stake in Deconstructing Women's History," *Journal of Women's History*, 2: 58-68.

Newton, Judith L., Ryan, Mary P. and Walkowitz, Judith R. (1983) "Editors' Introduction," in Judith L. Newton, Mary P. Ryan and Judith R. Walkowitz (Eds), *Sex and Class in Women's History: Essays from* Feminist Studies, London: Routledge & Kegan Paul, pp. 1-15.

O'Brien, Patricia (1989) "Michel Foucault's History of Culture," in Lynn Hunt (Ed.), *The New Cultural History*, Berkeley, CA: University of California Press, pp. 25-46.

O'Hanlon, Rosalind and Washbrook, David ([1992] 2000) "After Orientalism: Culture, Criticism and Politics in the Third World," in Vinayak Chaturvedi (Ed.), *Mapping Subaltern Studies and the Postcolonial*, London: Verso, pp. 191–219.

Olson, Mancur (1965) *The Logic of Collective Action: Public Goods and the Theory of Groups*, Cambridge, MA: Harvard University Press.

Omi, Michael and Winant, Howard ([1986] 1994) *Racial Formation in the United States: From the 1960s to the 1990s*, 2nd Edn, New York: Routledge.

Owusu, Kwesi (Ed.) (2000) *Black British Culture and Society: A Text Reader*, London: Routledge.

Pakulski, Jan ([1993] 1996) "The Dying of Class or of Marxist Class Theory?," in David J. Lee and Bryan S. Turner (Eds), *Conflicts About Class: Debating Inequality in Late Industrialism: A Selection of Readings*, London: Longman, pp. 60–70.

Pakulski, Jan and Waters, Malcolm (1996a) *The Death of Class*, London: Sage.

Pakulski, Jan and Waters, Malcolm (1996b) "The Reshaping and Dissolution of Social Class in Advanced Society," *Theory and Society*, 25: 667–91.

Palmer, Bryan D. (1981) *The Making of E. P. Thompson: Marxism, Humanism, and History*, Toronto: New Hogtown Press.

Palmer, Bryan D. (1987) "Response to Joan Scott," *International Labor and Working-Class History*, 31: 14–23.

Palmer, Bryan D. (1990) *Descent into Discourse: The Reification of Language and the Writing of Social History*, Philadelphia, PA: Temple University Press.

Palmer, Bryan D. (1994) *E. P. Thompson: Objections and Oppositions*, London: Verso.

Pandey, Gyanendra ([1982] 1988) "Peasant Revolt and Indian Nationalism: The Peasant Movement in Awadh, 1919–1922," in Ranajit Guha and Gayatri Chakravorty Spivak (Eds), *Selected Subaltern Studies*, New York: Oxford University Press, pp. 233–87.

Pandey, Gyanendra ([1984] 1988) "'Encounters and Calamities' The History of a North Indian *Qasba* in the Nineteenth Century," in Ranajit Guha and Gayatri Chakravorty Spivak (Eds), *Selected Subaltern Studies*, New York: Oxford University Press, pp. 89–128.

Pandey, Gyanendra ([1992] 1997) "In Defense of the Fragment: Writing About Hindu–Muslim Riots in India Today," in Ranajit Guha (Ed.), *A Subaltern Studies Reader, 1986–1995*, Minneapolis, MN: University of Minnesota Press, pp. 1–33.

Pinchbeck, Ivy ([1930] 1981) *Women Workers and the Industrial Revolution, 1750–1850*, 3rd Edn, London: Virago.

Prakash, Gyan (1994) "Subaltern Studies as Postcolonial Criticism," *American Historical Review*, 99: 1475–90.

Prakash, Gyan ([1990] 2000) "Writing Post-Orientalist Histories of the Third World: Perspectives from Indian Historiography," in Vinayak Chaturvedi (Ed.), *Mapping Subaltern Studies and the Postcolonial*, London: Verso, pp. 163–90.

Prakash, Gyan ([1992] 2000) "Can the 'Subaltern' Ride? A Reply to O'Hanlon and Washbrook," in Vinayak Chaturvedi (Ed.), *Mapping Subaltern Studies and the Postcolonial*, London: Verso, pp. 220–38.

Puranik, Allison (1993) "Celebrate the Many Shades of Black: Paul Gilroy, Sociologist, Guitarist and Former Disc Jockey Tells Allison Puranik Why It Is Time to Embrace the Diversity of Black Culture," *Times Higher Education Supplement*, 20 October.

Rabinbach, Anson (1987) "Rationalism and Utopia as Languages of Nature: A Note," *International Labor and Working-Class History*, 31: 30–36.

Race Traitor (no date) "What We Believe," *Race Traitor*, available online at: http://racetraitor.org/.

Rancière, Jacques (1983) "The Myth of the Artisan: Critical Reflections on a Category of Social History," *International Labor and Working-Class History*, 24: 1–16.

Rancière, Jacques (1988) "Good Times or Pleasures at the Barriers," in Adrian Rifkin and Roger D. Thomas (Eds), *Voices of the People: The Social Life of "La Sociale" at the End of the Second Empire*, London: Routledge & Kegan Paul, pp. 51–58.

Rancière, Jacques (1989) *The Nights of Labor: The Workers' Dream in Nineteenth-Century France*, Philadelphia, PA: Temple University Press.

Rawick, George P. (1972) *From Sundown to Sunup: The Making of the Black Community*, Westport, CT: Greenwood.

Reddy, William, M. (1987) *Money and Liberty in Modern Europe: A Critique of Historical Understanding*, Cambridge: Cambridge University Press.

Reddy, William M. (1992) "The Concept of Class," in M. L. Bush (Ed.), *Social Orders and Social Classes in Europe since 1500: Studies in Social Stratification*, London: Longman, pp. 13–25.

Reed Jr., Adolph (2001) "Response to Eric Arnesen," *International Labor and Working-Class History*, 60: 69–80.

Reid, Donald (1989) "Introduction," in Jacques Rancière, *The Nights of Labor: The Workers' Dream in Nineteenth-Century France*, Philadelphia, PA: Temple University Press, pp. xv–xxxvii.

Reid, Donald (1993) "Reflections on Labor History and Language," in Lenard R. Berlanstein (Ed.), *Rethinking Labor History: Essays on Discourse and Class Analysis*, Urbana, IL: University of Illinois Press, pp. 39–54.

Robinson, Cedric J. ([1983] 2000) *Black Marxism: The Making of the Black Radical Tradition*, Chapel Hill, NC: University of North Carolina Press.

Rodríguez, Ileana (2001) "Reading Subaltern across Texts, Disciplines, and Theories: From Representation to Recognition," in Ileana Rodríguez (Ed.), *The Latin American Subaltern Studies Reader*, Durham, NC: Duke University Press, pp. 1–32.

Roediger, David R. (1994) *Towards the Abolition of Whiteness: Essays on Race, Politics, and Working Class History*, London: Verso.

Roediger, David R. ([1991] 1999) *The Wages of Whiteness: Race and the Making of the American Working Class*, Rev. Edn, London: Verso.

Rose, Sonya O. (1992) *Limited Livelihoods: Gender and Class in Nineteenth-Century England*, Berkeley, CA: University of California Press.

Rose, Sonya O. (1997) "Class Formation and the Quintessential Worker," in John R. Hall (Ed.), *Reworking Class*, Ithaca, NY: Cornell University Press, pp. 133–66.

Rosenberg, Carolyn Smith (1975) "The Female World of Love and Ritual: Relations between Women in Nineteenth-Century America," *Signs*, 1: 1–29.

Rowbotham, Sheila (1972) *Women, Resistance and Revolution*, London: Allen Lane.

Rowbotham, Sheila (1973) *Hidden from History: 300 Years of Women's Oppression and the Fight Against It*, London: Pluto Press.

Rowbotham, Sheila (1997) *A Century of Women: The History of Women in Britain and the United States in the Twentieth Century*, New York: Penguin Books.

Ryan, Mary P. (1981) *Cradle of the Middle Class: The Family in Oneida County, New York, 1790–1865*, Cambridge: Cambridge University Press.

Said, Edward W. ([1978] 1995) *Orientalism*, London: Penguin.

Sarkar, Sumit (1984) "The Conditions and Nature of Subaltern Militancy: Bengal from Swadeshi to Non-Co-operation, c.1905–22," in Ranajit Guha (Ed.), *Subaltern Studies III*, New Delhi: Oxford University Press, pp. 271–320.

Sarkar, Sumit ([1996] 2000) "The Decline of the Subaltern in *Subaltern Studies*," in Vinayak Chaturvedi (Ed.), *Mapping Subaltern Studies and the Postcolonial*, London: Verso, pp. 300–23.

Saussure, Ferdinand de ([1907–1911] 1959) *Course in General Linguistics*, New York: Philosophical Library.

Saxton, Alexander (1990) *The Rise and Fall of the White Republic: Class Politics and Mass Culture in Nineteenth-Century America*, London: Verso.

Schechter, Ronald (Ed.) (2001) *The French Revolution: The Essential Readings*, Malden, MA: Blackwell.

Scott, Joan Wallach (1974) *The Glassworkers of Carmaux: French Craftsmen and Political Action in a Nineteenth-Century City*, Cambridge, MA: Harvard University Press.

Scott, Joan Wallach (1987) "On Language, Gender, and Working-Class History," *International Labor and Working-Class History*, 31: 1–13.

Scott, Joan Wallach (1988) *Gender and the Politics of History*, New York: Columbia University Press.

Scott, Joan Wallach (1992) "Experience," in Judith Butler and Joan Wallach Scott (Eds), *Feminists Theorize the Political*, New York: Routledge, pp. 22–40.

Scott, Joan Wallach (1993) "The Tip of the Volcano," *Comparative Studies in Society and History*, 35: 438–43.

Scott, John ([1994] 1996) "Class Analysis: Back to the Future?," in David J. Lee and Bryan S. Turner (Eds), *Conflicts About Class: Debating Inequality in Late Industrialism: A Selection of Readings*, London: Longman, pp. 127–35.

Seabrook, Jeremy (2002) *The No-Nonsense Guide to Class, Caste and Hierarchies*, London: New Internationalist Publications in association with Verso.

Seddon, Mark (2005) "Kapital Gain," *Guardian*, 14 July.

Sewell, William H., Jr. (1974) "Social Change and the Rise of Working-Class Politics in Nineteenth-Century Marseille," *Past and Present*, 65: 75–109.

Sewell, William H., Jr. (1980) *Work and Revolution in France: The Language of Labor from the Old Regime to 1848*, Cambridge: Cambridge University Press.

Sewell, William H., Jr. (1983) "Response to J. Rancière 'The Myth of the Artisan,'" *International Labor and Working-Class History*, 24: 17–20.

Sewell, William H., Jr. (1986) "Artisans, Factory Workers, and the Formation of the French Working Class, 1789–1848," in Aristide R. Zolberg and Ira Katznelson (Eds), *Working-Class Formation: Nineteenth-Century Patterns in Western Europe*, Princeton, NJ: Princeton University Press, pp. 45–70.

Sewell, William H., Jr. (1990) "How Classes Are Made: Critical Reflections on E. P. Thompson's Theory of Working-Class Formation," in Harvey J. Kaye and Keith McClelland (Eds), *E. P. Thompson: Critical Perspectives*, Philadelphia, PA: Temple University Press, pp. 50–77.

Sewell, William H., Jr. (1993) "Toward a Post-Materialist Rhetoric for Labor History," in Lenard R. Berlanstein (Ed.), *Rethinking Labor History: Essays on Discourse and Class Analysis*, Urbana, IL: University of Illinois Press, pp. 15–38.

Sewell, William H., Jr. (1994) *A Rhetoric of Bourgeois Revolution: The Abbé Sieyès and "What is the Third Estate?"*, Durham, NC: Duke University Press.

Sewell, William H., Jr. (2001) "Whatever Happened to the 'Social' in Social History?," in Joan Wallach Scott and Debra Keates (Eds), *Schools of Thought: Twenty-Five Years of Interpretive Social Science*, Princeton, NJ: Princeton University Press, pp. 209–26.

Shaikh, Nermeen (2003) "Towards a Postcolonial Modernity: *AsiaSource* Interview with Partha Chatterjee," *AsiaSource*, available online at: www.asiasource.org/news/special_reports/chatterjee.cfm.

Spivak, Gayatri Chakravorty (1988) "Can the Subaltern Speak?," in Cary Nelson and Lawrence Grossberg (Eds), *Marxism and the Interpretation of Culture*, Urbana, IL: University of Illinois Press, pp. 271–313.

Spivak, Gayatri Chakravorty ([1985] 1988) "Subaltern Studies: Deconstructing Historiography," in Ranajit Guha and Gayatri Chakravorty Spivak (Eds), *Selected Subaltern Studies*, New York: Oxford University Press, pp. 3–32.

Stansell, Christine (1987) "A Response to Joan Scott," *International Labor and Working-Class History*, 31: 24–29.

Stearns, Peter N. (1998) "Social History," in D. R. Woolf (Ed.), *A Global Encyclopedia of Historical Writing*, Vol. 2, New York: Garland Publishing, pp. 844–49.

Stedman Jones, Gareth (1972) "History: The Poverty of Empiricism," in Robin Blackburn (Ed.), *Ideology in Social Science: Readings in Critical Social Theory*, London: Fontana, pp. 96–115.

Stedman Jones, Gareth (1982) "The Language of Chartism," in James Epstein and Dorothy Thompson (Eds), *The Chartist Experience*, London: Macmillan, pp. 3–58.

Stedman Jones, Gareth (1983) *Languages of Class: Studies in English Working Class History, 1832–1982*, Cambridge: Cambridge University Press.

Stedman Jones, Gareth ([1971] 1984) *Outcast London: A Study in the Relationship Between Classes in Victorian Society*, Harmondsworth, England: Penguin.

Stedman Jones, Gareth (1996) "The Determinist Fix: Some Obstacles to the Further Development of the Linguistic Approach to History in the 1990s," *History Workshop Journal*, 42: 19–35.

Stedman Jones, Gareth (2001) "History and Theory: An English Story," *Historein: A Review of the Past and Other Stories*, 3: 103–24.

Steedman, Carolyn (1986) *Landscape for a Good Woman: A Story of Two Lives*, London: Virago.

Steedman, Carolyn (1992) "Culture, Cultural Studies, and the Historians," in Lawrence Grossberg, Cary Nelson and Paula A. Treichler (Eds), *Cultural Studies*, New York: Routledge, pp. 613–22.

Steedman, Carolyn (1994) "The Price of Experience: Women and the Making of the English Working Class," *Radical History Review*, 59: 109–19.

Steedman, Carolyn (2002a) "Lord Mansfield's Women," *Past and Present*, 176: 105–43.

Steedman, Carolyn (2002b) "Service and Servitude in the World of Labor, 1750–1820," in Colin Jones and Dror Wahrman (Eds), *The Age of Cultural Revolutions: Britain and France, 1750–1820*, Berkeley, CA: University of California Press, pp. 124–36.

Steedman, Carolyn (2004) "The Servant's Labour: The Business of Life, England, 1760–1820," *Social History*, 29: 1–29.

Stoianovich, Traian (1976) *French Historical Method: The* Annales *Paradigm*, Ithaca, NY: Cornell University Press.

Stowe, David W. (1996) "Uncolored People: The Rise of Whiteness Studies," *Lingua Franca*, September–October: 68–77.

Szelényi, Szonja and Olvera, Jacqueline (1996) "The Declining Significance of Class: Does Gender Complicate the Story?," *Theory and Society*, 25: 725–30.

Taylor, Barbara (1983) *Eve and the New Jerusalem: Socialism and Feminism in the Nineteenth Century*, New York: Pantheon Books.

Taylor, Miles (1996) "Rethinking the Chartists: Searching for Synthesis in the Historiography of Chartism," *The Historical Journal*, 39: 479–95.

Tester, Keith (1992) *Civil Society*, London: Routledge.

Thompson, Dorothy (1971) *The Early Chartists*, Columbia, SC: University of South Carolina Press.

Thompson, Dorothy (1976) "Women and Nineteenth-Century Radical Politics: A Lost Dimension," in Juliet Mitchell and Ann Oakley (Eds), *The Rights and Wrongs of Women*, Harmondsworth, England: Penguin, pp. 112–38.

Thompson, Dorothy (1984) *The Chartists: Popular Politics in the Industrial Revolution*, New York: Pantheon Books.

Thompson, Dorothy (1987) "The Languages of Class," *Bulletin of the Society for the Study of Labour History*, 52: 54–61.

Thompson, Dorothy (1990) *Queen Victoria: The Woman, the Monarchy, and the People*, New York: Pantheon Books.

Thompson, Dorothy (1993) *Outsiders: Class, Gender, and Nation*, London: Verso.

Thompson, E. P. (1960) "Revolution Again! Or Shut Your Ears and Run," *New Left Review*, 6: 18–31.

Thompson, E. P. ([1963] 1968) *The Making of the English Working Class*, Harmondsworth, England: Penguin.

Thompson, E. P. ([1955] 1977) *William Morris: Romantic to Revolutionary*, Rev. Edn, New York: Pantheon Book.

Thompson, E. P. (1978a) "Eighteenth-Century English Society: Class Struggle without Class?," *Social History*, 3: 133–65.

Thompson, E. P. (1978b) *The Poverty of Theory and Other Essays*, London: Merlin Press.

Thompson, E. P. (1978c) "The Poverty of Theory or an Orrery of Errors," *The Poverty of Theory and Other Essays*, London: Merlin Press, pp. 1–210.

Thompson, E. P. ([1965] 1978) "The Peculiarities of the English," *The Poverty of Theory and Other Essays*, London: Merlin Press, pp. 245–301.

Thompson, James (1996) "After the Fall: Class and Political Language in Britain, 1780–1900," *Historical Journal*, 39: 785–806.

Tilly, Charles (1985) "Retrieving European Lives," in Olivier Zunz (Ed.), *Reliving the Past: The Worlds of Social History*, Chapel Hill, NC: University of North Carolina Press, pp. 11–52.

Tilly, Louise A. and Scott, Joan Wallach ([1978] 1989) *Women, Work, and Family*, New York: Routledge.

Tocqueville, Alexis de ([1856] 1987) *The Old Regime and the French Revolution*, Chicago, IL: University of Chicago Press.

Touraine, Alain (1992) "Is Sociology Still the Study of Society?," in Peter Beilharz, Gillian Robinson and John Rundell (Eds), *Between Totalitarianism and Postmodernity: A Thesis Eleven Reader*, Cambridge, MA: MIT Press, pp. 173–98.

Tucker, Robert C. (Ed.) (1978) *The Marx-Engels Reader*, 2nd Edn, New York: Norton.

Turner, Bryan S. (1996) "Capitalism, Class, and Citizenship," in David J. Lee and Bryan S. Turner (Eds), *Conflicts About Class: Debating Inequality in Late Industrialism: A Selection of Readings*, London: Longman, pp. 254–61.

University of Birmingham, Centre for Contemporary Cultural Studies, Women's Studies Group (1978) *Women Take Issue: Aspect of Women's Subordination*, London: Hutchinson.

University of Birmingham, Centre for Contemporary Cultural Studies (1982) *The Empire Strikes Back: Race and Racism in 70s Britain*, London: Hutchinson.

Vernon, James (1993) *Politics and the People: A Study in English Political Culture, c.1815–1867*, Cambridge: Cambridge University Press.

Vernon, James (1994) "Who's Afraid of the 'Linguistic Turn'? The Politics of Social History and its Discontents," *Social History*, 19: 81–97.

Vernon, James (1997) "Review of Anna Clark, *The Struggle for the Breeches: Gender and the Making of the British Working Class*," *Journal of Social History*, 30: 1002–4.

Vickery, Amanda (1993) "Golden Age to Separate Spheres? A Review of the Categories and Chronology of English Women's History," *Historical Journal*, 36: 383–414.

Vovelle, Michel (1990) "Reflections on the Revisionist Interpretation of the French Revolution," *French Historical Studies*, 16: 749–55.

Wahrman, Dror (1992a) "National Society, Communal Culture: An Argument About the Recent Historiography of Eighteenth-Century Britain," *Social History*, 17: 43–72.

Wahrman, Dror (1992b) "Virtual Representation: Parliamentary Reporting and Languages of Class in the 1790s," *Past and Present*, 136: 83–113.

Wahrman, Dror (1995) *Imagining the Middle Class: The Political Representation of Class in Britain, c.1780–1840*, Cambridge: Cambridge University Press.

Walker, Pamela J. (2000) "Interview with Dorothy Thompson," *Radical History Review*, 77: 4–19.

Weber, Max ([1920] 1976) *The Protestant Ethic and the Spirit of Capitalism*, New York: Scribner.

Weedon, Chris, Tolson, Alexander and Mort, Frank (1980) "Theories of Language and Subjectivity," in Stuart Hall, Dorothy Hobson, Andrew Lowe and Paul Willis (Eds), *Culture, Media, Language: Working Papers in Cultural Studies, 1972–79*, London: Hutchinson in association with the Centre for Contemporary Cultural Studies, University of Birmingham, pp. 195–216.

West, Cornel (1988) "Black Radicalism and the Marxist Tradition," *Monthly Review: An Independent Socialist Magazine*, September: 51–56.

Whelehan, Imelda (1995) *Modern Feminist Thought: From the Second Wave to "Post-Feminism"*, New York: New York University Press.

Williams, Raymond (1961) *The Long Revolution*, London: Chatto & Windus.

Williams, Raymond (1977) *Marxism and Literature*, Oxford: Oxford University Press.

Williams, Raymond (1983) *Keywords: A Vocabulary of Culture and Society*, London: Fontana Paperbacks.

Winkler, Karen J. (1998) "Robin Kelley's Work on Race and Class Explores Culture, Politics, and Oppression," *Chronicle of Higher Education*, 6 February.

Wright, Erik Olin (1978) *Class, Crisis, and the State*, London: NLB.

Wright, Erik Olin (1985) *Classes*, London: Verso.

Wright, Erik Olin (1996) "The Continuing Relevance of Class Analysis: Comments," *Theory and Society*, 25: 693–716.

Index

Wittgenstein, Ludwig 71
women *see* feminism; gender
working class 5, 11, 17, 18, 33, 43, 52, 53, 55, 89,
    94–5, 101, 109, 112, 220
  absence of in post-industrial society 71–2
  affluence 39–40
  and Chartism 107, 108, 111, 114
  decline in militancy 69, 76
  gendering the 154–61
  and Marx 27, 29

supplanting of industrial proletariat with
    postindustrial 72–3
  and Thompson *see* Thompson, E.P.
  see also labor history
World Bank 2
Wright, Erik Olin 5, 37, 41–4, 79, 83, 214
  Class, Crisis and the State 43
Wright, Richard 177

Zulus 177